1992

THE GREAT REPORTERS

An Anthology of News Writing at Its Best

ON THE COVER: Reporters and policemen investigate the scene of a crime in the 1880s.

THE GREAT REPORTERS

An Anthology of News Writing at Its Best

❦

By Wm. David Sloan, Julie K. Hedgepeth,
Patricia C. Place, & Kevin Stoker

ISION PRESS

P.O. Box 1106	3230 Mystic Lake Way	Northport, AL 35476

Vision Press
P.O. Box 1106
3230 Mystic Lake Way
Northport, Alabama 35476

Library of Congress Cataloguing-in-Publication Data

The Great Reporters / by Wm. David Sloan ... [et al.].
        p.   cm.
    ISBN 0-9630700-2-9 : $16.95
    1. Journalists--United States--Biography. 2.
Reporters and reporting--United States--Biography.
I. Sloan, W. David (William David), 1947-   .
PN4871.G74   1992
070'.92'273--dc20
    [B]   92-9110
                                                      CIP

Printed in the United States of America

Acknowledgments

A number of people helped us in the preparation of this book. We first would like to thank those individuals who aided us in obtaining permission to reprint copyrighted material: Ms. Peggy Walsh and Mrs. Rose Cervino of the New York *Times*; Ms. Kathryn A. Ritchie and Mrs. John Hay Whitney for stories from the New York *Herald Tribune*; and Ms. Mary Lou Marusin, executive director of the Scripps Howard Foundation.

We owe special appreciation to Joanne Sloan and Cheryl S. Watts for their diligent job of editing and vastly improving the manuscript.

For assistance in preparing the manuscript, we especially thank Lisa Bailey.

CONTENTS

THE GREAT
REPORTERS

An Anthology of News Writing at Its Best

1

GREAT REPORTERS
AND GREAT WRITING

"THE BEST WAY TO WRITE WELL IS TO READ GOOD WRITING"

Journalism textbooks and professionals warn against the use of adjectives because they make value judgments difficult to measure. These same authorities probably would argue, however, that if the word fits, use it.

In the case of the reporters included in this anthology, the word *great* applies. They proved that writing done quickly does not have to be done poorly. Of the thousands of reporters who have paraded through American journalism, they wrote in such a way that set them apart from the rest. Although most of the stories were written more than a half-century ago, even today they still maintain their ability to transport the reader to the exact time and place the news events occurred. Readers still come away from them feeling as if they experienced the events themselves.

Therein lies the motive behind this book.

What journalist is unfamiliar with the maxim, "The best way to write well is to read good writing"? It is so true and so oft repeated that it has become a cliché. Poets recite it. Short story writers repeat it. So do novelists. Why don't more journalists? Reporters who are known widely for excellence in writing do advocate the principle. The answer for others perhaps is that in journalism we commonly assume that the principle is applicable to "creative" writing but not to journalistic writing. Nothing, though, could be further from the truth. The problem is that many journalists think that news writing is good only for the day and has no lasting value. They forget about a piece of writing once it is tossed out with yesterday's newspaper. What a disservice they do themselves, their readers, and the profession of journalism!

Journalistic writing can be wonderful! It can be engrossing. It can be poignant. It can be dramatic and moving. Not only *can* it be—much of it has been. If there appears to be a shortage of great writing, the reason is not that there is. The problem is that many journalists—probably not those now reading this book—generally are not aware of it. The authors of this anthology hope that our little volume will help journalists who wish to appreciate good writing by bringing together in a convenient collection some of the best journalistic writing ever done.

One wonders how the stories are able to exercise the power that they do. There are many reasons, but one thing the reader of this anthology will notice immediately is that most of the reporters operated by some measure other than simple adherence to mechanical dicta. None of them gained their quality by slavishly following, for example, a set of Associated Press style rules. Journalistic rules may properly have a place in newspaper writing—to assure, let us say, consistency in the use of the word "Ms." or of digits for certain numbers—but it is apparent that the greatest reporters did not think that relying on such rules would assure excellent writing. Rather, they did whatever worked best to make their stories come alive for readers.

Just as evident is the fact that they did not believe that reporters must be dissociated from their story. Many of them wrote with a clearly personal approach. They would have agreed with Charles Dana, the famous editor of the New York *Sun*, who in the late 1800s complained that "Men with actual capacity of certain sorts for acceptable writing have been frightened off from doing natural and vigorous work by certain newspaper...doctrinaires who are in distress if...the temper and blood of the writer actually show in his work." There are legitimate reasons in the standard practices of journalism for reporters to keep themselves removed from their stories, to be detached and "objective." News reporting should provide an honest, informative, fact-based account for readers. The principle of objectivity also is use-

ful in protecting readers from the tripe of mediocre reporters. One can only imagine the results if every reporter
were let loose to exercise his or her "creativity" unre-
strained. Despite such potential disaster for the future, it is
true that the best stories that ever have been done were those
in which the reporter got immersed.

The great journalists, though, were not mere fiction
writers looking for an easy paycheck in between novels.
They were reporters who made a habit of scooping the competition. They were diligent gatherers of facts. In their work
can be seen clearly the principle that the basis of good writing is good reporting. No story of average quality can be
constructed from nothing, and no truly superior story can be
written without painstaking and exhaustive collection of
facts, figures, concrete details, background, and other relevant matters. No would-be reporter should fool himself into
thinking that excellent journalistic writing is "creative"
writing that can grow from or excuse sloppy reporting.

Where and how does one find "great" reporters? This
anthology does not claim to include them all, only eighteen
of them. Journalism history is filled with fine writers,
many of whom worked in relative obscurity. Some of the best
news writers plied their craft on newspaper rewrite desks,
taking jumbled notes from reporters on the scene and turning them into sparkling stories. The writers in this anthology, however, worked on the front lines, gathering the news
as well as reporting it. Some of them believed in making
news themselves by covering battles or helping investigate
crime. Others wanted to experience the events for themselves, risking their lives to lead military charges or defy-
ing political dangers to cover domestic issues. Most of them
just wrote about people, capturing the human experience in
memorable prose rivaling classic works of fiction.

Selecting only eighteen reporters to include in this anthology proved difficult because many journalists qualified
as exceptional in either reporting or writing. However,
since—as anyone who has read much journalistic writing
knows—fantastic reporting does not assure great or even
good writing, the main criterion used for selecting reporters
for inclusion was their writing talent. No matter how exceptional the newsgathering efforts of other reporters might
have been, we had no wish to bore readers with tedious sto-

ries.

It is evident, however, that the writing quality of some great reporters grew principally from their exceptional reporting ability.

Herbert Bayard Swope, for instance, possessed better than ordinary writing talent, but the fact that he was an extraordinary reporter was the reason that he was able to create irresistible stories. He found wonderful material. He had, according to one observer, "illusions of grandeur," but his recklessness allowed him to obtain information others failed to get. Bold and brash, he may have been in a class by himself when it came to crashing in on news stories, gathering all the details, and then packing them into a riveting story. He also had boundless energy and a dynamic personality. He made his writing irresistible by filling it with so much important information that readers struggled to put his stories down.

Another who excelled mainly because of her reporting skill was Marguerite Higgins. She defied male bureaucrats who attempted to hold her back and then wrote stories filled with compassion for victims of tragedy. Her ability to scoop her male counterparts repeatedly and her tireless energy in pursuing stories imbued her writing with a dramatic storytelling quality.

Although many journalists of today have names recognizable in the field, most notable reporters worked in an earlier time. Because of both the less confining nature of journalism and their own unique talents, they enjoyed greater freedom to describe and interpret the news than does the average reporter of today. Freedom alone, however, never assures superior performance. Constraints may restrict talent, but freedom from convention does not lead automatically to quality. Such freedom, if not tempered with rigor and a mastery of writing style, may lead simply to sloppiness.

The reporters that we now think of as the greatest ones were not typical of their own generation. They may have worked within the same constraints; but, nevertheless, they were the standard-bearers of their time. As such, their writing and reporting served as models for generations of journalists. Thus, the primary purpose of this anthology, by emphasizing the works of the greatest journalists, is to provide models for the present and the next generation of journalists.

Because outstanding reporters often had exciting careers, one can be tempted to concentrate more on a reporter's exploits than his or her writing style. Indeed, several of the reporters in this anthology have been the subjects of highly readable biographies. While chronicling the fascinating aspects of the reporters' personalities and careers, however, this book is intended primarily as a study of writing style, and it continually attempts to answer the questions, "What made these reporters good writers? What was their philosophy of reporting? What can we learn from their writing."

What accounts for good newspaper writing, and is good newspaper writing different from good writing in other genres?

There are, indeed, some peculiarities that set newspaper writing apart. Unlike good writing in magazines and books, most newspaper prose has not benefited from extensive rewriting. Indeed, journalism has been called "literature in a hurry."

The reporters included in this anthology had a knack for getting the facts as well as writing them. Icy water dripped from a shivering Floyd Gibbons as he cabled the story about his rescue from a passenger liner torpedoed by a German U-boat. Meyer Berger gathered his information and wrote his Pulitzer Prize-winning account of the rampage of a berserk killer in less than six hours. The New York *Times* printed the 4,000-word story without changing a word. Under the pressure of deadline, Grantland Rice churned out his epic sports story on Notre Dame's "Four Horsemen of the Apocalypse." Most of the reporters included in this anthology worked under tight deadlines that did not allow for extensive editing and rewriting.

On the other hand, good writing in any genre bears certain similarities to that in other genres. Thematic focus, structural and stylistic unity, intensity of writing, and economy of language are but a few.

Despite such universal characteristics, there are differences among reporters' writing styles. The great reporters' approaches to journalism were as diverse as the subjects they wrote about. Even writers who covered the same types of news events tended to focus on different aspects of the story.

Except for the similarity in their first names, Ernie Pyle and Ernest Hemingway had little in common in covering wars. Pyle, a travel writer before World War II, wrote about the life of ordinary foot soldiers, capturing the details of lives in simple, unassuming prose. Hemingway, on the other hand, was an arm-chair general who tried to understand the overall scope of the battle. Instead of remaining detached from the people and events he covered, he became a part of them. He led troops, drummed up support for causes, and wrote in the first person. Yet, despite the differences in approaches, both reporters succeeded in writing memorable stories about war and warriors.

With such diversity, are there any common characteristics that accounted for the superior quality of writing done by these eighteen *Great Reporters*? Was it their ability to capture the essence of an event and tell it in a lively way, or was it their tenaciousness at gathering lively facts and information?

All the best reporters have been energetic and diligent in gathering information. Most of the great ones were tenacious. When they locked on to a story, they refused to let go until they had gathered every available detail and reported it before anybody else. Although some would help fellow reporters and others resorted to questionable means to cover their stories, most just outworked and outsmarted the competition. Generally, the great reporters exhibited as much creative ability in getting stories as they did in writing them.

For some, bold bravado and creative methods for snooping out the news offset their ordinary literary talent. Other reporters, Ernie Pyle and Alexander Woollcott, to name two, had the uncanny ability to sniff out a story that less observant journalists might overlook. Floyd Gibbons and James Creelman exhibited a dogged tenacity, going after a story no matter where it was and no matter what the cost—even if to the point of endangering their lives.

Contrast that approach with that of the astute observers. This group had a gift for interpreting complex events. Their news accounts, relying on an incisive ability to understand the essence of events, captured the tone and texture of what was happening around them. Anne O'Hare McCormick became known as a benevolent teacher because she filled her reports about important international events with insight and instruction as well as news. South African-born journalist William Ryall Bolitho's stories probed deep into the meanings behind the news. Bolitho could "see through a brick wall," according to long-time New York *Times* reporter Walter Duranty.

The writing of these great reporters also shared certain structural and stylistic qualities that made their writing stand out above that of their peers. Here are the most obvious.

Human drama. Perhaps the key to effective journalistic writing is to capture human drama. News is important almost solely because it involves people. The stories written by the best reporters in American journalism have presented the characters as real, full-dimensioned people. They focused on the effect events had on people, how the people coped, how they struggled, how they lived, and sometimes how they died. In one story included in this anthology, for example, Anne McCormick focused on a woman sweeping up the mess after World War II; and in another, during the Spanish Civil War, Ernest Hemingway wrote about a wounded soldier from Pennsylvania, "where once we fought at Gettysburg." The feature that draws the reader into these human dramas is the emotion and intensity with which the writing tells the people's stories.

To show the human drama, the reporters did not always honor the rules of objectivity. They placed a greater emphasis on revealing the character of the people in the stories. That often required personal interpretation and analysis rather than detached accounting. Indeed, the reader will find that several of the best stories in this anthology are in first person. Many of those that are not still reflect the personality of the writer. First-person can be dangerous in the hands of an undisciplined writer, and avoiding it is a useful device for trying to force the writer's biases out of a story. In some instances, however, it is more honest than third-person is, for it clearly lets the reader know that the story is being told from a particular point of view.

The great reporters instilled in their stories the excitement, the fear, and the emotion they felt as they covered events ranging from boxing matches to peace conferences. They had a personal style characteristic of good narrative writing, the kind that normally is associated with fiction rather than news. By re-creating the scenes, the sights, the sounds, and smells, they propelled readers vicariously into events that were shaping world history. Their descriptions probed deeper—past surface details of what people did or said—to explain why people acted as they did and why they said what they said. Through their descriptions, the reporters did more than tell what happened. They showed how people acted and reacted to events ranging from sports glory to national tragedy.

Storytelling. The best writers had a knack for relating a good story. They wrote in chronological order, weaving, when necessary, background and explanation into the fabric of the story without ruining the dramatic flow of the narrative. Some news accounts do not lend themselves to storytelling; some require exposition. Many of the most effective, however, have a narrative structure. Some news events lend themselves to plot development, characterization, conflict, rhythm of pacing, and denouement. Such a structure shows up with obvious frequency in the works by the best reporters. Their stories have a beginning, a development of the action, and a chronological ending. Normally, they are told through the actions of characters, showing interesting people doing interesting things.

Curiosity. The great reporters had—and continue to have—an abiding curiosity. They were willing to go to great lengths to gain a firsthand understanding and knowledge of the subject. They were not just clever word technicians sitting at a desk in the newsroom and molding canned material into readable prose.

On the contrary, most of them experienced the news for themselves. That is why many of the stories included in this anthology are eyewitness accounts. Having seen an event themselves, the reporters were able to recount the experience as it occurred, thus allowing readers also to live through the experience.

Even on occasions when the reporters did not witness the event, they provided the reader with as close a reconstruction as possible. They were able to do that conducting exhaustive investigation and research to allow them to reconstruct the event as if they had witnessed it. Through their firsthand experience or their exhaustive gathering of material, they breathed life into historical leaders, army privates, and starving peasants, capturing their experiences and emotions.

Providing context. The reporters in this anthology recognized the importance of explaining the context within which events occurred. They tried to explain the political, economic, and historical forces that merged or diverged to create news events. They tried to give more than a superficial account of what happened. Again and again, they sought to answer the questions: What do these events mean, and what effect do they have on people? Answering the questions required them to probe beyond the obvious—to peel back the layers and identify the patterns and trends that may have caused people and nations to behave the way they did. It was as if they were constantly asking, "Why? How does this affect me? How does this affect my readers? What is the worldwide impact?" The reporters were vicarious representatives of their readers, and they took their responsibility seriously.

Respect for readers. The reporters respected their readers. They did not write down to them, but wrote about what they perceived to be the most consequential issues. For the most part, they also understood their readers, providing them with information they needed as well as what they wanted to know. They had an unwritten contract with readers to meet their informational needs. That meant going to great lengths, occasionally even risking danger, to get the best story possible.

Thematic unity. The best stories always have a central theme. The theme acts as a helm, preventing the writer from drifting away from the story's central purpose. This ability to focus the facts, people, and events around a central theme stands out as a key element in making a story readable and relevant.

Two structural points are especially important in the principle of thematic unity. The first is the definition of what a "theme" is. A theme is not simply the topic of a particular story. It is the *point that the story makes about that topic.* Thematic unity, furthermore, requires that a news story be structured around *one* central idea, or theme. If a story flits among several, it will go off in various directions, losing the reader and any force that it might otherwise have had to concentrate on a central point.

Without a unifying theme, a story falls apart. If it is no

more than a collection of details or an odd, unintegrated assortment of pieces of information, it will work poorly or not work at all. The great stories, those that have an impact, did more than pull together a group of facts, quotes, dates, places, names, and other bits of "news." All of their parts worked together to create a unified whole focused around a central concept.

Elements of style. The best news writing has an intensity that derives in part from stylistic devices. The most important are the following: (1) Style is natural, not artificial. It suits the writer naturally and is determined by the writer's personal approach and talent rather than by mechanical rules. (2) It employs concrete details. Physical descriptions of people and scenes help readers grasp characteristics better and visualize where and how actions took place. (3) News stories are—and must be—clear. All types of writing should be clear, but clarity in news writing is especially important because of the nature of newspaper reading. It must be easily understandable to the average person on a first reading. (4) Effective writing is precise. Words are chosen for their exact meaning. (5) It is economical—meaning not only that it is concise, but that it uses terse words and pointed sentences, simplicity of phrasing, and exact word choice. (6) Nouns and verbs outnumber adjectives and adverbs. The former are stronger. Active verbs are preferred over passive ones. (7) Good writing uses variety. Sentence structures, for example, and word choice vary; and sentence length and rhythm change.

Desire to improve. The great reporters were intent on improving their craft. They wanted to be exceptional at what they did. Even Ernest Hemingway, whose comments did not always reveal a high esteem for journalism, sought out the best journalists and learned from them. In addition, his journalistic writing reveals qualities apparent in his best fiction. Despite his literary achievements, he worked as a journalist throughout the most productive years of his writing life. Some of the other great reporters also plied their talents as non-fiction book writers and novelists. Most of them, however, stuck with the profession of journalism until the day they died.

The most important principle of good writing to be learned from this anthology may be that the great reporters of the past have a lot to teach us. Journalism today is unforgivably negligent when it ignores the wonderful and valuable contributions of history's great reporters. News people sometimes suffer from the illusion that anything that happened yesterday is old news and not worth reading. How much can be learned, however, when we simply *read*! The qualities inherent in yesterday's great reporting and writing continue to apply to those who would like to write today's great journalism.

2

CHARLES ANDERSON PAGE

A KEEN EYE FOR DETAIL

The neophyte Civil War reporter had just witnessed one of the fiercest battles of the war when he saw a horse gallop past him. All that remained of the rider was his booted leg—still in the stirrup. When the reporter relayed the sight to the more seasoned reporters back at camp, they told their own horror stories, besting one another with a tale more terrible than the one before.

Charles Anderson Page observed the horrible incident and the reporters' apparent callousness and reported to his readers: "During the stampede, for a moment the attention of hundreds was attracted to a horse galloping around carrying a man's leg in the stirrup—the left leg, booted and spurred. It was a splendid horse, gaily caparisoned."

The managing editor of the New York *Tribune*, Sydney Howard Gay, said in an understatement: "...Page shows a nice eye for the grotesque."

This was one of many compliments paid to the most brilliant of the Civil War reporters. He was highly regarded by editors and soldiers, truly one of the "Bohemian Brigade," as northern Civil War reporters were called.

Although Page did not begin reporting on the war until 1862, he had an auspicious beginning. Horace Greeley, publisher-editor of the *Tribune*, took notice of Page from the first and awarded him the rare privilege of a byline. He was forever after known to *Tribune* readers as "C.A.P., our special correspondent."

Page was born in 1838 in Illinois, the son of farmers.

While working for the Mount Vernon, Iowa, *News,* he was a staunch Lincoln supporter and so was awarded a clerkship in the Treasury Department when Lincoln won the presidency. It was in Washington that he caught the eye of Adams Hill, the *Tribune's* Washington editor. He began to write for the *Tribune* in 1862.

Page was with the U.S. Army in the East and became famous for his coverage of the Wilderness Campaign. His was the first account of the campaign to be printed, and the *Tribune* sold 15,000 copies of that day's edition four hours before its competitors. The account demonstrated his eye for detail, his perception of soldiers, his ability to understand and explain military maneuvers, and his sense of humor. Hill referred to Page as "a cool, brisk, quick-eyed young man."

His style has been called "off-hand." Simpler and less flowery, his writing was different from that of his peers. He wrote in a diary style, which was similar to the other dispatches from correspondents. However, he wrote to the reader, using illustrations and language with which they could identify.

Page's quick eye caught sight of details like the left boot remaining in the stirrup, and his keen ear heard such remarks as "There are cheers and yells, for our men *cheer,* while they [the Confederate soldiers] *yell.*"

He also had a command of the language, as when he described the heat of battle at Mechanicsville, Virginia: "The tornado swept right and left as if one current of electricity had discharged every man's musket." James Gilmore, editor of an anthology of Page's work, said that Page was "an accomplished word-painter, who so vividly described the clash of the contending forces that his reader became, like him, a spectator looking on at the terrific conflict. Some of his battle-pictures are scarcely equalled by those of the most famous war-correspondents of this country or England." Page wrote with a realism and a simplicity of language that his counterparts often did not have. He himself said, "It is somewhat the habit to represent a body of troops...as 'eager for the fray,' 'burning to be led against the foe,' or, less elegantly, 'spoiling for a fight.' Writers who indulge the use of such phrases know nothing of armies, or do not state what they know, unless indeed they know it to be false. The soldiers themselves laugh at these expressions when they see them. They are not conscious of...any amorous inclination toward bullets."

Page was a tireless reporter. He was one of the first three correspondents in Richmond after its capture. The War Department had prohibited correspondents from going into Richmond, but Page earlier had received a pass from Gen. Ulysses Grant, and he used it to sneak into the city.

He chartered steamboats and trains for his own use and spent freely to get a story, prompting Greeley to say: "We are greatly pleased with your work; you are quick and graphic, and give us the news early, and we must have it early; but Mr. Page, you are the most expensive young man the *Tribune* has ever employed." Page responded: "Early news is expensive news, Mr. Greeley; if I have the watermelons and whiskey ready when the officers come along from the fight, I get the news without asking questions."

Greeley did not object to spending money because he admired Page's reputation for being accurate. "If Page says something," Greeley said on several occasions, "it is so."

Page reported on not only the war, but also the background of the war, from horses to sanitation. In one account, he described the use of ether:

Dr. Morton of Boston, one of the first discoverers, if not indeed the first discoverer of the anaesthetic properties of ether, has been with the army the last week, working and observing in his capacity with all his might. During this time he has, with his own hands, administered ether in over 2,000 cases. The Medical Director, when asked yesterday in what operations he required ether to be used, replied, "In every one."

I believe the division of labor in the manufacture of any given article has now reached the point where 25 different men help make a pin. Science is scarcely behind art in this particular, as the following incident will show.

Day before yesterday some 300 Rebel wounded fell into our hands. Of these, 21 required capital operations. They were placed in a row, a slip of paper pinned to each man's coat collar telling the nature of the operation that had been decided upon. Dr. Morton first passes along, and with a towel saturated with ether puts every man beyond consciousness and pain.

The operating surgeon follows and rapidly and skillfully amputates a leg or an arm, as the case may be, till the 21 have been subjected to the knife and saw without one twinge of pain. A second surgeon ties up the arteries, a third dresses the wounds. The men are taken to a tent near by and wake up to find themselves out in two without torture, while a windrow of lopped off members attest the work. The last man had been operated upon before the first wakened; nothing could be more dramatic and nothing could more perfectly demonstrate the value of anaesthetics. Besides, men fight better when they know that torture does not follow a wound, and numberless lives are saved that the shock of the knife would lose to their friends and the country. Honor, then, to Morton and Jackson, the men who so opportunely for this war placed in our hands an agent that relieves the soldier.

Page was popular with his readers, consistently turning out interesting stories. He felt that it was "the business of a correspondent to report certain events, facts, and news...." He wrote on May 18, 1864, about the Army of the Potomac:

Early yesterday it was determined to attack this morning. At first the decision was to try a movement upon the left, with the view of turning the enemy's right; but late in the afternoon, it being apparent that the enemy must have seen us moving troops to mass upon the left, and the line of attack not proving as favorable there as had been expected, the plan of attack was recast, and the 2d and 6th Corps were moved during the night to the extreme right. The assault was to be at sunrise, Wright at the right, Hancock joining with his left, and Barnside and Warren still further to the left, in the order they are named. The struggle actually began soon after daybreak. It has proved abortive. The losses of the day I estimate at 1,000, and we hold no more ground than in the morning. The day's work has been unsuccessful.

He knew his readers, giving them more than just an account of a battle. The following passage illustrates his technique:

The Corcoran legion suffered most severely; witness the accompanying partial list of casualties. By far the largest loss was inflicted by the enemy's artillery, which he has had ample time to place in position. I have never before seen such terrible wounds as those of today, and have never heard of so many hair-breadth escapes. Horses seemed to be particularly unlucky, and men particularly lucky.

Four days these armies have been maneuvering—little fighting, but a contest of generalship. The enemy is quiet, and hits back only when hit. He is sullen, and purely on the defensive. Nevertheless, I am convinced there are more things in Grant's philosophy than he dreams of. Await the development of these things and possess your souls in patience.

After the war, Page was named to the consulate in Switzerland. While there, he founded an evaporated milk company, quit the consulate, and made his fortune with the company that later became Nestle's. He died in London on a business trip in 1873.

◆

UNION FORCES ATTACK ON BEWILDERING BATTLEFIELD

The coverage of the Battle of the Wilderness gained fame for Page. The *Tribune* sold out of copies, and reprints were published in newspapers throughout the country. Page's horse was shot out from under him as he returned to wire his story to the paper. He commandeered another horse and sent a short wire to the *Tribune* in New York. Unfortunately, the telegrapher sent the dispatch to Washington. So Page then jumped on a train to New York. He wrote all night, turning in the first accounts of the story of this great battle. Notice how he described the troop movements in language every reader could understand.

THE BATTLE OF THE WILDERNESS
Charles Anderson Page
New York *Tribune*
May 6, 1864

Wilderness Tavern, Heart of the Wilderness.
8 a.m., Thursday, May 5, 1864.

Late of Tuesday the whole army became aware that it would be moved within a few hours. During the night and the first daylight of the next morning everything was put in motion. Gregg's Division of Cavalry crossed Ely's Ford, without opposition, at daybreak. Wilson's Division (late Kilpatrick's) crossed Germania Ford. Hancock's Second Corps followed Gregg, and Warren's Fifth Corps followed Wilson. Long before night Hancock had posted his corps and established headquarters at Chancellorsville, while Warren had pushed on to Wilderness Tavern and occupied the ridges facing Mine Run and the enemy. By sunset Sedgwick, with the Sixth Corps, had crossed Germania Ford, and last night encamped along the road in rear of Warren. Sheridan, with the Cavalry Corps, thoroughly scoured the country in all directions. He intercepted despatches [sic] from the Rebel General Rhodes to Ewell, stating that Meade had effected a crossing, and asking instructions. Another intercepted despatch apprised us that Stuart was having a cavalry review at Hamilton's Cross-Roads. Sheridan was anxious to assist at the spectacle, but it was not thought expedient.

General Grant left Culpeper and General Meade Brandy early yesterday morning, and early in the afternoon pitched headquarters just this side of Germania Ford.

At daybreak this morning Sheridan moved with all his force with two purposes,—to find and fight Stuart, and to push a reconnaissance far to our left on the enemy's right flank. The order of march to-day, as fixed since midnight, is for Warren to advance to Parker's Tavern, five miles toward Mine Run, for Hancock to take a road leading him from Chancellorsville, that will enable him to establish a line on the left of Warren, connecting with the latter, while Sedgwick is to move up and assume Warren's present position.

It is possible, however, that Lee may cause a change in the programme. General Griffin reports the enemy menacing his position on the ridge south of this point, and not a mile away. Warren orders him not to move off toward Parker's Tavern until Sedgwick can come up and relieve him. General Meade rode up ten minutes ago and said to Warren, "If the enemy comes near you, pitch right in with all you've got!" The dispositions necessary to sustain an attack, if such be Lee's purpose, have caused a halt of the columns, and now we are listening for the first gun. If the enemy does not choose to precipitate the battle here, our army before night will hold the position contemplated by the morning order. On the other hand, we can well afford to fight him now. It is six miles back to the Rapidan [River]; if we are attacked it will be with the hope of breaking through the moving columns by a vigorous assault upon the flank. Generals Grant and Meade and Warren and Sedgwick will see to it that what the enemy supposes to be a weak flank he shall find to his cost is nothing less or else than a formidable front.

I have never seen the army move with more exact order, with a less number of stragglers, and with so little apparent fatigue to the men. All had a full ration of sleep last night—which is a better augury of victory than a re-enforcement of thousands. The roads are in excellent condition, the weather delightful, and so warm that whole divisions abandoned their overcoats and extra blankets on the march. At one point I noticed some hundreds of overcoats had been thrown into a stream to improve the crossing. Overcoats and blankets are decidedly better for the purpose than rails.

I understand that Burnside marched last night to join this army, and will reach Germania to-day. It is understood that General Butler is making a simultaneous "Onward to Richmond," and will first occupy City Point, James River. That these two movements are being made is generally known in the army, and has a most inspiring effect.

Rest your confidence, not only in what may be predicted upon the records of its generals as to how this army will be handled, but in this: *the rank and file will fight this fight with more than the élan of the French, with more than the pluck of the British.* They feel it in their bones,—that *something* allied to these, but better than either or both.

Wilderness Battle-Field,
Thursday, May 5, 2 p.m.

How perfect have been the combinations, how completely on time they have been executed, how well in hand the army has been every hour and is now, how masterly and successful thus far has been the movement,—all this is so clearly apparent that I can but notice it here, even while a spirited battle is being fought only half a mile from where I write.

Let me here pay a tribute to the first soldier killed in this campaign. Let Charles Wilson, of Franklin, Mass., private in Co. I, Eighteenth Mass., Col. Jos. Hayes commanding, be remembered as the first man to give his life in this (God willing) last grand campaign of the war.

Immediately after "writing up" this morning, I rode out to Griffin's lines, then reported to be menaced by the enemy. His division was in line of battle at right angles with and on either side of the Old Turnpike. The enemy had evidently despatched a force from his lair on Mine Run to worry and delay our march by threatening in flank. General Griffin had sent the Eighteenth Massachusetts and Eighty-third Pennsylvania, under Colonel Hayes of the former, to feel well out on the turnpike. It was here that Charles Wilson fell, the Rebel skirmish line opposing a vigilant front. Finally, after some little firing, General Warren, who had come up in person, ordered an advance down the road in force. Ayres' Brigade moved on upon the right of the road, and Bartlett's upon the left, with each flank well supported.

Field officers were obliged to dismount, so dense was the growth of dwarf pines. An advance of less than half a mile, and a smart fusillade opened the action. The two brigades carried the first eminence, and were pushing up a second, who, owing to a failure of the commands right and left to connect and form a continuous line, the Rebels flanked them on both sides. Colonel Hayes, Eighteenth Massachusetts, finding himself in command of several regiments and the enemy all around him, formed a line facing to the rear and fought in both directions. At length he gave the order to fall back, and the movement was being executed when he was hit on the scalp and fell. The brigade bugler brought him safely off. Meanwhile fresh troops were put in and the Rebels slowly driven along, the whole front then fighting. In this action our loss is probably 300 or 400. At this hour the enemy has ceased to make demonstrations, and we are waiting for Hancock to join on our left. General Grant is smoking a wooden pipe, his face as peaceful as a summer evening, his general demeanor indescribably imperturbable. I know, however, that there is great anxiety that Hancock should fall into position, for it is believed that the entire Rebel force is massing upon us.

Wilderness Battle-Field
9 p.m., Thursday, May 5.

Heavy fighting since three o'clock, mostly at the extreme left, under Hancock. Getty's Division, Sixth Corps, was at the right of the Orange Plank road, fronting toward Mine Run, where Carr's Division, Second Corps, joined him on his left. The other divisions of Hancock's Corps were pushing up; in the twinkling of an eye the Rebels were upon him in great force, with the evident purpose of turning our left. The ground was fearfully overgrown with shrub trees, thick as one sees shoots from the same root. In a few minutes urgent requests came back for re-enforcements. The enemy was repeating his tactics at Chancellorsville of falling with tremendous force and super-human *vim* upon one wing. This time he was not repulsed, but foiled. The battle raged for three hours precisely where it began, along a line of not more than half a mile. Fast as our men came up they were sent in—still no ground gained, none lost. It was all musketry, roll surging upon roll,—not the least cessation. We were fighting 20,000 men, and such was the nature of the country but two guns could be planted bearing upon the enemy. Hayes's Brigade of Birney's Division became warmly engaged soon after the ball opened. A little while and he asked for re-enforcements. Hancock sends back word: "I will send a brigade within twenty minutes. Tell Gen. Alex. Hayes to hold his ground. He can do it. I know him to be a powerful man." Within that time General Hayes was killed and his body brought to the rear. The work was at close range. No room in that jungle for maneuvering; no possibility of a bayonet charge; no help from artillery; no help from cavalry; nothing but close, square, severe, face-to-face volleys of fatal musketry. The wounded stream out, and fresh troops pour in. Stretchers pass out with ghastly burdens, and go back reeking with blood for more. Word is brought that the ammunition is failing. Sixty rounds fired in one steady, stand-up fight, and that fight not fought out.

Boxes of cartridges are placed on the returning stretchers, and the struggle shall not cease for want of ball and powder. Do the volleys grow nearer, or do our fears make them seem so? It must be so, for a second line is rapidly formed just where we stand, and the bullets slip singing by as they have not done before, while now and then a limb drops from the tree-tops. The bullets are flying high. General Hancock rides along the new line, is recognized by the men, and cheered with a will and a tiger. But we stay them. The Second Corps is all up, and it must be that troops will come up from Warren or Sedgwick, or else they will divert the enemy's attention by an attack upon another quarter. Yes, we hold them, and the fresh men going in will drive them. I ride back to General Headquarters, and learn that an advance has been ordered an hour ago along the whole line. General Meade is in front with Warren, and Grant is even now listening for Wadsworth's Division or Warren's Corps to open on Hill's flank, for it is Hill's Corps that is battling with Hancock. The latter reports that he shall be able to maintain his ground. The severe fighting for the day is over, and it is sunset.

I write now at 10 p.m. Since dark there has been brisk firing at intervals at different points along the line. The enemy has been splendidly foiled to-day in his intention of beating us before we should be ready to fight. To-morrow we shall be altogether ready. Our line to-night extends, perhaps, six miles from northeast to southwest, the right being a little advanced.

General Burnside has come up 25,000 strong, and will probably be the reserve to-morrow. Our loss to-day may be estimated at 3,000 or 4,000. The main battle, probably a decisive one, must be to-morrow. To-day we have fought because the enemy chose that we should. To-morrow, because we choose that he shall.

●✧

THE LIFE OF A CIVIL WAR CORRESPONDENT

In June 1864, Page wrote: "Your correspondent is sick with

fatigue. The sun broiled his brains, and he was last night placed in hospital, where this has been written." While recovering, he wrote the following story. In it he described the feelings of every active person who has been made inactive because of illness. He also talked about the hardships of reporting a war. This story illustrates his keen sense of observation, as well as his command of the language. Notice his use of such devices as repetition, variations in sentence length, and imagery. He employed his brisk sense of humor to enliven the whole composition.

AN INVALID'S WHIMS
Charles Anderson Page
New York *Tribune*
June 25, 1864

With the Army of the Potomac,
Saturday, June 25, 1864.

Invalids are proverbially querulous and unreasonable, and because they are invalids it is forgiven them. Their whims and vagaries are humored. They may fret and scold, abuse their toast and their friends, scatter their maledictions and the furniture, and who shall cry them "Nay"? The reader of this, if any there be, is informed respectfully but firmly that the writer, being an invalid, proposes to avail himself of all the privileges which attach to the character. Released from the bonds of the proprieties, for him there are no improprieties. Careless of consequences, careless in rhetoric, altogether careless of everything, this letter that is to be shall write itself. I am an invalid. If any thin stratum of sense or news should happen to crop out between underlying and overlying strata of nonsense, such formation will be accidental, abnormal, unaccountable.

Imprimis: It is hot. It is hotter than yesterday. Yesterday was hotter than the day before. The day before hotter than its immediate predecessor, and it than its, and so on indeterminately. Purgatory is at least a week back, and hell itself not far ahead. How hot it is now, no thermometer of words will begin to indicate. The boy who extended the comparison of the adjective from hot to hottest, then began again with Hottentot and ended with Hottentotest, made a creditable effort, but failed. In other climates he may be thought to have succeeded. But in the light and heat of this locality I denounce the ambitious youth as unequal to his attempt. It is hot. Has the lower world invaded the confines of this, or is Virginia a part of that world?

This indescribable hotness is a part of the misery of correspondents.

It is dusty. I wrote the de-apotheosis of dust the other day (did you see it in the "Daily ———"?), but failed in the deep damnation commensurate with the subject. Did you ever smile and smile, and feel like a villain? We down here do, whenever we come in dusty from a long ride. Did you ever grit your teeth in rage? We do, whenever we shut our mouths—else we shouldn't shut 'em. Water, I adore thee; soap, thou art my benefactor; towels, ye are blessed!

Tertiary deposit, good for growing potatoes, but contempt is bred of familiarity with thee—behind me, Satan!

Dust is a part of the misery of correspondents.

A Scene: Three "specials" of metropolitan journals, smoking meerschaums, and conning letters [news stories] yet to be. Mail arrives with New-York papers. Each reads one of his own letters.

Reading their own letters is a part of the misery of correspondents.

"Herald" special swears oaths both loud and deep: "They have rewritten my despatch!" "Times" special finds something he spoke of as "impudent" pronounced "important." "Tribune" special is amused. He had said certain troops were "handled skilfully"; he is made to say that they "were travelled skilfully." In another place, where he had described foliage as of the "densest, deepest green," it appears that it was of the *direst* green! "Magnificent" is transformed into "magnified" and destroys the point of a quarter of a column of elaborate rhetoric.

Verily, reading their own letters is a part of the misery of correspondents.

Mr. Winser of "The Times" had his horse shot under him at Cold Harbor. Mr. Anderson of "The Herald" was hit in the arm at Wilderness. Richardson and Browne of "The Tribune" have been sixteen months in Rebel prisons. All have had their hairbreadth 'scapes.

Constant danger, without the soldier's glory, is a part of

the misery of correspondents.

Abstractly considered, horseback exercise is a good thing. I have known it to be recommended by physicians. Taken in moderate quantities not too long after sunrise, or not too long before sunset, I have myself found it not unpleasant. In imagination I see myself, September next, indulging in flowing rein on smooth beach roads to the murmur of ocean waves, or in the back country, where the foliage is crimson and there are cider-presses in the orchards, following where there are

"Old roads winding, as old roads will,
Here to a ferry, and there to a mill."

That is one picture. Now look on this: Virginia wastes, where only desolation swells, arid with summer heats, and now four weeks without sprinkle of rain. The sky is brass, heated to a white fervor; the air you breathe heated like the blast of a furnace, and laden with dust that chokes you. A fierce, pitiless sun sheds rays like heated daggers; these impalpable daggers stab you. You broil; you pant; you thirst; your temples throb with thrills of mighty pain; you are threatened with *coup de soleil* [sunstroke], you wish yourself anywhere—anywhere out of such torment.

Pooh, man! you forget that you are a "special," and therefore not supposed to be subject to the laws which govern other mortals. You are a Salamander. You are Braireus. You are Argus. You are Hercules. You are Mark Tapley. Be jolly. Ride your ten, fifteen hours; your twenty, thirty, forty, fifty miles. Fatigue is your normal condition. Sleeplessness ditto. "Tired nature" is yours; the "sweet restorer" somebody else's. "Balmy sleep" is for babies. You are a "special," I tell you.

Incessant riding in the sun is a part of the misery of correspondents.

Composition is pleasant, sometimes. I don't mean the mighty joy of creation of the great author, but the simple pleasure of ordinary mortals writing ordinary things. With dressing-gown elegance, and beslippered ease, a fair prospect out of the window, fragrance stealing through from the garden beneath, tempered by the fragrance of a rich Havana between your lips, a well-ordered desk before you, quill pens, and clear, white paper, a snug bookcase in the corner, a basket of fruit and a bouquet at your elbow, a good dinner in prospect, and a drive at sunset with somebody, your friends to see in the evening, and only a column to write—under such circumstances, "by St. Paul, the work goes bravely on!"

But you are a "special." It is far into the night when you begin. You rode all day and a part of the night, and have only now had your ablution and your supper. You begin,— "squat like a toad" before a camp-fire; a stumpy lead-pencil, and smoke in your eyes, dingy paper, and ashes puffed in your face; no part of you that has not its own special pain and torment. Your brain is in a state of "confusion worse confounded." Your eyes will shut, your pencil will drop from nerveless fingers, but I say unto you, Write! Do you forget that you are a "special," and must write? Force yourself to the rack, tug away, bear on hard, and when you are done, do not read it over, or you will throw it into the fire. Now arrange with the guard to have yourself awakened at daybreak, an hour or two hence, and then lie down, wondering who would n't be a "special."

The necessity of writing just so much every day is a part of the misery of correspondents.

You will inevitably write things that will offend somebody. Somebody will say harsh things of you, and perhaps seek you out to destroy you. Never mind. Such is a part of the misery of correspondents.

Was your horse stolen last night? Are your saddle-bags and all that they contain missing this morning? No matter. It is a thing of course. It is a part of the misery of correspondents.

You are a "special," and who would n't be?

There is news at the front, for I hear great guns; but I am too sick to ride till the sun is lower down the sky. Now, "sweet restorer," now is your time!

3

JAMES CREELMAN:

THE REPORTER WHO CREATED HISTORY

James Creelman had studied the layout of the land long and hard, and he had a plan.

If the troops would attack the fort at El Caney from the right direction, they would be completely concealed from the Spanish enemy by a crease in the hill. Loss of life would be minimal if at all, and the fort would be taken for the glory of a free Cuba. He was sure the strategy would work. He consulted with the soldiers. Captain Walsh agreed that the attack was possible but not advisable because of a shortage of ammunition. Neither was Captain Clark enthusiastic. General Chaffee seemed mildly interested and said he'd mull it over. Finally, Captain Haskell agreed that the battle plans were good. Creelman himself volunteered and was appointed to lead the charge up the hill. As he quietly led the advancing Americans to the trench, he discovered it was already filled with dead and dying Spaniards. Creelman ordered those who were still alive to surrender. They did so calmly. Moments later he burst into the fort and ordered the men there to surrender. They gave up, and Creelman threw their rifles from the fort.

"Suddenly I thought of the flag," Creelman recalled. He meant to fulfill every fighting man's dream—to capture the flag. Even though a bomb had torn the Spanish flag from the fort, Creelman found the banner and waved it high, causing a flurry of gunshots. But the flag was his. The battle was his. The surrender was his. The fort was his. The glory was his.

The irony was that Creelman was not a soldier. He was

a newspaper reporter, writing at that moment for the New York *Journal*. He was living up to his philosophy that "the modern [reporter] is seldom contented unless he feels that he is making history as well as writing it."

To Creelman, who was the talk of the news world in the 1890s, news reporting was far more than mirroring events. It meant creating events, influencing their outcomes, and making sure everything was tied up neatly at the end. Objectivity? Creelman would have laughed. Why be objective when the whole point of newspapers was to stir up society and guide it carefully in the right direction?

Because of such an outlook, Creelman's reports were peppered with his own colorful impressions, analyses, opinions, and actions. Often he was as much a part of his stories as were his characters. As a result, his stories burned with the fire of someone who went beyond mere caring. They were the great works of his life; they meant everything. Each story was, to Creelman, part of a larger good to help society accomplish some great work—at any cost. "The modern newspaper and its thirsty presses take no account of the amenities of life," he said. "It has one supreme law—send the news and send it first. Friendship, home, health, and life itself, if necessary, must be sacrificed in the effort."

Creelman wanted to free Cuba through the Spanish-American War. As he admitted, his boss, William Randolph Hearst, had actually dreamed up and provoked the war, when war otherwise might have not existed. Creelman felt that newspaper involvement in the conflict was vital. He wrote from the battlefield in order to spark the flames of Cuban patriotism and to discredit Spain. In fact, he told readers, his whole point in taking the flag at El Caney was that it ought to be a trophy for his newspaper. He had hopes for a free Cuba, and he wrote toward that end. He had cast Spain as the villain, both with description and editorial-style comment, before America entered the war.

Creelman was not bashful about pointing out the role of both himself and his newspaper in liberating Cuba, smashing evil business rings, or whatever the latest reporting/editorial project was. He and the New York *World* had undertaken a project in early 1896 to bail the United States out of a financial crisis by raising $1 million in gold. The *World* demanded that certain financial interests be demolished. "The President has taken the whole financial question into his own hands, and it is likely that he will follow the suggestion of The *World's* now historic editorial and 'Smash the Ring,'" Creelman told his readers. "The *World's* declaration that the gold syndicate was being organized against the Government under a pretense of coming to the relief of the Treasury is absolutely accurate." Later on in the article Creelman quoted a U.S. senator as praising the newspaper's offer of gold and said that President Grover Cleveland should "heed the advice of the *World*."

Of course, Creelman's praise of the newspaper and of his own work did not exactly make bewitching reading. His comments, though, revealed his deep involvement in his stories, an involvement that often gave his work a haunting quality beyond mere description.

Creelman's descriptions were captivatingly realistic, even sickening. Readers back home read about "a horrible, blood-splashed thing, and an inferno of agony. Many men lay dead, with gleaming teeth, and hands clutching their throats. Others were crawling there alive." Subscribers also read about the death of a defenseless Cuban who screamed, "You won't kill me this way!" but "was shot down and then killed with the machete." His story of the impending battle of Santiago, Cuba, which is included in this anthology, demonstrates his use of vivid, horrid description.

If readers were queasy at such descriptions, that was just what Creelman wanted. He felt it was of the utmost importance to tell things exactly as the troops felt them. To achieve that, he did not allow himself a change of clothes during battle. "For days I never knew what it was to have dry clothes on, so great was my desire to understand clearly the nature of the action that was about to occur," he wrote. In turn, he wanted to pass on such feelings clearly to his readers.

Eventually, Spanish authorities expelled Creelman from Cuba. In a first-person piece for the front page of the New York *World*, he used his characteristic realism and his typical strong opinions to chastise Spanish General Valeriano Weyler for his behavior:

A hundred corpses with bound arms lie within eight miles of your palace....The neighbors of the victims are there to tell you how they were dragged from their homes or their fields by your soldiers and shot on the roadside without trial or accusation.

...Is this your conception of honorable warfare? If so, why try to prevent the world from knowing how your triumphs are accomplished? A soldier should not be ashamed of his deeds.

My offense as *The World* correspondent is that I have refused to print false news issued by the general staff of the Spanish army in Cuba, or to hide the blunders and defects of the Spanish forces in the field. I have told the truth and you know it.

That attitude was present in all his stories, whether he was interviewing the Pope, covering a Japanese massacre in China, or forcing Tolstoy to explain his opinions on marriage. Creelman intended to tell the truth as he saw it. As he told Pope Leo XIII, his only faith was journalism, the truth, letting the public know. Consequently, he felt free to write his journalism "gospel" as he saw it. For instance, commenting on the financial crisis, he said bluntly, "The situation is hopeless. The silver men, who are in control by consent of the Republicans, seem to be without patriotism or common sense. Their methods are the methods of blackmailers." Furthermore, Creelman sized up President Cleveland as a loser in the matter. "The President knows little of the principles of finance, and is doubly handicapped by his obstinate self-confidence," Creelman wrote. "This being the case, the keen New York bankers prey upon his ignorance and upon his assumption of knowledge with disastrous results to the Treasury."

Creelman did not hesitate to speculate in his stories. To him, feelings were just as concrete as blood-covered men and ought to be reported. Conversely, he used ordinary episodes as a means to provide broad perspective as he perceived it.

It was not that Creelman was an egomaniac about his own point of view. Instead, he seemed to feel that rational readers in the same situation would have the same reaction that he did. Although he did not see another side to the story, he did see the news as he thought his readers ought to see it. For instance, in a story describing the nightmarish ruin of Port Arthur, China, he did not give the Japanese reasons for the attack. Rather, he explained actions from an opposing perspective. It was as though he realized that no report could be completely divorced from the writer's point of view. He accepted his own point of view and told the story from that angle:

> The Japanese troops entered Port Arthur on November 21 and massacred practically the entire population in cold blood.
>
> The defenseless and unarmed inhabitants were butchered in their houses, and their bodies were unspeakably mutilated. There was an unrestrained reign of murder which continued for three days. The whole town was plundered with appalling atrocities.
>
> It was the first stain upon Japanese civilization. The Japanese in this instance relapsed into barbarism.
>
> All pretense that circumstances justified the atrocities are false. The civilized world will be horrified by the details.
>
> The foreign correspondents, horrified by the spectacle, left the army in a body.

The use of his own point of view had great power. As officials would later do in Cuba, the Japanese officials tried to suppress Creelman's reports. His brutal honesty was doing too much, in the government's view, to stir up Americans. His countrymen immediately became antagonistic to Japan after his report. The United States halted a treaty with Japan. Japanese officials went so far as to offer Creelman a bribe to keep his story out of the papers.

Creelman, however, would not be stopped. He went forth to shape history by telling his version of the truth. He gave his analysis, his opinion, in hard-hitting, carefully calculated words. "Everywhere we saw bodies torn and mangled, as if by wild beasts," he later wrote of the Port Arthur massacre. "Dogs were whimpering over the frozen corpses of their masters. The victims were mostly shopkeepers. Nowhere the trace of a weapon, nowhere a sign of resistance. It was a sight that would damn the fairest nation on earth."

Likewise, Creelman would not be bridled a few years later in Cuba. As he was being expelled from the island, he filed a report from Tampa. It amounted to a battle cry for

American intervention:

> Out of this red, blazing whirlwind of battle and murder there rises a strong, insistent cry for the intervention of some power that can force peace and prevent Cuba from being utterly destroyed.
>
> Spain has lost control of this land. Gen. Weyler's campaign is a failure. His boasted trocha is a grave eighteen miles long that will presently be filled with brave Spanish soldiers when the rains fall and fever stalks from camp to camp. His toy forts, ditches and barbed-wire fences are a mockery of war.

Although Weyler expelled Creelman as a correspondent for the *World*, that didn't stop the reporter from returning to Cuba as a correspondent for the New York *Journal*. In that job, he decided he would lead the charge to El Caney for a good story and capture the flag of the fort in the name of his newspaper.

True to his declaration that a newsman should be prepared to give his life for his job, Creelman nearly did that after the El Caney raid. He was shot in the arm. As he later recalled, his delirious thoughts as he writhed in pain were, "Copy! copy! an hour to spare before the paper goes to press!"

He managed to dictate his story to William Randolph Hearst, who, like Creelman, had a belief that a newspaper should shape history, not just report it. Hearst was risking his life, too, on the battlefield. He got Creelman's story out of him and wired it to New York. "I'm sorry you're hurt," Hearst bubbled to his star reporter, "but wasn't it a splendid fight?"

●◆

POLITICAL UNDERCURRENTS
CHILL WHITE HOUSE GALA

On New Year's Day, 1896, President and Mrs. Grover Cleveland hosted a reception at the White House for various Washington dignitaries.

The gala could have made a run-of-the-mill feature

story. But Creelman wanted his story to be more. He wanted to put the event into its proper context. The reception was a glittering social event, but it had strong political undercurrents. Creelman deftly described both. Not only did he keenly observe what was visible to the eye, but he also observed what was visible only to the intuition. The result was a story rich in color and characters and brimming with political speculation.

WHITE HOUSE AGLOW
James Creelman
New York *World*
January 2, 1896

WASHINGTON, JAN. 1.—Mr. Cleveland looked careworn as he took his place in the famous blue room this morning with the sweet-faced mistress of the White House at his right hand, the grim countenances of Secretaries Olney and Carlisle peering over his shoulders and a glittering pageant of diplomats waiting at the door for the signal to enter—glorious and gorgeous beyond words to describe, blue and scarlet, steel and gold, cross and star, strange, picturesque and mediaeval.

The big, strong, square-toed President seemed out of place in the presence of this dazzling flummery. And yet his tremendous and aggressive personality dominated the room. A stranger would have picked him out at once as the master of the place. Every civilized nation of any consequence had a representative there to wish him a happy new year, but it is no secret that the President looks forward to the most embarrassing year of his life, with pits dug on every side for his feet, a year full of dangers and difficulties, largely of his own making.

It was a scene of rare beauty. Stretching across the room beyond the President were the ladies of the Cabinet, and behind this line of glimmering silk and smiling faces were marshalled the feminine friends of the White House, the Cabinet officers and Vice-President Stevenson. Great palm branches arched overhead, the sparkling crystal chandeliers were draped with tender green vines, and the faint breath of flowers filled the air.

But in spite of it all there was not a member of the Government who looked as if he were in a mood for play. Politically speaking, the White House is not a place of pleasure just now. There are elements of loneliness evident.

While the President squared himself on his heels and the ladies grouped themselves according to the order to precedence, regardless of height or breadth or barbaric rivalry of color, the great multitude was assembling in front of the grounds in preparation for the general handshaking. Within the gates was a huge semi-circle of official carriages backed up on the curving path like a black border on a gigantic green fan fringed with horses' heads. Policemen scurried hither and thither. Detectives prowled about the place. The Marine band made the air dance with the music of all nations.

A Happy New Year—with the President urging the country to war against its peaceful inclinations; with silver Senators damning the financial credit of the country and blocking the path to relief in the hope of levying blackmail upon Congress; with the Government's financial policy immersed in a fog of mystery and a handful of New York bankers conspiring to bleed the Treasury; with confusion, division and muddle-headedness rampant in the Capitol. A Happy New Year!

Sir Julian Pauncefote, tall, ponderous, gleaming with gold and the scarlet sash of the Order of the Bath slanting across his massive bosom, was the first to greet the President. The British Ambassador towered up, the incarnation of bland courtesy. His strong, grave face is the window of an alert and self-confident mind. As he grasped the hand of the President and smilingly wished him joy, with one hand resting lightly on the gilded hilt of his harmless sword, it was hard to believe that this was the representative of the nation for whose blood the President thirsts. Mr. Cleveland beamed, and retained the stalwart diplomat's hand in his own for a minute, looking straight in his eyes. Then Sir Julian, with a bow, retreated three paces and stood opposite to the President, for it was his duty, as Dean of the diplomatic Corps, to formally present his colleagues.

Strangely enough, the next man to enter was Señor De Lome, effulgent in gold lace and brimming over with smiles, the uneasy agent of another nation with whom the

United States has grave matters to settle. It was easy to see that the searching glance which the Spanish Minister cast at Mr. Cleveland was the indication of an inquiring and not-too-confident spirit. Would the President recognize the Cuban rebels? The President's face is not an easy book to read. He smiled down upon Señor De Lome as he had smiled up at Sir Julian Pauncefote. A gentle genuflexion, and the keen Spaniard passed on to the ladies. Lady Pauncefote looked at her husband and smiled.

Then along came the Turkish Minister, with a curved sword clinging at his side and the green sash of Islam crossing his rotund person. Another agent with a bright, inquisitive eye. There is trouble in store for Turkey, too. But Mavroyeni Bey smiled, as Sir Julian had smiled, and as Señor De Lome had smiled, and swept down the line of ladies, bowing and whispering glibly like a true little Oriental diplomat.

So the bright procession passed on, with rattling swords and flashing orders, plumes, ribbons, quaint jewels and the strangest medley of queer coats and baggy trousers, blue bodies and red legs, green bodies and white legs. Now came the Chinese Minister, Yang Yu, many-colored and tripping along in stilt shoes; by his side the daintiest little Chinese lady the sun ever shone upon, with a wonderful silk robe hiding her little feet, a fantastic headdress rising above her dainty face, and on the summit of it a sort of roof adorned with...curious shining jimcracks from the far-away East. And presently Mr. Kurino, the Japanese Minister, short, swart and swelling with the pride that fills the souls of all true sons of Dai Nippon in this year of victory. Anon Pak Yung Hyo, representing poor, gentle, foolish, down-trodden Korea, the victim of all nations. Then came Germans, Frenchmen, Italians, Russians, Mexicans, Brazilians, Australians, Danes and Portuguese, phalanxes of South American plenipotentiaries, envoys from islands in the sea, all gilded and embroidered to the very heels.

The President's arm worked with the regularity of a piston-rod. Mrs. Cleveland was radiant. There is a charm about this lovely woman that never fails her, and she seemed to enchant the atmosphere around her.

The dazzling train moved on its path into smaller chambers on its way to the great East Room, and here the diplomats saw the most marvellous sight of all—a double rank of daintily costumed women with notebooks and pencils, the newspaper women of Washington. There must have been a hundred of them. And there was not one among their high mightinesses who did not stop and shake hands with some writer.

Next came the Justices of the Supreme Court, some with gray hair and some with white and some without any hair at all. Chief Justice Fuller halted at the head of the line and presented his colleagues. The most remarkable in this group was Chief Justice Brewer, who, it is said, will serve on the commission to decide whether we shall go to war with Great Britain.

Hardly had the hoary tributes passed the President before the officers of the army and navy marched into the White House, two by two, headed by Gen. Miles, the handsomest man in the army, and...an undulating stream of blue and gold and good-looking, manly faces, adorned with hair of every color, kind, length and shape imaginable, for there is not much uniformity in such matters in the American army. The procession halted for a moment before entering the reception room, and the officers shivered, for they had been waiting in the cold for a long while.

High up on the dim staircase leading to the President's private apartments sat little Ruth Cleveland and her doll, surrounded by a group of children, the little Carlisles, the little Lamonts and other little greatnesses of the upper realms of governmentalism. It was a pretty sight to see the children stare and clap their hands as the brilliant cortege of warriors trod the carpeted corridor on their way to the tired and unhappy Commander-in-Chief.

Old Gen. Van Vleet, snowy-headed and rosy, the father of the retired list and the champion diner of Washington, was so excited by the scene that he allowed one of his huge epaulets to fall in the presence of the President, carrying it in his hand.

While the military stretched across the corridor, the British Ambassador hurried along. He had drawn his sword from his belt and was carrying it in his hand like a cane. Without a moment's hesitation he plunged through the line laughingly.

Next came the officers of the Navy, with still more massive epaulets, more gold, more muscle, more dash. After them filed the Grand Army of the Republic. Then Dr. Talmage, the hero of the moment. But when the glitter and glare of officialdom had vanished from the line, when the Senators and the Representatives had shaken the President's hand, there came thousands of the plain people, shuffling in black coats, with their hats posed daintily in their left hands, each one imitating the man in front of him; and finally the doors were shut, the band played one last terrific fanfare, and the President went back to his babies.

◆

AMERICAN SOLDIERS CONFRONT TROPICAL ELEMENTS OF CUBA

After Creelman returned to Cuba as a reporter for the New York *Journal*, he essentially became a soldier. Although he was not in the Army, he traveled with it. He saw the same sights that the soldiers did. He marched with them. Ultimately he would lead a charge and capture a fort and its flag.

He wrote the following piece while on the road with American soldiers. He filled it with haunting descriptions of the harsh Cuban landscape and the hardships the Americans endured. He also saw heroism in the men and duly recorded it. Having helped persuade America to join the war, he wanted to do his part to applaud the American presence in Cuba.

AMERICAN TROOPS PREPARE FOR BATTLE IN CUBA
James Creelman
New York *Journal*
July 1, 1898

WHEELER'S HEADQUATERS AT THE FRONT, JUNE 28, BY THE *Journal's* DISPATCH BOAT Simpson TO KINGSTON, JUNE 30—We are almost ready for the last dread scene of agony on the intrenched green slopes that guard the doomed Santiago.

Two barriers of barbed wire surround the city on the land side, with six heavily guarded openings. The American army is gradually stretching out across the hills on the eastern side of Santiago, within five miles of the cannon-crowded hillside which must be taken before the city can be captured.

No man who has not gone over this trail, no man who was not in the terrible downpour of rain which drenched our army to the skin this afternoon, can understand the suffering of our troops and the heroism with which they bore it.

Cavalrymen dismounted; infantrymen from Colorado, Michigan, and Massachusetts toiled hour after hour through jungles of cactus, poisonous vines, and high grass that cuts like razor edges.

The blistering tropic sunlight makes the skyline of distant hills shimmy and waver prismatically before the eyes. From the stagnant pools strange gray mists float upward, and vultures with outstretched wings look greedily down from above vegetation torn and trampled underfoot by our troops.

A horribly sour breath rises from the earth. Curious stenches steal from hidden places in the jungle.

Thousands of gigantic land crabs, splotched with yellow and red, wriggle and twist themselves along the sides of the roads with leprous white claws clicking viciously—a ghastly, dreadful sight to young soldiers fresh from New York, Boston, and Detroit.

Ragged Cubans skip noiselessly through the undergrowth or sprawl under the shade of huge gossamer trees, watching with childish pleasure the steady on-push of their American defenders.

The heat is almost intolerable. The sun is like a great yellow furnace torturing everything living and turning everything dead into a thousand mysterious forms of terror.

A fierce light swims in waves before the eyes of the exhausted soldiers. This morning a young infantryman reeled and fell in the road almost under my mule's feet. When I helped him to his feet he smiled and said:

"It's all right. I never struck such a place as this, but I must get to the front before the fight begins. I had to lie to get into the army, for I am only seventeen years old."

Five minutes later he was trudging along gallantly.

Two hours later the first great tropical rainstorm we encountered fell from the sky, not slantwise, but straight down. It was the first actual test of the army in the most dreadful experience of the tropics. For three hours the great, cold torrent swept down from the clouds, drenching the soldiers to the skin, soaking their blankets and carrying misery into all our vast camps reaching out on either side of the trail, extinguishing campfires and sending rivers of mud-red water swirling along the narrow road, dashing over rocks where the trail inclined downward. Through this filthy flood our army streamed onward, splashing in the mud and water or huddling vainly for shelter under trees.

An hour before, the heat was so great that men reeled and swooned, but now came one of the mysterious transitions of the tropics.

The whole army shivered. As I rode along I could see robust men shaking from head to foot, their skins turned gray and white. Millions of land crabs came chattering and squirming from under poisonous undergrowth, and the soldiers crushed them under their heels.

Every man who had quinine swallowed a dose. Officers, splashed with mud to their hips, hurried here and there, urging the men to strip naked when the rain was over and dry their clothes at the campfires.

Presently thousands of men were standing about naked, while the sun drew up the thick vapors from the earth and vicious tropical flies stung their white skins.

One thought which seemed to run like an electric current through the army was anxiety to get to the front.

Soldiers everywhere begged to have their regiments put in the first line of attack. The weather is nothing to them. The possibility of disease is nothing to them. Exposure and hunger do not trouble them. You can see it in their faces. You can hear it in their talk.

The most wonderful thing is that, in spite of the surroundings, less than one per cent of the army is sick. This, I believe, is the lowest death record of any army in the world.

I saw a touching scene during the great storm today. While the giant gusts of rain were beating down on the earth, groups of soldiers stood unsheltered around the graves of Rough Riders on the little trail where they died so heroically. There may be a monument erected to these men, but there can never be a nobler tribute than this.

As the poor fellows pressed around Hamilton Fish's grave, the rain cataracted from their hat rims and ran in little rivulets over the mound.

4

DAVID GRAHAM PHILLIPS

A DANDY KNIGHT IN QUEST OF TRUTH

At the beginning of the twentieth century, several journalists turned their talents toward fiction. Of them, few had the single-mindedness of purpose that David Graham Phillips had. He had set his mind to writing fiction from the beginning of his journalistic career.

He knew from the time he was in college at Princeton that in order to write realistic fiction, he had to observe people in every walk of life. The best place for this experience was in the newspaper business. With that in mind, he took advantage of his friendship with the sons of publisher Murat Halstead and got a job with the Cincinnati *Times-Star*. Phillips was lucky; although he had few friends, the ones he had, proved to be profitable. They included not only the Halstead brothers, but later Joseph Pulitzer and William Randolph Hearst.

Although one friend claimed that Phillips was a born writer, he learned about journalism by first observing the work at the *Times-Star* beginning in 1887. His first editor, James A. Green, initially was suspicious of the college man who dressed well and smoked incessantly. He did not give Phillips an assignment for several weeks. Later Green said, "As I remember, David Graham wrote a legible hand and he was able to turn out copy rapidly. This I do remember. He had the ability to fill any space that was demanded, a column if you wanted that, or a stickful if that was all that was needed....Everything he did he did well. And he did it with joy. He flung his whole heart into his work, brilliantly and yet laboriously."

Soon Phillips was wooed to the Cincinnati *Commercial-Gazette*. His reputation increased, and he expressed his desire to become a foreign correspondent on a New York daily. He tried to cover as many political events as possible and spent long hours at the newspaper. He developed his observation of human events and what one source called his "larger view." He wrote not only news but also what was to become his forté—feature articles. He took news events and then expanded and personalized them, going beyond the story to the real causes and effects. He stored these personal vignettes in his memory for future use as a novelist.

At the *Commercial-Gazette*, he wrote columns as well, including a famous one about shaking hands that read:

> Start out in the morning some time and notice the different hands you will shake in the course of the day. Broad, flat hands; tough, calloused hands; hairy hands and smooth ones; white, black, brown, gray, yellow, red, blue and even green hands; hands that clutch you like a drowning man clutches at a straw; and again little white gloved hands that rest in yours for a moment and then are taken away, drawing your heart with them.

Versatile and prolific, Phillips also wrote editorials and a special editorial column entitled "Lagniappe." It was short, pithy, and immensely popular. Critics said he had "a glib flair for the timely and the 'human interest.'" He also wrote a gossip column, "Notes About Town." It featured humorous, yet thought-provoking sayings. The most famous was "A bank is a great place for taking cold—so many drafts passing through all the time."

Although his writing was popular, Phillips was not. He had few friends. Even though people enjoyed listening to him talk at parties and other social functions, he was aloof, always observing people around him. A dandy, he dressed in the latest fashion. Although he was from an affluent family, wealthy people had the impression that he mocked them. They were right, as he was later to prove.

One friend said that he had "a type of secretiveness, especially about his own affairs, purposes, and hopes....He outlined his plans and purposes thus: He intended to get all he could out of newspaper work, not as an end in itself, but as a training in the study of men and social conditions. When he had gotten all the understanding of that sort which newspaper life could give him, he would then make a big name for himself as a writer of books, that is, novels with a purpose, a purpose not solely or even with the major object of making money, but with the intent to shed a lot of light on certain phases of the national life, which as he then admitted, he did not know much about, but which he intended to know a lot about as a basis for his books."

In 1890, Phillips joined the staff at the New York *Sun*. There he further developed his philosophy of journalism: "a call which demanded the sharpening of all the faculties; the service of truth and right and human betterment, in daily combat with injustice and error and falsehood; the arousing and stimulation of the drowsy minds of the masses of mankind." Phillips had a passion for Truth. He later took this passion into his work as a reformer, transferring the truth he had learned about politicians, insurance companies, and the role of women in society into stories that helped to change the social order.

The story that made him stand out in New York was about a three-year-old boy, Dayton Weaver, who was lost in the Catskills. Phillips wrote the news story like a work of fiction. He explored the father's sense of duty, the mother's helplessness and guilt, the swamp and the way the sun penetrated through the woods, and the special relationship between the boy and his dog. The story is included in this anthology. With it, Phillips established his reputation as a journalist.

He continued to write for the *Sun*, storing images for use in his novels. "He developed a vivid, striking style," said one critic, "and likewise a great facility for putting life and color into what he wrote." He also began to write magazine pieces while at the *Sun*. His first was for *Harper's Weekly*, entitled "The Rescue of the Jeansville Miners." It was originally a newspaper assignment and, as usual, provided the stuff of fiction.

Phillips developed an amazing capacity for hard work. He would leave the *Sun* about midnight, go home, and write other pieces until dawn. Writing all night was a practice he would continue in his fiction-writing days.

In the spring of 1893, he met Joseph Pulitzer, publisher of the *Sun*'s rival New York *World*. Pulitzer was impressed with Phillips from their first meeting and said the magic words to the young reporter: "How would you like to go to London as a correspondent of the *World*?" Phillips answered, "Nothing could suit me better."

One of Phillips' lifelong dreams was finally fulfilled. However, his work at the *World*, although often spectacular, was stymied by Pulitzer's fiery temperament and inconsistent behavior. Although Pulitzer said several times that he was grooming Phillips for a higher position, he often limited Phillips' coverage and pulled or edited stories that did not suit his emotions or ambitions at the moment. Furthermore, Pulitzer did not allow his reporters to write "outside stories."

Foreign correspondents were not given bylines; so most of Phillips' London work is not known. One story that did earn a "D.G.P." was about the sinking of the British warship *Victoria*, with the loss of 400 men, in a collision with the *Camperdown* during maneuvers in Tripoli in 1893. Phillips was the only correspondent to recognize the importance of the disaster, and London papers were forced to reprint the *World*'s account.

During this time, Phillips wrote to a friend about preparing oneself for newspaper work. His advice is still timely:

> I should say that a man needs, first of all, the best education a college can give him; and by that I do not mean a profound knowledge of the contents of a few books, but rather a broad and intelligent insight into all kinds of learning. He must have read widely—history, novels, essays, poetry, these of the best, and I might say everything that the great writers have written. This would not mean any more reading than one should do in the leisure of a college course.
>
> Then in his essay work he should try to get at short, clear and simple words, expressions of actual thought—short words, Anglo-Saxon words, words that the laboring man and humble people will not stumble over.
>
> I should say that a man should learn to be simple, natural, and absolutely unaffected in his intercourse with his fellowmen—learn to judge men and things fairly, charitably and without considering what other people think of

them.

The newspaper business today is not what it was a few years ago. Its tending is toward higher requirements. Nor is it a business in the ordinary sense of the word. It will require necessarily each year a man who knows a great deal about many subjects, who can turn his mind to many phases of life, can change his style to suit each phase. These things do not require genius—they do require education and aptitude.

As in all other occupations, men without any qualifications appear to succeed. There are liars and frauds as elsewhere—and ignoble men. But the real and satisfactory results come, I think, to the man I have outlined. Summary—wide reading, knowledge and use of simple words, unaffectedness of mind and manner.

In 1897, Phillips returned to New York to write editorials for Pulitzer. He was Pulitzer's special pet. Not knowing that Phillips planned to leave newspaper work for novel writing, Pulitzer continued to groom him for an editorship. Pulitzer's brand of journalism—exposés of political corruption and crusades against social wrongs—appealed to Phillips' sense of seeking the truth. It was fodder for his novels. Indeed, Pulitzer was thought to be the inspiration for the main character of Phillips' first novel, *The Great God Success*, written in 1901. The following year, Phillips left the *World* and became a free-lance writer, finally giving himself more time to write novels. In the next nine years he churned out more than twenty novels and wrote hundreds of magazine articles.

The most famous was the series "The Treason of the Senate," published in *Cosmopolitan* in 1906. It was Phillips' journalistic masterpiece, earning him the title "muckraker." Although Theodore Roosevelt, who coined the word, meant it to be pejorative, Phillips and his fellow muckrakers wore it like a badge. For Phillips, it was a point of honor. He was writing the Truth. He wanted change. Old moralities would have to broken down and replaced with new ones.

Phillips wrote with an eloquence that caught the attention of the people in power. His "Treason" series was one of the great achievements of muckraking. At that time the Senate was elected by state legislators, not the populace. Often, powerful figures in the various states held senators in their pockets. Corruption was rampant, but many felt the Senate was above reproach. Only Phillips had the boldness and the ability to write a full-scale indictment of this elite group.

The editor of *Cosmopolitan*, Bailey Millard, said that only Phillips "could indict the Senate. What writer had the power, as well as the courage, to limn the Senators and recount the outrages they had perpetrated, in such form as to win that writer the support of the public?" The answer, of course, was David Graham Phillips.

Billboards in Washington publicized the series. Hearst wrote an introduction saying that no one was to be spared. Several newspapers requested reprints before the stories came out. The senators became nervous. In March 1906, the series appeared. Magazine stands were emptied of copies, and hundreds of readers begged for more issues and subscriptions. *Cosmopolitan's* circulation increased from 300,000 to 450,000.

The articles presented fact after fact, gradually bringing in senator after senator in a web of conspiracy of deliberate corruption. One source said that Phillips "prepared a veritable storehouse of facts, as well as living descriptions of Senators and their careers, which was long to serve as an arsenal for reformers throughout the West." Horace Lorimer, editor of *Saturday Evening Post*, said after the "Treason" series came out: "Some of Phillips' friends are saying of him that he has a 'message' to deliver, and that is pretty tough, for when an author gets an idea he has a message to deliver, usually he finds the wires are crossed. Phillips is sane and level-headed—barring a tendency now and then to enthusiasms that have not so many piles driven under them as would be well—and it is quite likely that he will get over the message business and will continue as a novelist." One reader wrote in a letter to the magazine: "Glory Hallelujah! You have found a David who is able and willing to attack this Goliath of a Senate."

Phillips was criticized also. Partisan newspapers denounced him. He received threatening letters; and the Senate castigated him. After ten of the articles, Phillips became so discouraged by the attacks that he quit writing them.

Nevertheless, after "Treason" there was freer discussion of the Senate and of the House of Representatives as well. Several Congressmen were unseated in the next elections, and by 1912 the composition of the Senate had changed. In 1913 the U.S. Constitution was amended to provide that senators be elected directly by the people, not the state legislators.

Phillips continued his muckraking, exploring not only the practices of businessmen and politicians, but also the role of women in society. He felt that most social ills were due to the inferior position of women and that in order for those ills to be cured, the role of women would have to be changed. His literary masterpiece, *Susan Lenox*, was about a woman forced into prostitution. Some of his novels shocked his readers, but he continued to write them, because he believed in "popular education" through books and magazines.

In 1911, he was shot and killed by a manic-depressive who thought that one of his novels, *The Fashionable Adventures of Joshua Craig*, was about him and his family.

◆

THE DRAMATIC STORY OF A LITTLE BOY LOST

One morning in 1890 three-year-old Dayton Weaver wandered from home with his dog and became lost. Phillips had written other features about children with a dramatic touch and was assigned to this story. In a simple, straightforward narrative, he introduced the boy and his dog, his mother, and his father. As the story developed, all became real, multidimensional characters, rather than cardboard news subjects. Through them Phillips built tension as he unfolded the story of Dayton's fondness for his dog, the parents' first discovery that their son was lost, and the long search to find him. The story made Phillips a star on the New York *Sun*, the newspaper that was regarded as the epitome of excellent journalistic writing.

LOST BABY FOUND
David Graham Phillips
New York *Sun*
1890

George Weaver, a spinner in the knitting mill of William Harder, lives in Greenport Township, about two miles from here. His is a shabby, small house, 100 feet from the road, and but a few hundred yards from the wild, rough and tangled forests of the "mountains," as the more heavily rolling upland of this region is called. He has a wife and two children. The younger child is a six weeks' baby. The older is a boy, born on August 15, 1887, and therefore three years old. His name is Dayton Weaver. Until six weeks ago he was the only child in the family, and as there were no children in the neighborhood, his life was lonely. So when a boy down the road offered Mr. Weaver a mongrel puppy, three months ago, Mr. Weaver accepted the offer, because he thought it would be a companion for his child. The dog was called Frank and soon became thoroughly domesticated at Weaver's

The little boy was always fond of animals and before long made Frank his inseparable companion. As soon as he would get up in the morning he would ask for Frank, and he would not go to sleep unless the dog was near him. Frank was not very pretty to look at, plainly betraying his base origin and having a low look about his black, hanging ears and pinkish white muzzle. The short hair on his body was white, except a large black spot on his back, near the root of his tail, and a few smaller spots scattered among his ribs. But he made up in affection what he lacked in beauty. As for Dayton, he was a handsome boy, not so handsome as a year ago, when he had long, golden curls, but still a comely tow-headed child with big hazel eyes and a mouth that was always laughing, to show some white, even teeth.

He and the dog played in the open air all summer; and Dayton was, therefore, tanned in the face, while his chubby legs were burned quite brown. There never was a better natured child or one less given to weeping. Having been so long alone, he had learned to amuse himself. Early in the summer he began to make long trips of exploration and discovery. Frank, of course, was always with him. These trips were toward the cultivated and settled parts of the country; and after a few hours, some neighbor would bring him back. Since the birth of the baby, Mrs. Weaver has not been able to look after him closely. Last Saturday Dayton and Frank disappeared in the morning.

At noon Lawyer William Brownell, living a mile from the Weavers, found the boy and the dog fast asleep on a pile of hay in his barn-yard. The boy had watched and talked to the chickens that went clucking and chirping about. Then he fell asleep. His arm was about the dog's neck, and one of the dog's big drooping ears shielded his eyes from the light.

Tuesday morning was clear and bright. Frank was up early, playing about the yard. Dayton's mother partly dressed him at seven o'clock and then gave him his breakfast. He was still trying to swallow the last mouthful when he left the table and ran out to see Frank. He was bareheaded and barefooted.

Mrs. Weaver was clearing away the breakfast table when she saw from the kitchen window the boy and the dog down at the fence along the front of the lot. "Dayton!" she called. Dayton did not answer. Generally he replies to this call with "Here I be, mamma!" But when his brain is busy with the plan for a tour of exploration, he refrains from answering. Mrs. Weaver knows this, and when she called again she added a threat of punishment. Just then there was a wild wail of rage and hunger from the crib, and Mrs. Weaver had no further time to talk to Dayton.

At ten o'clock she thought of him again, but he was nowhere to be seen. She started out in search of him, but gave it up at noon and decided to wait until one of the neighbors brought him back. The afternoon wore on, but Dayton and his dog did not return. The sky clouded, and at five o'clock a heavy rain began to fall. Mrs. Weaver was alone in the house and, although frantic with anxiety, could do nothing until her husband returned. He came at eight o'clock and at once started in search of the missing boy. He inquired at every house within a radius of half a mile, but no one had seen Dayton or Frank. The night was perfectly dark, and the rain was falling in torrents. At eleven o'clock Mr. Weaver returned and began to upbraid his wife. After a while he went to bed. She sat all night by the window, sleepless and without weeping.

In the gray of the morning she awoke her husband, and he started forth. The rain was still falling as it had fallen all night. The roads were miry and half covered with water. All the creeks and brooks were swollen beyond their banks. Mr. Weaver went to the mill and told Mr. Harder that the boy was lost. Mr. Harder at once shut down the mill and started thirty-five men out with Weaver. They were joined by a number of men from the neighborhood. All day Wednesday and until far into the night they scoured the country around, but found no trace of boy or dog. Stories of bands of gypsies were soon afloat, and wild rumors of all kinds. But no band of gypsies could be found or traced reliably, and no rumor developed anything....

Among those who started out, partly to search and partly to hunt, were Fred Coons, son of the grocer of Greenport, and his friend, Giles D. Van Deusen, an electrician, living at No. 705 Gates Avenue, Brooklyn. They separated from the hundred or more who were searching Jones' back mountain. They went to Newman's woods, two miles from Weaver's. They searched through Newman's and then began to look into the dense and tangled swamp woods belonging to Mr. Delamatyr. There is not a wilder or more untrodden place about Hudson. The light scarcely penetrates the foliage even on a bright day. The ground is rough and sometimes precipitous, closely covered with brush and trailing vines. Van Deusen and Coons had penetrated some distance into this forest and came to the edge of a swamp surrounded by cedars. They were now three miles from Weaver's house.

"Let's look in here," said Van Deusen.

He handed Coons his gun and began to make his way through the edge of the swamp. All at once he stopped in astonishment. There was a clear bit of firm ground a few yards in front of him. In the midst of it was a cedar tree. Under the tree, seated upon the ground, was the lost boy. His bare, brown legs, torn and bleeding, were stretched straight in front of him. His bare feet were bruised and cut. His brown gingham apron was wet and dirty, as was also the blue gingham dress under it. His hands were torn and smeared with blood. He was quietly sitting there playing with a tin can. He had put a stone in it and was making a great rattling. Frank, the dog, was running to and fro about him, seemingly enjoying the noise. The boy's face was tear-stained, and his eyes were swollen. But he was not crying then, and there was a little laughter lurking in his face, which was thin and hollow and flushed with fever. His head was bare and his hair was badly mussed.

Van Deusen was astonished at this scene when he, with everybody else, supposed that the boy was dead after three days and nights of exposure to rain and cold. He went toward the child. The pup ran at him savagely and began to bark and snap. But the boy looked at him with frank, questioning eyes, and said:

"Want mamma. I'se hungry."

Van Deusen picked up this prodigy of endurance. The gingham apron and dress were soaked through and through.

"You're hungry?" he inquired.

"'Ess. An' I'se wet. It wained an' wained." Then the child began to sob a little and said, "It was dark and cold. I want mamma."

But he soon stopped crying and began to shiver and shake as though cold. The child has always made friends with strangers easily. He was soon at home with the man in shooting clothes, who assured him that he was being taken to his mother. Dayton gave a sigh of relief as they came from the damp, dark forest into the clear sunlight of the afternoon.

Mrs. Weaver's face had not changed as she watched the parties go out to search for her baby boy. Crowds of men stood in the door and stared curiously at her or asked to see the picture, which was the only one she had. Finally she was left with the baby and with a neighbor, Mrs. Kesselburgh. It was well on toward three o'clock. Mrs. Kesselburgh walked to the kitchen door and stood there looking down the road. Suddenly she screamed. Then she said:

"My God! There's Dayton."

The mother was out of the door at a bound. Yes, there was Dayton, in the arms of the man in shooting clothes. Frank was trotting wearily behind.

"Dayton! Dayton!" she called.

The baby boy turned his head quickly and then stretched out his arms. By this time Mrs. Weaver was at the gate, laughing, screaming, crying. The man quickened his pace, and soon the boy was with his mother, safe again after enduring hunger and cold and rain and dampness and fatigue that few grown men would care to risk. His first words were:

"Hungry, mamma!" and then he began to cry softly.

●◆

PHILLIPS MUCKRAKES THE U.S. SENATE

In the first two installments of "The Treason of the Senate," Phillips introduced to the readers the chief wrongdoer in the Senate, Chauncey Depew of New York. He also pointed out the corruption of the ringleader of these senators, Nelson Aldrich of Rhode Island, the "monster." In the third installment, reprinted here, Phillips continued to draw in other senators of both parties who had misled the people of the United States, pinpointing the Democratic Senate leader. Notice how Phillips used clear logic and presentation of a mass of facts to implicate Sen. Arthur Gorman and other corrupt senators.

THE TREASON OF THE SENATE
CHAPTER III
LEFT ARM OF THE MONSTER
David Graham Phillips
Cosmopolitan Magazine
March - December, 1906

We have now seen,

First: That there has been in the past quarter of a century an amazing and unnatural up-piling of wealth in the hands of a few; that there has been an equally amazing unnatural descent of the masses, despite skill and industry and the boundless resources of the country, toward the dependence of wages and salaries; that the massing of wealth and the diffusion of dependence are both swiftly increasing.

Second: That these abnormal conditions have come with, and out of, the development of a small group of controllers of railways and, through them, of finance and manufactures; that this little group controls and freely levies upon and trims the twenty thousand millions of our annual internal commerce, three-fourths of which is interstate and therefore subject to the supervision of Congress only.

Third: That this little group owes its power and its wealth, in part to legislation favoring it, but in the main to the failure of Congress to safeguard the people in the possession of the fruits of their labor by enacting the laws in regulation of interstate commerce which the public welfare has clearly demanded and which the Constitution clearly authorizes.

Fourth: That the responsibility both for legislation in favor of "the interests" and for failure to legislate in restraint upon their depredations rests wholly and directly upon the United States Senate.

Fifth: That as the Senate's legislation for "the interests" and its failure to legislate against them have not been frank and open, but tricky, stealthy and underhanded, the Senate cannot plead in its own defense either ignorance or honest motives; that its conduct has been and is deliberate, has been and is an intentional betrayal of the people, has been and is treason.

Sixth: That the right arm of this treason has been and is Senator [Nelson] Aldrich.

But the monster has a left arm, also. And the left arm, almost as powerful and quite as useful as the right, is Arthur P. Gorman, of Maryland.

The common enemy, "the interests," dominate the political as well as the industrial machinery of the nation. In the political machinery of both parties they have at the important points faithful, well-paid agents, shrewd at fooling the people or at selecting those who can fool the people. Their control of state legislatures is such that they determine nearly three-fourths of the senators. Whoever may be, "for appearance's sake," in charge of the Republican machine, Aldrich is really in charge. Whoever may be nominally at the head of the Democratic machine, Gorman is really there. For only to men approved by them or their lieutenants will "the interests" supply the "oil" indispensable to a machine. Popular movements and heroes and spasms of reform rage and pass; but the machine abides, and after the storm it resumes; indeed, it works exceeding well even through the roughest cyclones. To our national political machine, with its label that reads "Republican" on the one side and "Democratic" on the other, Aldrich and Gorman are as the thumb and forefinger to a skillful hand.

Gorman was born in Maryland sixty-seven years ago. After a few years at public school, he, at the age of thirteen, entered politics; his father, a contractor and lobbyist in a small way, got him a place as page in the United States Senate. This is the way, as in 1852, when the slave oligarchy, then in the heyday of its haughtiness, was using the same methods of sophistries about alleged "constitutional law" and alleged jealousy for the "grand old Constitution," that the industrial oligarchy is using in this heyday of its haughtiness. The slave oligarchy, to maintain and strengthen itself, was strenuous for the state as paramount over the nation; to-day, we have the doctrine resurrected by alleged Republicans from its grave under the battlefields of the Civil War, rehabilitated and restated to make the nation impotent before enemies far worse than the slave oligarchy. And under the renovated banner of "states' rights," "the blue" and "the gray," the "bloody shirt" Forakers and Spooners and the Confederate Baileys and Stones march shoulder to shoulder in protecting "the interests" in their lootings.

Gorman, the brightest of bright boys, absorbed and assimilated all the mysteries of the Senate—all its crafty, treacherous ways of smothering, of emasculating, of perverting legislation; how to thwart the people and shift the responsibility; when to kill a just bill in committee and when to kill it in open Senate in the midst of a wild scrimmage among "honest patriots contending only for the right but conscientiously differing in views." For the Senate, not elected by the people, not responsible to them, and containing a controlling nucleus of men who have their seats as securely and for as long a period as the members of any hereditary legislative body in the world—the Senate has almost from the beginning been the bulwark of whatever form of privilege happened to be struggling to maintain itself against the people.

Gorman continued his invaluable education in the Senate throughout the stormy, corrupt days of the Civil War. In 1866 he received from a Republican President the internal-revenue collectorship for the Fifth Maryland District. It has been charged that he was in those days a Republican, and that this appointment is proof of it. But the charge is foolish. He was no more a Republican then than he is a Democrat now. Such men have no politics of principle; and no one will think they have if he will take the trouble to glance from the badge to the man and his deeds. In the spring of 1869, Gorman ceased to be a Republican officeholder; in the fall he was elected to the lower house of the Maryland legislature by the Democratic party. There, at the age of thirty, he entered upon his real career.

Aldrich's simple home problem has been to rule Rhode Island by means of an aristocratic old constitution which puts all the power in the hands of the ignorant and cheaply purchasable voters of a few sparsely populated rural townships. Gorman's has been less easy, yet far from difficult. Maryland, being a border state, has a great many white Republicans; and there is a negro vote large enough to hold the balance of power. It has been Gorman's cue to keep "negro domination" ever before the eyes of the Maryland voter, to make the whites feel that, rotten though his machine is, it is yet the only alternative to "rule by and for the black." When the Republican machine, usually his docile dependent, would, in some brief spasm of reform, cease to play his game, he has sometimes lost; not always, because the uncertain conditions in Baltimore compelled the machine to maintain at all times an army of thugs, repeaters, ballot-box stuffers and the like, and several times the lost day has been saved to him by a carnival of ballot-box debauchery and blood rioting.

In a speech in Baltimore, on October 15, 1895, Theodore Roosevelt said, "I caught Mr. Gorman in an ugly falsehood, one that might be termed better in the plain Anglo-Saxon word of three letters."

Mr. Bonaparte, the present secretary of the Navy, said on March 31, 1904:

"A good many years ago Mr. Gorman was described on good Democratic authority as a 'generalissimo of the lobby.' Senator Gorman calls me a professional reformer. Whether it is more commendable to be a professional reformer or a professional lobbyist, I must leave each to judge for himself. But I must own that Senator Gorman's 'profession' has had one advantage over mine—it has been vastly *more profitable*. Although the senator seems to think *honesty* is of minor importance in determining a man's qualifications for high public office, it is certainly true that a *conspicuous absence of this qualification* has not proved fatal to at least one man holding a high office and aspiring to a higher." (Gorman was then a seeker of the nomination for President.)

On October 22, 1888, Henry E. Wooten, a distinguished Marylander living at Ellicott City, issued an open letter to Gorman in which he challenged him to sue for libel on the following statements:

"That you, with your own hands, assisted by others, distributed three thousand dollars among the ruffians that thronged the city in 1875.

"That you were an active participant in the fraud of 1879. You had Higgins at your headquarters in Baltimore, and he was in this county at least upon two occasions closeted with you and other conspirators against the rights and liberties of the people, perfecting the details of conspiracy, conferring as to what names should be dropped and what names misspelled, and by which route the negro repeaters should be sent out.

"That you are *steeped in corruption and saturated with official perjury.*"

Gorman did not sue Mr. Wooten for calling him a briber and perjurer. Nor did he sue Mr. Roosevelt for calling him a liar, nor Mr. Bonaparte for calling him a notoriously dishonest professional lobbyist. Nor did he sue Bernard Carter, the eminent lawyer and Democrat, who denounced him as "generalissimo of the lobby" when he was handing over the streets of Baltimore to the Baltimore and Ohio Railroad, which was the section of "the interests" he chiefly represented in those days.

The original basis of Gorman's power in Maryland was the state-built and state-owned Chesapeake and Ohio Canal, connecting the coal regions with tide water. This canal had two values for a boss: It offered an indefinitely large number of "soft snaps"—good for heelers of all grades—and it enabled corrupt and highly profitable negotiations with the railways, which would be prevented from looting the people through extortionate freight rates if it were honestly administered. Gorman appreciated both of these values to the uttermost. In 1872, at the very outset of his career, he had himself made president of the canal company, and that soon enabled him to make himself boss of the party and of the state, at first a levier upon the corrupt controllers of big corporations, then a partner and promoter of those controllers in "milking" both the corporations and the people. In 1880, a suit was brought by Daniel K. Stewart to enjoin Gorman and his gang in control of the canal from entering into contracts to give the railroad companies rebates. The testimony revealed Gorman as a grafter, great and small. There was the big side to the scandal—the huge loot in rebates, and in packing the service with idle heelers. Then there was the minor stealing revealed in expense accounts, of which this is only one typical specimen from a mass offered in evidence:

Dec. 13, 1874.

Gorman—

Board and rooms	$13.50
Boy, 25 cts.; fire, $1.50; cash, 50 cts.	2.25
Fires in two rooms	1.50
Two carriages, $4; telegram, 30 cts.	4.30
Champagne, $2; hack, $1	3.00
Cash to waiters	10.00
	$34.55

Despite scandal and outcry, Gorman, giving Maryland a choice between thug domination and "nigger" domination, was able to hold on to the canal until it had been "milked dry," had been rendered worthless and had been turned over by Gorman's legislature to the Baltimore and Ohio and the Western Maryland Railways. And with it went the people of Maryland's protection against railway-rate extortion through the necessities of life.

It was by stupendous open frauds that the gang elected the legislature which put Gorman into the United States Senate in 1881. Several of the heelers afterwards confessed. Harrig, for instance, told how "Gorman and Higgins called the body of men [repeaters] together to meet them at a certain hotel in this city [Baltimore]. He [Gorman] wanted a certain man in Howard County defeated for the legislature." Charlie Goodman, who had twenty-eight entries in the criminal docket against him, told how "Higgins paid me five dollars apiece for forty men." He told about various Baltimore elections—the gangs of roughs sent by the political machines of New

York, Philadelphia, etc., in exchange for similar services from the Gorman gang. "Those repeaters," said he, "have been put in my hands forty strong. I was ordered not to put in less than five thousand votes; but I usually put in fifty-eight hundred."

So diligently did Gorman reward the assiduity of his humble allies who lifted him to the Senate by these methods that the Independent Democrats of Maryland, in a public address in 1887, said, "Of twenty-three state and federal employees in one ward (of Baltimore) we have found nineteen whose names appear on the criminal records." There were money rewards also; these, of course, came chiefly from the Baltimore and Ohio Railroad, which financed the Gorman machine and which had the first call upon Gorman himself until the Pennsylvania Railroad bought control of the Baltimore and Ohio. Then, naturally, Gorman passed to the service of that powerful section of "the interests" called the "Pennsylvania."

We may not linger upon Gorman's home record—upon the treachery to the people of Maryland, equal proportionately to Depew's and Platt's in New York, to Aldrich's in Rhode Island—the hundreds of millions of loot, the great licenses to loot in perpetuity handed over, with no public compensation, to railway companies, gas companies, traction companies, or, rather, to the greedy few who "milk" those companies and, through the companies, the people. The distinction between the corporation and the thief who seizes and robs it and uses it as a tool for robbing others should not be lost sight of. It is precisely that abysmal but too often overlooked distinction which makes the men in control of our industrial machinery, not leaders and developers of the national resources, but looters and national enemies, parasites upon prosperity, and upon the producers of prosperity.

Gorman entered the Senate as a senator twenty-five years ago this spring. He already knew the mysteries of the Senate. He had been studying and practicing the black art of politics for nearly thirty years. Inevitably he was soon a leader, the trusted counselor of those of his party who wished to be led skillfully in the subtle ways of doing the will of "the interests" without inflaming the people against them. He, of course, entered the Senate primarily as an agent of the eminently respectable among his pals and sponsors, the interstate looters through the railway corporations of his state. Every traitor senator, whatever else he represents in the way of an enemy to the people, always represents some thief or group of thieves through railways. For the railway, reaching everywhere, as intimate a part of our life now as the air we breathe, is the easy and perfect instrument of the wholesale looter of investors and of the public, and is also the natural nucleus and subsidizer of a political machine. And, as the railways have merged—even Aldrich now publicly concedes that competition has almost been abolished—the senators have "merged" also. And peace reigns in the Senate Chamber under a "community of interest" in treason corresponding to the "community of interest" in spoliation.

But it is with the "merging" of the Republican and Democratic political machines that we are now concerned. And let no one be distracted by the roaring eloquence and the sham battles of the Senate or by the "eminent respectability" of the senators into losing sight of the central fact that the machines, drawing their revenues from the one power, ruled by the twin agents of that power, are the property of that power—never more so than when the politicians, wearing and disgracing official robes, beat the air and "jam the wind" to make the people confuse party and party principle with party machine. To appreciate the Senate, look, not at its professions, not at the surface pretenses of the measures it permits to become laws, but at the effect of those laws—how plutocracy and plunder thrive under them. And to understand why the laws always somehow fail to serve the people, always somehow relicense the people's enemies, look at Aldrich and Gorman and their band—how they got, how they keep their seats; whom they associate with; their private fortunes; how their fortunes are invested. "Where a man's treasure is, there will his heart be also."

Rarely does the Senate hold a session without there cropping out some indication of the existence of this secret "merger" of the two party machines under which they work together in harmony wherever "the interests" are interested—befogging the responsibility for acts hostile to the public interest, lining up senators from both parties for a debate or a vote, and releasing to perfunctory, though always perfervid opposition, senators who have "insuperable conscientious objections" in the particular matter or dare not offend the people of their state in that particular crisis. For, while many of the "merged" senators can all but leave out of account the feelings of "my people," there are more who have to be "conscientious" and careful and crafty, except during the first two or three years after they have been elected, and when they have three or four years before they come up for election again. Occasionally the evidences of the existence and smooth working of the "merger" are so plain that only the very stupid or the stone-blind partisan would fail to see.

5

RICHARD HARDING DAVIS

So far as the world was concerned, the coronation of Czar
Nicholas II of Russia and Czarina Alexandra was *the* event
of 1896. Everyone in Europe intended to be there. Every
newspaperman in the world begged for the right to cover the
biggest news story of the year. The New York *Journal* had
advertised for months that star reporter Richard Harding
Davis would cover the story.

Now, though, he was in a bind. He was having trouble
getting into the ceremonies.

He appealed to a diplomatic official "and begged him to
represent me as a literary light of the finest color," Davis
told his brother. The appeal worked. Davis was admitted
and was one of the few American reporters allowed to cover
the coronation ceremony.

Davis was not exaggerating in his description of himself as a literary figure. His reporting was so popular with
readers that he had established an international celebrity
status. He had built his writing success on his ability to create shimmering images with words. Like paintings, his
news stories glowed with light and color. He enhanced his
glowing, glittering descriptions with sound, texture, touch,
and smell. He used all his senses to set rich and powerful
scenes.

Davis was destined to be a writer from the very start, but
he didn't let that get in the way of being glamorous. He was
born in 1864 to a novelist mother and newspaper editor father. He never had any notion of doing anything but writ-

ing, whether it be short stories or newspaper reports or plays. He tried his hand at them all. He was an adventurer, a traveler, an American hero, a household word. He was handsome. Before the time when there were movie idols, women swooned at the sight of him, and envious men tried to imitate him, their swashbuckling hero. He was also a fashion model. Richard Harding Davis, the "Gibson Guy," was everyone's dream man.

One of the reasons so many admirers fancied him was that he was the world's eyewitness. He saw, he felt, he reported subjects from travel to wars to glittering festivals. The world was at his feet, and he brought the world to his readers.

In his news accounts, Davis did far more than tell people what was going on. He put his readers on the scene with him by describing every nuance of light, color, sound, and feeling. He described the foreign by comparing it to the familiar. He kept his senses sharp and communicated his impressions clearly. The coronation story demonstrated his technique, early building a climate of suspicion as a backdrop to the event. "The visiting stranger [in Russia]," Davis wrote, "likes to believe that he is giving no end of trouble to a dozen of the secret police; that, sleeping or waking, he is surrounded by spies. It adds an element of local color to his visit and makes a good story to tell when he goes home."

No little detail escaped Davis in creating the exact mood for readers. In doing the coronation story, he was amazed at the constant prayers of the Russians. He described the religious, yet busy and harried, atmosphere with characters and comparisons readers would readily understand:

You will see a porter who is staggering under a heavy burden stop and put it down upon the pavement and repeat his prayers before he picks it up again, and he will do this three or four times in the course of half an hour's walk; troops of cavalry come to halt and remove their hats and pray while passing a church; and when the bells ring, even the policeman standing in the middle of the street, splattered by mud and threatened by galloping droschkas, crosses himself and repeats his prayers bareheaded, while you try vainly to imagine a policeman on Broadway taking off his helmet and doing the same thing. In restau-

rants there is a like show of devotion on the part of the waiters, who stand beside your table muttering a prayer to
themselves, while you allow your food to grow cold rather
than interrupt them.

Such sharp attention to detail pervaded Davis' work. In
describing a violinist in Hungary, for instance, Davis not
only made sure his readers saw the violinist, but also felt the
power of his music:

He has curious eyes, like those of a Scotch collie—sad, and
melancholy, and pleading—and when he plays they grow
glazed and drunken-looking, like those of an absinthe
drinker, and tears roll from them to the point of his short
beard and wet the wood of his violin. His music probably
affects different people according to their nerves, but it is
as moving as any great passage in any noble book, or in
any great play, and while it lasts he holds people absolutely
in a spell, so that when the music eases women burst into
tears, and I have seen men jump to their feet and empty the
contents of their pockets into his lap, and they are so sure to
do this that their servants take their money away from
them....

Davis made sure his readers were able to travel with him
by seeing and hearing and feeling what he did. He made
keen use of all of his senses and expected his readers to do
the same. He made sure they could sense what he sensed by
translating the sense into clear, uncomplicated, beautiful
words. He found that color created a clear image, and he
used it lavishly. Describing a Moscow cathedral, he wrote,
"These walls are overlaid from the floor to the dome above
with gold-leaf, upon which are frescos of the saints in dark
blues and reds and greens, each saint wearing around his
head a halo of gold studded with precious stones." The adjoining screen wall featured "rows of pearls and [was] hung
with emeralds, rubies, and diamonds." Nearby was a curtain of purple velvet rimmed with ostrich feathers in orange,
black, and white. The royal family's thrones were just as
colorful. "His was of silver inlaid with great blue
turquoises; the Czarina's of ivory, carved with scenes of the
chase; that of the Dowager Empress was of silver studded

with all manner of precious stones, including eight hundred and eighty diamonds."

Davis' use of colors is evident in the stories included in this anthology. In his account of the the execution of a Cuban freedom fighter, the colors are eerie and dark, in contrast to the lavish color of the Russian coronation. Davis described Cuban palm trees that "showed white in the moonlight" and "tiny camp-fires" that sparkled brightly. "But as the light grew stronger," he wrote, "and the moonlight faded, these were tamped out, and when the soldiers came in force the moon was a white ball in the sky, without radiance, the fires had sunk to ashes, and the sun had not yet risen." In his story of the German army's invasion of Belgium, he described a hideous gray uniformed machine. The German uniform, he wrote, "is a gray green, not the blue gray of our Confederates. It is the gray of the hour just before daybreak, the gray of unpolished steel, of mist among green trees....Like a river of steel [the army] flowed, gray and ghostlike."

Even more important to Davis than color was the play of light. Perhaps unconsciously, he included the shadows and glimmers and outright glares of illumination in nearly every story. Light told a tale; so he observed and communicated powerful pictures, dramatic with incandescence. During the coronation of the Czar, he noticed:

Around the platform itself were the princes and granddukes glittering with the chains and crosses of the imperial orders, and between the screen and the platform the priests moved to and fro in jeweled mitres as large as a diver's helmet, and in robes stiff with gold and precious stones, their vestments flashing like the scales of goldfish. For five hours the sun shone dimly through the high open doors on this mass of color and mixture of jewels, so that the eye grew wearied as it flashed from sword hilts and epaulets or passed lightly from shining silks and satins to touch tiaras and coronets, falling for one instant upon the white hair of some red and grizzled warrior, or caressing the shoulders and face of some beautiful girl.

Over and over again, Davis caught the glimmer of light and described it. His writing flashed with the brilliance of sun and moon and gemstone and electricity and anything else that might shimmer and glow in his readers' imaginations. The results were lasting impressions of rich tone. In describing the inaugural ball for President William McKinley, Davis couldn't help but notice that "the effect of the electric lights against the soft white folds of the challis was that of yellow diamonds shining through spun silver...and hidden among the sturdier palms and palmettoes on the floor were hundreds of tiny electric globes glowing like red and green fire-flies."

On a less festive occasion, a war in Greece, he noticed that cartridges from guns "reminded one of corn-cobs jumping out of a corn-sheller, and it was interesting...to see a hundred of them pop up into the air at the same time, flashing in the sun....They rolled by the dozens underfoot, and twinkled in the grass."

Similarly, as the Germans entered Brussels in 1914, Davis observed a spooky illumination in the dying daylight. "Then," he said, "as dusk came and as thousands of horses' hoofs and thousands of iron boots continued to tramp forward, they struck tiny sparks from the stones, but the horses and the men who beat out the sparks were invisible."

While sight and light provided the essence to Davis' writing, he also considered other senses to be deeply important to telling the whole story. In writing of President McKinley's inauguration, he heard the "shoosh-shoosh" sound of the Supreme Court justices arriving as they "came rustling forward in black silk robes." He also heard the disconcerting sounds of weapons in Greece:

Then there began a concert which came from just overhead—a concert of jarring sounds and little whispers. The "shrieking shrapnel," of which one reads in the description of every battle, did not sound as much like a shriek as it did like the jarring sound of telegraph wires when someone strikes the pole from which they hang, and when they came very close the noise was like the rushing sound that rises between two railroad trains when they pass each other in opposite directions and at great speed....The bullets were much more disturbing....They moved under a cloak of invisibility....The bullets sounded like rustling silk, or like humming-birds on a warm summer's day, or like the wind as it is imitated on the stage of a theatre.

Davis also made use of the sense of smell, noting that when Londoners built hasty bleachers to accommodate spectators at Queen Victoria's Jubilee, the scent of London changed dramatically. "The smell of soft coal, which is perhaps the first and most distinctive feature of London to greet the arriving American," he wrote, "was changed to that of a green pine, so that the town smelt like a Western mining-camp."

He likewise could use words to make readers feel disgusted and grimy. "The bath-tub is the dividing line between savages and civilized beings," he said forthrightly in a story from Cuba. "And when I learned that regiment after regiment of Spanish officers and gentlemen have been stationed in that town—and it was the dirtiest, hottest, and dustiest town I ever visited—for eighteen months, and none of them had wanted a bath, I believed from that moment all the stories I had heard about their butcheries and atrocities...."

Davis was not afraid to give assessments of situations or offer his opinions, such as he did about bathing. He was, after all, an eyewitness with as much right to an opinion about the goings-on as anyone else. He made the most of his position to critique events as he reported them. Deploring the behavior of members of Congress as they sought the best seats for the McKinley inauguration, he complained:

Common courtesy and the convention which exists in other countries enjoin...a government to give the diplomatic corps the precedence of the local administrators, just as a host gives the better place at dinner to the visiting stranger, and not to members of his own family. If a thing is worth doing, it is worth doing correctly....Neither the members of the Senate nor of the House gained any credit or additional glory by shoving themselves into places which should by right and courtesy have been given to the foreign ministers.

He also, however, criticized the foreign diplomats, who had their feelings crushed over the situation, for not acting more mature. "But to go away pouting like a parcel of children with their toys under their arms," Davis fussed, "was distinctly disrespectful to the President, and was hardly the act of gentlemen, not even of diplomats."

In a similar vein, Davis criticized the Greek royal family for maintaining its soft lifestyle in wartime and wished that the princes of the nation could show the gumption of the common soldier. He interviewed a courageous young soldier on the battlefield and then commented wryly, "It would be an excellent thing for Greece if someone discovered that, in spite of the twenty years discrepancy in their ages, he and the Crown-Prince had been changed at birth."

One of Davis's most powerful and emotionally charged eyewitness accounts was that of the German army burning Louvain, Belgium. The army held him prisoner in a railroad car, but still he could observe the ghastly scene through the window, and still he could assess the situation. "The Germans sentenced Louvain on Wednesday to become a wilderness," he wrote bitterly, "and with the German system and love of thoroughness they left Louvain an empty and blackened shell." He was not afraid to show his contempt for the German army's determination to destroy:

> No one defends the sniper [who shot at the Germans and helped touch off the rampage]. But because ignorant Mexicans when their city was invaded fired upon our sailors, we did not destroy Vera Cruz. Even had we bombarded Vera Cruz, money could have restored it. Money can never restore Louvain. Great architects, dead these six hundred years, made it beautiful, and their handiwork belonged to the world. With torch and dynamite the Germans have turned these masterpieces into ashes, and all the Kaiser's horses and all his men cannot bring them back again.

Davis' account of the apparent Hun barbarism helped incite American public sentiment to shift in favor of going to war against Germany.

Despite taking his position as the eyewitness and giving his honest opinions about situations, and despite his claim to be a "literary light" of fine color, Davis was not always cocky about his work. He longed to make the events he wrote about more real, more true to life than his fumbling pen would allow. Speaking of his coronation report, he told his brother, "The story I sent is not a good one....I ought to have made a great hit with it, but there was no time, and there was so much detail and minutia that I could not treat it right." Another time, after sending back a report on the Spanish-American War from Cuba, he chided himself, "I had to write the story in fifteen minutes, so it was no good except that we had it exclusively."

Even if, as he claimed, he reported events badly, he was especially concerned that news of big events got out to the public. His job, he believed, was to tell the world. Despite his "poor" writing of the coronation story, he said, "after the awful possibility...we...had to face of not getting any story at all, I am only too thankful" for having been able to do *any* story of the event.

Ultimately, he believed, he had to describe events well enough that his stories would last. "[I]t is as an historian and not as a correspondent," he told his family, "that I get on over those men who are correspondents for papers only."

●◆

CUBAN FREEDOM FIGHTER BRAVELY FACES EXECUTION

Davis was sympathetic to native Cubans who wished to free their island from the yoke of Spain.

One such freedom fighter in the insurrection of 1896 was 20-year-old Adolfo Rodriguez, the only son of a Cuban farmer. Although captured by the Spanish army, he was tough to bring down, managing to wound three Spaniards with his machete. Tried by a military court for bearing arms against the government, he was sentenced to be shot before dawn on January 19, 1897.

Davis' sympathetic account of the execution included his trademark descriptions of eerie light and careful details. This story and others by Davis helped stir up the American public against Spain's troops in Cuba.

The story took up an entire front page and half of a second in the New York *Journal*. It is abridged here.

THE DEATH OF RODRIGUEZ
Richard Harding Davis
New York *Journal*
January 20, 1897

There had been a full moon the night preceding the execution, and when the squad of soldiers marched from town it
was still shining brightly through the mists. It lighted a
plain of two miles in extent, broken by ridges and gullies
and covered with thick, high grass, and with bunches of
cactus and palmetto. In the hollow of the ridges the mist lay
like broad lakes of water, and on one side of the plain stood
the walls of the old town. On the other rose hills covered with
royal palms that showed white in the moonlight, like hundreds of marble columns. A line of tiny camp-fires that the
sentries had built during the night stretched between the forts
at regular intervals and burned clearly.

But as the light grew stronger and the moonlight faded,
these were stamped out, and when the soldiers came in force
the moon was a white ball in the sky, without radiance, the
fires had sunk to ashes, and the sun had not yet risen.

So even when the men were formed into three sides of a
hollow square, they were scarcely able to distinguish one
another in the uncertain light of the morning.

There were about three hundred soldiers in the formation. They belonged to the volunteers, and they deployed
upon the plain with their band in front playing a jaunty
quickstep, while their officers galloped from one side to the
other through the grass, seeking a suitable place for the execution. Outside the line the band still played merrily.

A few men and boys, who had been dragged out of their
beds by the music, moved about the ridges behind the soldiers, half-clothed, unshaven, sleepy-eyed, yawning,
stretching themselves nervously and shivering in the cool,
damp air of the morning.

Either owing to discipline or on account of the nature of
their errand, or because the men were still but half awake,
there was no talking in the ranks, and the soldiers stood
motionless, leaning on their rifles, with their backs turned
to the town, looking out across the plain to the hills.

The men in the crowd behind them were also grimly
silent. They knew that whatever they might say would be

twisted into a word of sympathy for the condemned man or a protest against the government. So no one spoke; even the officers gave their orders in gruff whispers, and the men in the crowd did not mix together, but looked suspiciously at one another and kept apart.

As the light increased, a mass of people came hurrying from the town with two black figures leading them, and the soldiers drew up at attention, and part of the double line fell back and left an opening in the square.

With us a condemned man walks only the short distance from his cell to the scaffold or the electric chair, shielded from sight by the prison walls, and it often occurs even then that the short journey is too much for his strength and courage.

But the Spaniards on this morning made the prisoner walk for over a half-mile across the broken surface of the fields. I expected to find the man, no matter what his strength at other times might be, stumbling and faltering on this cruel journey; but as he came nearer I saw that he led all the others, that the priests on either side of him were taking two steps to his one, and that they were tripping on their gowns and stumbling over the hollows in their efforts to keep pace with him as he walked, erect and soldierly, at a quick step in advance of them.

He had a handsome, gentle face of the peasant type, a light, pointed beard, great wistful eyes, and a mass of curly black hair. He was shockingly young for such a sacrifice, and looked more like a Neapolitan than a Cuban. You could imagine him sitting on the quay in Naples or Genoa lolling in the sun and showing his white teeth when he laughed. Around his neck, hanging outside his linen blouse, he wore a new scapular.

It seems a petty thing to have been pleased with at such a time, but I confess to have felt a thrill of satisfaction when I saw, as the Cuban passed me, that he held a cigarette between his lips, not arrogantly nor with bravado, but with the nonchalance of a man who meets his punishment fearlessly, and who will let his enemies see that they can kill but not frighten him.

It was very quickly finished, with rough and, but for one frightful blunder, with merciful swiftness. The crowd fell back when it came to the square, and the condemned man, the priests, and the firing squad of six young volunteers passed in, and the line closed behind them.

The officer who had held the cord that bound the Cuban's arms behind him and passed across his breast, let it fall on the grass and drew his sword, and Rodriguez dropped his cigarette from his lips and bent and kissed the cross which the priest held up before him.

The elder of the priests moved to one side and prayed rapidly in a loud whisper, while the other, a younger man, walked behind the firing squad and covered his face with his hands. They had both spent the last twelve hours with Rodriguez in the chapel of the prison.

The Cuban walked to where the officer directed him to stand, and turning his back on the square, faced the hills and the road across them, which led to his father's farm.

As the officer gave the first command, he straightened himself as far as the cords would allow, and held up his head and fixed his eyes immovable on the morning light, which had just begun to show above the hills....

The officer had given the order, the men had raised their pieces, and the condemned man had heard the clicks of the triggers as they were pulled back, and he had not moved. And then happened one of the most cruelly refined, though unintentional, acts of torture that one can very well imagine. As the officer slowly raised his sword, preparatory to giving the signal, one of the mounted officers rode up to him and pointed out silently that, as I had already observed with some satisfaction, the firing squad were so placed that when they fired they would shoot several of the soldiers stationed on the extreme end of the square.

Their captain motioned his men to lower their pieces, and then walked across the grass and laid his hand on the shoulder of the waiting prisoner.

It is not pleasant to think what that shock must have been. The man had steeled himself to receive a volley of bullets. He believed that in the next instant he would be in another world; he had heard the command given, had heard the click of the Mausers as the locks caught—and then, at that supreme moment, a human hand had been laid upon his shoulder and a voice spoke in his ear.

You would expect that any man, snatched back to life in such a fashion, would start and tremble at the reprieve, or would break down altogether, but this boy turned his head steadily, and followed with his eyes the direction of the officer's sword, then nodded gravely, and, with his shoulders squared, took up the new position, straightened his back, and once more held himself erect.

As an exhibition of self-control, this should surely rank above the feats of heroism performed in battle, where there are thousands of comrades to give inspiration. This man was alone, in sight of the hills he knew, with only enemies about him, with no source to draw on for strength but that which lay within himself.

The officer of the firing squad, mortified by his blunder, hastily whipped up his sword, the men once more levelled their rifles, the sword rose, dropped, and the men fired. At the report, the Cuban's head snapped back almost between his shoulders, but his body fell slowly, as though some one had pushed him gently forward from behind and he had stumbled.

He sank on his side in the wet grass without a struggle or sound, and did not move again.

It was difficult to believe that he meant to lie there, that it could be ended so without a word, that the man in the linen suit would not rise to his feet and continue to walk on over the hills, as he apparently had started to do, to his home; that there was not a mistake somewhere, or that at least someone would be sorry or say something or run to pick him up.

But, fortunately, he did not need help, and the priests returned—the younger one with tears running down his face—and donned their vestments and read a brief requiem for his soul, while the squad stood uncovered, and the men in the hollow square shook their accoutrements into place, and shifted their pieces and got ready for the order to march, and the band began again with the same quickstep which the fusillade had interrupted.

The figure still lay on the grass untouched, and no one seemed to remember that it had walked there of itself, or noticed that the cigarette still burned, a tiny ring of living fire, at the place where the figure had first stood....

Everyone seemed to have forgotten it except two men, who came slowly towards it from the town, driving a bullock-cart that bore an unplaned coffin, each with a cigarette between his lips, and with his throat wrapped in a shawl to keep out the morning mists.

At that moment the sun, which had shown some promise of its coming in the glow above the hills, shot up suddenly from behind them in all the splendor of the tropics, a fierce, red disk of heat, and filled the air with warmth and light.

The bayonets of the retreating column flashed in it, and at the sight a rooster in a farm-yard nearby crowed vigorously, and a dozen bugles answered the challenge with the brisk, cheery notes of the reveille, and from all parts of the city the church bells jangled out the call for early mass, and the little world of Santa Clara seemed to stretch itself and to wake to welcome the day just begun.

But as I fell in at the rear of the procession and looked back, the figure of the young Cuban, who was no longer a part of the world of Santa Clara, was asleep in the wet grass, with his motionless arms still tightly bound behind him, with the scapular twisted awry across his face, and the blood from his breast sinking into the soil he had tried to free.

●◇

AN ARMY THAT HAD "LOST THE HUMAN QUALITY"

The German army swept into Brussels, Belgium, on August 20, 1914, beginning World War I. Davis witnessed the continual marching, marching. He was first excited, then bored with the machine-like monotony, and last disturbed by the threatening, humanless quality of the juggernaut.

After writing the story, he went to great lengths to get it out. The Germans forced him to remain in Brussels until their army had moved. Davis, however, got in touch with E. A. Dalton, an Englishman, who agreed to act as courier. Dalton dressed in dark clothes and left under cover of darkness, occasionally getting rides in cars or wagons. When he felt his journey was becoming dangerous, he hid in underbrush alongside the road. He crawled for a mile in order to stay hidden. Finally he reached the coast and hitched a ride to England on a refugee boat.

Davis later said this was his favorite piece of writing from World War I. It exhibits his use of color and light, and it uses the motif of the German army as a modern gray machine to hold the entire story together.

[GERMAN ARMY FLOWS LIKE A RIVER OF STEEL]
Richard Harding Davis
London *News Chronicle*
August 23, 1914

BRUSSELS, FRIDAY, AUGUST 21, 2 P.M.—The entrance of the German army into Brussels has lost the human quality. It was lost as soon as the three soldiers who led the army bicycled into the Boulevard du Régent and asked the way to the Gare du Nord. When they passed, the human note passed with them.

What came after them, and twenty-four hours later is still coming, is not men marching, but a force of nature like a tidal wave, an avalanche or a river flooding its banks. At this minute it is rolling through Brussels as the swollen waters of the Conemaugh Valley swept through Johnstown.

At the sight of the first few regiments of the enemy we were thrilled with interest. After they had passed for three hours in one unbroken steel-gray column, we were bored. But when hour after hour passed and there was no halt, no breathing time, no open spaces in the ranks, the thing became uncanny, inhuman. You returned to watch it, fascinated. It held the mystery and menace of fog rolling toward you across the sea.

The gray of the uniforms worn by both officers and men helped this air of mystery. Only the sharpest eye could detect among the thousands that passed the slightest difference. All moved under a cloak of invisibility. Only after the most numerous and severe tests at all distances, with all materials and combinations of colors that give forth no color, could this gray have been discovered. That it was selected to clothe and disguise the German when he fights is typical of the German staff in striving for efficiency to leave nothing to chance, to neglect no detail.

After you have seen this service uniform under conditions entirely opposite, you are convinced that for the German soldier it is his strongest weapon. Even the most expert marksman cannot hit a target he cannot see. It is a gray green, not the gray blue of our Confederates. It is the gray of the hour just before daybreak, the gray of unpolished steel, of mist among green trees.

I saw it first in the Grand Palace in front of the Hotel de Ville. It was impossible to tell if in that noble square there was a regiment or a brigade. You saw only a fog that melted into the stones, blended with the ancient house fronts, that shifted and drifted, but left you nothing at which you could point.

Later, as the army passed below my window, under the trees of the Botanical Park, it merged and was lost against the green leaves. It is no exaggeration to say that at a hundred yards you can see the horses on which the uhlans ride, but you cannot see the men who ride them.

If I appear to overemphasize this disguising uniform, it is because, of all the details of the German outfit, it appealed to me as one of the most remarkable. The other day when I was with the rear guard of the French Dragoons and Cuirassiers and they threw out pickets, we could distinguish them against the yellow wheat or green gorse at half a mile, while these men passing in the street, when they have reached the next crossing, become merged into the gray of the paving stones, and the earth swallows them. In comparison, the yellow khaki of our own American army is about as invisible as the flag of Spain.

Yesterday Major General von Jarotsky, the German Military Governor of Brussels, assured Burgomaster Max that the German army would not occupy the city, but would pass through it. It is still passing. I have followed in campaigns six armies, but excepting not even our own, the Japanese, or the British, I have not seen one so thoroughly equipped. I am not speaking of the fighting qualities of any army, only of the equipment and organization. The German army moved into this city as smoothly and as compactly as an Empire State Express. There were no halts, no open places, no stragglers.

This army has been on active service three weeks, and so far there is not apparently a chin strap or a horseshoe missing. It came in with the smoke pouring from cookstoves on wheels, and in an hour had set up post-office wagons, from which mounted messengers galloped along the line of columns, distributing letters, and at which soldiers posted picture postcards.

The infantry came in in files of five, two hundred men to each company; the Lancers in columns of four, with not a pennant missing. The quick-firing guns and fieldpieces were one hour at a time in passing, each gun with its caisson and ammunition wagon taking twenty seconds in which to pass.

The men of the infantry sang Fatherland, My Fatherland. Between each line of the song they took three steps. At times two thousand men were singing together in absolute rhythm and beat. When the melody gave way, the silence was broken only by the stamp of iron-shod boots, and then again the song rose. When the singing ceased, the bands played marches. They were followed by the rumble of siege guns, the creaking of wheels, and of chains clanking against the cobblestones and the sharp bell-like voices of the bugles.

For seven hours the army passed in such solid columns that not once might a taxicab or trolley car pass through the city. Like a river of steel it flowed, gray and ghostlike. Then, as dusk came and as thousands of horses' hoofs and thousands of iron boots continued to tramp forward, they struck tiny sparks from the stones, but the horses and the men who beat out the sparks were invisible. At midnight pack wagons and siege guns were still passing. At seven this morning I was awakened by the tramp of men and bands playing jauntily. Whether they marched all night or not, I do not know; but now for twenty-six hours the gray army has rumbled by with the mystery of fog and the pertinacity of a steam roller.

6

HERBERT BAYARD SWOPE

THE REPORTER WHO SCOOPED THE WORLD

Minutes before 2 a.m. on a midsummer night in 1912, Herman Rosenthal, owner of a small-time gambling shop in New York City, finished eating dinner with friends at the Hotel Metropole. He had promised his wife he would return home early. She feared something might happen to him because he was to testify before a grand jury the following day and reveal a tale of rampant graft and corruption within the city's police department. It was an appointment Rosenthal failed to keep.

As he prepared to leave the hotel, someone approached him, telling him a man wanted to see him at the front entrance of the restaurant. Rosenthal stepped through the door and probably recognized the four gunmen as they fired the fatal bullets. Several policemen who were standing nearby watched as the assassins escaped in a getaway car. They wrote down numbers, but none matched the set on the license plate. However, a bystander jotted down the correct number, carried it to the nearest police station, and was locked up in a jail cell. Rosenthal appeared to have met the same fate as others who had attempted to unravel New York City's powerful coalition of crooked cops, politicians, and gamblers.

Then Herbert Bayard Swope, a gangly, red-haired reporter for the New York *World*, arrived on the scene. He had scooped every newspaper in the city with his page-one story of Rosenthal's statement to the district attorney charging the city's police with corruption. He knew most of the characters involved in the Rosenthal case, having hung out for nearly ten years at the city's race track and gambling haunts. He was prowling in the vicinity when word of Rosenthal's murder reached him. Walking through the doors of the West 47th Street police station, he discovered the police were trying to find a way to discard the lone piece of evidence they had. Swope called District Attorney Charles S. Whitman and roused him out of bed.

"What do you think I should do?" Whitman asked Swope.

"Get your clothes on and get to the police station as fast as you can," Swope demanded.

Whitman's arrival prevented the police from disposing of the evidence. Investigators traced the license plate number to the killers, and all four were captured. Swope also made sure Whitman made a statement to the press.

Three months later, Swope wrote a lively account about the murder and the events that followed. His classic story represented the best qualities of his writing and personality—bold, brash, and eccentric. The prose rolled and thundered like a grand overture or a wild car ride, hardly giving the reader time to pause for a breath.

His writing was known for its pace and suspense. His sharp observation helped him pick out small details that brought life to stories. His stories often contained melodrama and irony. His characteristic style can be observed in a boxing story written in April 1915, in which he described the outcome of the 26-round championship bout in which the champion lost his crown. *World* editor Charles Lincoln called the story "a classic of sports writing." It read in part:

> The last ten seconds that Jack Johnson held the world's prize-fighting championship were the most dramatic of his career. He lay on his back with his mouth wide open, eyes staring straight into the sun, belly heaving convulsively, half hearing but not grasping the slow counts of Referee Welch that took away from him the great prize and gave it to the grinning, lean-faced, youthful Jess Willard, who stood over him, waiting for the "ten" that made him rich and famous.

A black man, Johnson was unpopular, partly because he had married a white woman. Swope included a description of the third wife in his account:

> She is of medium height, rather slender, with a thinnish face that breaks into a smile too readily and shows too much teeth and gums. She seemed to fairly enjoy her importance as she entered, and equally she seemed to bitterly resent her slide into obscurity as she left. Her transition was abrupt—from the wife of the world's champion, frowned upon and adulated, she had become merely the white consort of a fat and unusually homely, middle-aged and very dark negro. The women present had eyes for her and sneers for her as she left dethroned.

Even though Swope was an effective writer, he was known primarily as a reporter. If he lacked anything in literary finesse, he offset it with a remarkable assortment of intriguing and entertaining facts. Lord Northcliffe, the most famous publisher in England, called Swope "the greatest reporter in the world."

The way Swope swarmed over the Rosenthal story stood out as just one example. He did not simply cover stories. He burrowed into the events and sometimes dictated their outcome. The corrupt police lieutenant, Charles A. Becker, who ordered Rosenthal "croaked" was later indicted and executed. Swope helped dig up some of the evidence that led to his arrest and scooped the rest of the city's papers by printing the full text of Becker's confession.

As he covered Becker's trial, Swope placed his readers in the courtroom and held them spellbound. As Becker testified, Swope wrote, he had

> a hunted look in [his] eyes, and his hands gripped the rail before him when the boyish looking foreman, Meredith Blagden, pronounced the finding, but otherwise the bold-faced, stalwart Becker showed no stress. He had schooled himself well. His cheeks went just a trifle grey; his voice once broke on a whimpering little cough. There was a touch of the wistful as he answered "married" when his "pedigree" was taken, but it took close watch to catch these suggestions of despair, for on the first glance he appeared the coolest man in the room.

A touch of drama, yes, that was Swope's style. Along with his dominance of the Rosenthal story, that syle so aggravated New York *Times* reporter Alexander Woollcott that, it was said, he suffered a nervous breakdown. "I said then that I would never again be a daily reporter," Woollcott told Swope's son years later.

Frenzied, aggressive reporting made Swope famous, but it wasn't his first love. He most loved to gamble, and he spent his life hanging around horses and the race track. He started gambling long before he ever thought about reporting. Swope was born January 5, 1882, to German immigrants. His father, a watch maker, died when Swope was seventeen. As a boy growing up in St. Louis, he hitched rides on his uncle's shoe-delivery wagons. The drivers stopped regularly at the race track and had the perky youth place bets for them. He soon bet on horse races for himself. By the time he was in high school, he had bushy red hair topping a six-foot-one-inch frame. He was expelled from school more than once for poor behavior. When on good terms with the administration, he played football.

He first recognized his writing talent in 1897 when he won a $100 prize for writing an essay about a local department store. That led to a job on the St. Louis *Post-Dispatch* that ended a year and three suspensions later. He had been dismissed for fighting in the newsroom, arriving too late for work, and playing too much football. It didn't help that his team beat the editor's alma mater. Despite his lack of discipline, he had a burning competitive fire. He hated to lose on a story and rarely did. He moved to Chicago, worked as a copy reader for the *Tribune*, and reported for the *Inter-Ocean*. A New York *Herald* recruiter discovered him and took him to New York.

The Manhattan night life and horse racing appealed to Swope more than newspaper work. He was always late, managing to hold onto his job only because he wrote faster and better than most reporters. Leo Redding, the editor, complained when Swope strolled in hours after starting time. Swope replied, "Leo, admit it. Whenever I come in, I'm still worth more than any two other men you've got on your staff." That arrogant attitude, gambling, and late-night carousing with John Barrymore (before he achieved fame as an actor) led to a dismissal from the *Herald* in 1903. Swope bounced to

another paper and back to the *Herald* in 1904. His contacts
with the fashionable crowd at expensive cafes and the race
track proved valuable to a paper wanting stories that appealed to this group of readers. Most of the time, though, editors had to corner Swope to force him to apply his talent. His
years at the *Herald* were numbered, and in 1907 the paper
dropped him again. For two years he was out of work or did
odd jobs.

Those two years changed him. His former colleague
Sherman W. Morse was city editor for the New York *World*.
He knew that Swope possessed untapped talent and offered
him a job in 1909 at $7 a week, $1 less than he had made at the
St. Louis *Post-Dispatch* as a cub reporter. "This time, the
newspaper's going to have to be more than an avocation,"
Morse said. "There'll be no more hanging around the track
and gambling halls on the pretext of looking for stories.
You'll take the assignments I give you, and you'll do your
best with them."

Swope agreed. Applying his talents, he became within
two years the paper's top reporter. His main strength was an
ability to get good stories, write them quickly, and make
them readable. He had a knack for finding something significant in routine events and for gathering enough material to make his stories substantial. His criteria for a good
reporter were accuracy, judgment of news, a sense of public
duty, understanding, professional ethics, and an ability to
write. Journalists today might question Swope's ethics because he tended to become part of the story while reporting it.
Swope believed, however, that getting involved was his duty
as a citizen as well as a reporter. It also paid off and helped
push him to the top of his profession.

By 1910 Swope's aggressive style, unrelenting pursuit of
stories, and network of sources led to scoop after scoop. He
chased a corrupt city official to North Carolina and chartered a boat to go alongside the yacht on which the official
was hiding. In January 1910 he accompanied federal mar-
shalls escorting Charles W. Morse, a prominent New York
banker convicted of manipulating bank stocks, to the federal penitentiary in Atlanta. During the train ride, the
banker told Swope he had misplaced the poem, *Invictus*,
which had given him comfort since his trial. Swope knew
the poem by heart, wrote it down for the banker, and opened

his story with it, followed by this lead paragraph:

Ten minutes after the big steel door of the United States Penitentiary here swung shut behind Charles W. Morse, but yesterday a man of millions, he had ceased to exist socially. He had become convict No. 2814, and clad in an ill-fitting suit of rough blue clothes was marched into the big dining-hall and with negroes, Indians, Chinamen, and whites of every condition took his first meal under the roof that is to shut out his liberty for fifteen years.

Swope had captured the irony and included a bit of information that added melodrama to the account.

His stories coming out of New York City were no less remarkable. After arriving late at the office, he would have three copy boys tie up office phones calling his sources. He then moved from one source to another without losing time. Soon sources ranging from two-bit gamblers to political powerbrokers were calling him. He frequented places that cost more than he could afford, but that didn't stop him. He refused to dress sloppily like most reporters and looked more like a wealthy merchant than a journalist. The duty of reporters, he said, is to get to know news sources without making moral judgments about them. Thus, he knew many of the underworld characters who became principal players in his stories. Columnist Westbrook Pegler said Swope knew as many prominent people as anyone and that "aquaintanceship, which widens and widens with experience and extends like...the ripples in a pond," was his top asset.

Swope's air of pomp and authority propelled him over and through bureaucratic mazes that frustrated other reporters. In 1911 he covered a fire at the Triangle Shirtwaist Co. in New York. The ten-story building was filled with 700 workers, mostly young girls. Workers were trapped because the building had only one fire escape. Swope engineered a statement by District Attorney Whitman and later interrupted a Whitman press conference to get the official to go to the scene.

Swope's ability to manipulate Whitman generated numerous scoops. Many observers credited Swope for playing a major role in Whitman's successful campaign for governor of New York.

Whitman wasn't the only government official whom Swope manipulated. At 2 a.m. April 15, 1912, word reached New York about the sinking of the *Titanic*. Without waiting for the *World* to make an assignment, Swope caught the first train to Halifax, Nova Scotia, where it was rumored that the survivors would be taken. No survivors showed up, but a ship carrying 300 bodies arrived. Government officials barred reporters from the harbor area. Swope persuaded the commander of the port to give him full access to the docks. Alexander Woollcott, again competing against Swope for the story, protested the special treatment but to no avail. He finally gave in and worked with Swope. When Swope learned the location of the port in which the *Carpathia*, carrying 700 survivors and 1,200 dead, would arrive, he notified a presidential investigative commission coming from Washington, D.C., and soon the commissioners were en route to the port. Swope then raced ahead of the commissioners and met them at the train station. Arranging for the group's escort to the dock, he rode in the lead carriage. Police tried to prevent the commissioners from entering the area, but Charles Nagel demanded entry. "I am Secretary of Commerce and Labor," Swope reported him as saying, "and as such I am in command of the police on an occasion of this kind. I don't propose to be held up in this manner." The words had a Swopian air about them. It was not uncommon for Swope to put words in the mouth of his sources and have them agree to having said it. Nagle rescued about seventy survivors who lacked the proper papers for immigration and took care of their needs.

In 1914 Swope became city editor of the *World*, but the desk job was short-lived. He sailed across the Atlantic to report on an adventurer attempting a transatlantic flight, but, when war broke out in Europe, the flyer remained grounded. Never one to pass up a story while in the neighborhood, Swope traveled to Germany. His mother, who had moved back to her homeland in 1899 after Swope's father died, and two married sisters lived there. "He was the same dazzling Swope," wrote journalist Stanley Walker. "He treated German generals, admirals and chancellors exactly as he had treated policemen, judges and district attorneys in New York, and he got results."

One of the biggest news story in the early days of the war concerned the exploits of Otto von Weddigen, a German U-boat officer who had sunk three British cruisers in one battle. The young officer's exploit dealt a disastrous blow to English sea power. Swope discovered where von Weddigen was stationed and set out to interview him. The ranking German naval officer, Admiral Alfred von Tirpitz, rejected the idea. So Swope slipped out of Berlin to avoid other correspondents and telegraphed a congratulatory note to von Weddigen and asked for a chance to interview him. The officer refused, but Swope worked his connections. Through a friend of von Tirpitz, he persuaded the admiral to allow him to talk to von Weddigen. He interviewed von Weddigen over the phone and gained a first-person account of the battle. He maneuvered the story through German censors without changes. Then he appealed to "traditional English fair play" to get it through British censors with only minor revisions. The story hit New York like von Weddigen's torpedoes. The *World's* brash reporter had shown he could scoop the world press as well as he had the reporters in New York. After returning to New York from Germany, he became the *World's* city editor but continued to write stories and columns.

He returned to Germany in 1916 and wrote a series of stories that ran in the *World* in October and November. In 1917 the series was awarded the first Pulitzer Prize. It offered insight into Germany's perceptions of the war, the people's attitudes toward America, hopes for democratization of the government, a detailed look at the country's trade and unemployment, and the details of food rationing. The writing revealed a more mature and serious observer and proved Swope could grasp world politics as well as he did urban issues.

He next tackled Washington, serving as a special correspondent for the *World*. The connections he made in the capital, especially with President Woodrow Wilson, opened doors for him when he traveled to France to cover the Paris Peace Conference at the end of World War I.

Despite being limited by restrictions placed on reporters covering the conference, Swope still scored the biggest scoop in his typically brash fashion. Only nine journalists were selected to attend the ceremony for the signing of the treaty, and Swope lost when the press corps drew straws. That's why his story on the signing of the Peace Conference accord sparked controversy when it included a frontal description of the Germans unavailable to the nine correspondents sitting behind the German delegation. Swope had borrowed a car from a general who was chief of military police. With a few other correspondents, he drove up in the car, dressed like a diplomat, wearing his top hat. He sat among the dignitaries and got his story—much to the dismay of his fellow correspondents.

Later, as executive editor of the *World* from 1919 to 1928, he supervised some of the best journalistic writers in the country—Heywood Broun, Woollcott, William Bolitho, Walter Lippmann, and many more. Much of his effort was aimed—just as it had been when he served as city editor earlier—at getting reporters to write with the "sparkle" he had instilled in his stories. The *World* was as feisty as its editor. Swope believed a good reporter should not just stand in the waters but should stir them up. "I think too much emphasis these days is laid upon good writing instead of good getting," he wrote in 1949 in the preface of *A Treasury of Great Reporting.* "There are too many press agents who substitute for the reporter. And in the truer function of the reporter— swarming all over the story and making it wholly his—we had men who made journalistic history."

●◆

A MURDEROUS TALE OF POLICE CORRUPTION

In July 1912, Herman Rosenthal owned a small-time gambling shop. When corrupt policemen demanded more money from him for doing business, they had not figured he would go public with the story. He planned to reveal a tale of police graft and corruption to a grand jury, but he was gunned down before he could squeal. Swope helped to keep the police from suppressing evidence by getting District Attorney Charles S. Whitman to take charge of the investigation. A high-ranking policeman, Lieutenant Charles Becker, and the four killers died in the electric chair for the killing.

HOW POLICE LIEUTENANT BECKER PLOTTED
THE DEATH OF GAMBLER ROSENTHAL
TO STOP HIS EXPOSÉ
Herbert Bayard Swope
New York *World*
October 27, 1912

"Herman Rosenthal has squealed again."

Through the pallid underworld the sibilant whisper ran. It was heard in East Side dens; it rang in the opium houses in Chinatown; it crept up to the semipretentious stuss and crap games of the Fourteenth Street region, and it reached into the more select circles of uptown gambling where business is always good and graft is always high.

Rosenthal had squealed once too often.

This time his action was a direct affront to the "System." He had publicly defied it. He had set it, through its lieutenant, at naught. He had publicly thrown down the gantlet, and it was snatched up, to be returned in the form of four bullets crashing into his head while he stood in the heart of the city under the blaze of lights that enabled bystanders to follow every move of the four assassins, who, their job having been done, and well done, swarmed above the gray automobile that had brought them to their work, and fled, secure, as they thought, from successful pursuit because they were acting under the sheltering hand of Police Lieutenant Charles Becker, who had issued the order to Jack Rose:

"I want Herman Rosenthal croaked!"

But in his death Herman Rosenthal found a thousand tongues where he had been but one. His murder cried in accusation a thousandfold stronger than any he could have made. In his death he gave life to the grudge that he had been nursing in his heart. He vitalized the fierce hatred he felt for the powers that had preyed upon him, and now the people of the state of New York demand that two lives shall pay forfeit for every bullet fired at the man who was not permitted to tell his story.

In this drama of life, which reads so clearly that it would seem to be a work of art—an unreal thing rather than a real story lived by real people—three figures loomed.

Around them the plot is spun. Without them the action lags. Of them one is dead by murder, one is about to pay the penalty for this crime by death in the electric chair, and the third in fear and trembling awaits his summons—sure it will come—from the friends of those subordinate actors in the tragedy whom he surrendered to the law.

Rosenthal squeals; Becker, the police blackmailer, and Rose, his creature, enter upon the stage at the rise of the curtain and are never once away from it until the final fall.

And behind this trio hangs the vast impalpable spectacle, the "System," in whose Labyrinthian maze men are killed, others are robbed, and women are made slaves—each a sacrifice to the greater glory of the "System."

Becker was of the "System," by the "System," and for the "System." He lived and had his being through the grace he found in its eyes. Like Caesar, all things were rendered unto Becker in the underworld, and as it was his to take, so, too, was it his to give. Nothing escaped him. Like Briareus he had a hundred arms, and each of them reached into the pocket of whoever was engaged in an occupation that needed quiet and darkness rather than the light of day and the eyes of the public.

It was not a common type of man who could attain this position of power in the Police Department of the city of New York. He is big in girth and stature. He stands five feet eleven and weighs 190 pounds. His shoulders are broad and his chest deep. He is dark in hair and skin. His nose is straight and big, jutting out uncompromisingly over a long upper lip, a mouth like the cut of a knife, and a chin that sticks out squarely at the end of a jaw that looks like a granite block.

He is forty-two years old. He was born in Callicoon, New York, which was the place of nativity of the redoubtable Dr. Frederick A. Cook, the self-made hero of polar exploration. Becker joined the police force in 1893. His career has been a troublous one since then.

The System is many-sided. It can be gently kind as well as fiercely protective. It takes care of its own, and its own takes care of it. Becker wanted to be a hero. Becker was a good soldier in the System's cause; therefore Becker a hero should be.

He was presented with a medal of police heroism for rescuing James Butler from a rushing tide at the foot of West Tenth Street one July morning. Proudly Becker wore his medal and the accompanying bronze star on his sleeve for two years. Then came the expose.

Butler made an affidavit, fully corroborated, that he was an old lifesaver and an expert swimmer and that he had jumped into the river at the request of Becker, who promised him five dollars for doing so, but never paid the money.

Becker began to be talked about as a coming man in police circles.

On June 22, 1911, Charles Becker, who had been made a lieutenant four years before, was detailed to the command of Special Squad No. I, known as the "Strong-Arm Squad." From then on his history is written in blackmail and murder, in money and blood.

In ten months following his elevation to the most conspicuous position in the New York Police Department Becker, receiving a salary of $2250 and supporting himself and his wife in a luxurious manner, rolled up bank deposits approximating $100,000.

Here enters on the scene Jack Rose, Becker's man Friday—Rose, the humble; Rose, the obsequious; Rose, the fawning, who, at the last, was to turn and rend the man for whom he had committed blackmail, perjury, and murder.

Rose's real name is Jacob Rosenschwig. He is thirty-seven years old. He was born in Russian Poland, and he seems ashamed of it. He was reared on the East Side just at the time that that melon of the city had discovered that America was indeed an Eldorado—for those who wished to make it so. Money was to be had for the asking—if the asking was hard enough.

....Rosenthal was always a hustler. He was a money-maker. Rosenthal the loose-tongued, Rosenthal the babbler, in spite of his unpopularity, which was largely due to the fact that he often talked too much about things that he ought not to talk about at all, was credited with certain powers both in and out of the department.

He had watched Becker's rise closely. Rosenthal described himself as not being a "lover of cops." But he saw in Becker a chance to help himself and at the same time help Becker.

Like the little drops of water, one friction succeeded another between Rosenthal and Becker. Becker made a raid on a crap game during which his press agent, one Charles Plitt,

Jr., shot and killed a Negro named Waverly Carter. At the time Becker's money was pretty well tied up. Besides, he had heard that Rosenthal had made a "killing," so he told Rose to tell Rosenthal that he would like to get $500 for the purposes of Plitt's defense.

Rosenthal's refusal to give Becker the money, coupled with the pressure being put upon him at headquarters, caused the relations between the two to buckle, if not break.

Becker knew Rosenthal was dangerous, and he set himself a task of covering his enemy's every move. On a day late in June, Becker telephoned for Rose to hurry down to the Union Square Hotel, where the two were in the habit of meeting almost daily, either there or at Luchow's. Becker was much disturbed; he said:

"This ___ Rosenthal is going further than I ever thought he was. He is trying to prove that I was his partner. He is peddling the story to the newspapers. He is getting really dangerous. He must be stopped."

"That ought to be easy enough," Rose said, not realizing for a moment the sinister meaning that Becker sought to convey.

"Jack," responded the policeman, "I want you to go after this fellow Jack Zelig down in the Tombs. We framed him on a charge of carrying a gun. Give him a hundred dollars and tell him that if he wants to save himself you will get him out and that he is to send his gang after Rosenthal."

"What do you mean," asked Rose, "get them to beat him up?"

"No," answered Becker with scorn. "I don't want him beaten up. I want him croaked, murdered, his throat cut, dynamited, anything that will take him off the earth. There's a fellow who is too mean to live. There is no other way of handling the job. I want you to have him croaked!"

And as if realizing that the abruptness of his proposition had startled Rose, and fearing that a sufficient cause had not been presented to enlist the collector's sympathy in the undertaking, Becker went on, laying his hands on Rose's shoulders:

"Why, Jack, you haven't any idea the kind of man that Rosenthal is. I would be ashamed to tell you the things that he said about you and your wife and your children...."

Rose knew four of Zelig's men who traveled together—

Frank Muller, alias "Whitey" Lewis; Harry Horowitz, alias "Gyp the Blood"; Louis Rosenberg, alias "Lefty Louie"; and Frank Ciroficci, alias "Dago Frank." All were mankillers, if not in deed, then in spirit, and two of them had real notches on their guns. They knew he came from Zelig and that he had been responsible for getting Zelig out on bail to await trial on a second offense of carrying concealed weapons, which if substantiated meant imprisonment for fourteen years. They knew, too, that Rose, through Becker, could, if he wished, have the charge vitiated; so they felt grateful for what he had done for their chief, and eager to oblige him so that he could do more....

Here the details were supplied from Rose's narrative:

"Vallon, Schepps, and myself got in. The car was driven by Willie Shapiro. We went up to the Seventh Avenue place where 'Dago Frank' had moved. I often saw all the boys there. When we got in front of the house. I sent Schepps to ring the bell. A head popped out of the window, and I recognized 'Dago Frank.' He came downstairs and got in, and I asked him where the rest of the boys were, and he told me they had gone downstairs ahead.

"We drove down to Forty-third Street and Sixth Avenue. There, in front of the poker room, stood 'Bridgie' Weber, 'Lefty,' 'Whitey,' and 'Gyp.' We all went upstairs. Weber told the Negro waiter to bring us something to eat and drink. The rest did so, but I didn't seem to have any appetite. After giving the order to the waiter, Weber went out. We knew where he had gone and why. He had gone to find Herman Rosenthal and then he was coming back to tell us where he was.

"I found myself hoping that Weber wouldn't locate him. I wanted to give him another chance. I thought of his wife and how she was worrying every day about Herman, and it broke me all up.

"Just as I was trying to think of some way to stall it off for a little while, Weber came rushing back and leaned over the table and whispered,

"'Rosenthal is at the Metropole now.'

"Even if I had wanted to, before I could say a word, everybody got up and went out—'Gyp,' 'Lefty,' 'Whitey,' 'Dago,' Weber, and Vallon. Schepps started to, but I asked him to wait with me."

That Monday night there had been a heavy feeling about Mrs' Rosenthal's heart, and she sought to dissuade her husband from leaving her. "Don't go out, Herman," she said. "I'm dreadfully worried about you. Everybody tells me you're in great danger. So stay at home with me at least for tonight."

He was a marked man. Everyone in that neighborhood knew him, and everyone expected that those he attacked would square matters with him. He passed a group of gamblers who had just walked up from the Hotel Knickerbocker, and they stopped and told him that he had been the sole topic of conversation and that if he was a wise man he would go home.

With a cheery "Good night," which, if it were assumed, did not show it in the tone, Rosenthal went on. It was then about one o'clock. He entered the restaurant....

It has never been established whether Rosenthal was sent to or whether he walked to his fate, without being lured to it. He had returned to his table and thrown the newspapers down before him and said in a tone of pride: "That's what the newspapers think of me. Look at that!" and he showed his companions how his story had been given a prominent position on the front page.

Then, refusing another drink and saying that he promised his wife to be home early, Rosenthal threw a dollar down on the table to pay an eight-cent check and started out. Some of those present think that just at this time it was that a stranger approached him and said:

"Herman, somebody wants to see you outside."

Rosenthal passed through the opening formed by the folded back circular door, and as his foot touched the pavement four shots rang out. Four men had been standing on the sidewalk facing the cafe door. They stood close together. As Rosenthal emerged, they acted in unison. The right arms of three of them snapped up, the left arm of one, and as the pistols spoke Rosenthal topped forward and fell without a groan. As he was falling, the left-handed man pulled his trigger again and sent a bullet crashing into the top of the victim's head. The impact was so powerful that the body turned half around and fell on its side and the eyes stared straight up at the brilliant arc lights, the brows set in an expression of bewilderment, with the mouth parted in a fearful grin. There was a jagged hole in the left cheek, and the dropping jaw and relaxed muscles that let the joints twist horribly showed that medical assistance was unnecessary, and on the crown of his head was the great jagged wound made by the last bullet.

Seven policemen were within five hundred feet of the murder, yet the four men made their flight in safety.

Before the body had settled down, the four men had run to a gray car standing on the other side of the street in the shadow of the George M. Cohan Theater, pointing east, clambered aboard, and fled.

They were the adventurers, recruited by Jack Rose two hours earlier, who had come to the scene when "Bridgie" Weber gave the word that the trap had been baited.

Then they had piled out of the poker room, and the four had gotten into the same gray car that had brought them there and had moved on to the Metropole. Each of them knew Herman Rosenthal, and so the possibility of error was minimized. They had taken up their station not five feet from the cafe entrance, to be sure that their prey would not escape them, nor had he.

One officer had been in the Metropole all the time. He was Policeman File, who had jumped for the street at the flash of the first gun and who had stumbled over the body of the dead man, but from whom the murderers were able to escape because of the bystanders, who made it dangerous for file to shoot.

"They've murdered Herman Rosenthal!"

This time it was no whisper that spread through the underworld. It was a cry that staggered the city. It ran the length of Broadway and flashed through the East Side. It stirred the community as it had never been stirred before, for never had a crime of violence given such a direct defiance to law and order.

◦◇

INSIDE THE GERMAN EMPIRE

Before the United States entered World War I, American newspapers covered the conflict from both sides. The New York *World* sent Swope, the paper's city editor, to report on the war from behind German lines. Swope's reports provided insight into Germany, its people, and their feelings about the war. When he returned to the States, he compiled his stories into a book, *Inside the German Empire*. In 1917, he was awarded the first Pulitzer Prize for reporting for his dispatches from Germany.

GERMAN HATRED AIMS TO CRUSH WILSON'S POLICY
Herbert Bayard Swope
New York *World*
November 6, 1916

Throughout Germany today the hatred for America is bitter and deep. It is palpable and weighs you down. All the resentment, all the blind fury Germany once reserved for England alone have been expanded to include us, and have been accentuated in the expansion. The Germans have an outlet for their feelings against England—they express themselves on the battlefields and through the Zeppelins and submarines, but against America they lack a method of registering their enmity. And so the bitterness that cannot be poured out has struck in and saturated the whole empire.

The chagrin and humiliation of their failure to end the war before now through victory are visited upon America. The failure gave birth to hatred. Throughout the length and breadth of Germany the belief is certain and unqualified that had it not been for American moral and physical help to the allies the war would have been long since over. With magnificent disregard of the checks and reverses, both military and economic, Germany has suffered at the hands of the allies; her sons, from top to bottom, say that only America is to blame for the fact that the war is now well into its third year and the more pertinent fact that as time goes on the German chances are bound to grow less.

It is a common thing to hear in Germany that America has a secret alliance with England, under which she is operating now; it is even more of a commonplace to be told that America is deliberately seeking to prolong the war and circumvent peace for the "blood money" she is making out of the struggle. Germany's fear of defeat and loss of prestige are laid at our door; we are made the sacrificial goat offered on the altar of self-glory.

Hate may have no boundaries, but it has beginnings, and it is not hard to classify the grounds from which the German hatred of America springs. There are five, possibly six. They are, as the Germans put them: First—The supply of munitions to the allies. Second—The illegal blockade, for which we are responsible since we have not stopped it. Third—The interference with neutral mails. Fourth—The allies world-wide commercial blockade. Fifth—The submarine doctrine we have compelled Germany to accept. And the sixth may be one that is not so frequently expressed, but which is nevertheless a considerable factor—that America is out of the war and prospering: for what is more usual than for envy to breed hate? Perhaps this sixth cause of German hatred might with equal truth be applied to the resentment said to exist against us in the other countries at war, for surely Germany is not the only one who resents our peace and prosperity.

To the list I have given, I might add as one of the contributory causes our interpretation of neutrality, for this is made the object of bitter recrimination in Germany, and it is a subject on which even those placed in the highest positions speak with utmost candor. Von Jagow, Chief Secretary of State for Foreign Affairs, and Zimmermann, the Chief Under Secretary, in discussing the American attitude, phrased the sentiments of their country when they said to me: "The American neutrality toward Germany is one of the head; toward the allies it is one of the heart. What America does for the allies she does voluntarily and gladly—what she does for Germany she does because she must.

This is a mild view compared to the popular idea. The resentment against America has been cumulative in its growth, while that against England is perhaps less today than it was at the beginning. Because her military activity is against the English, it has wrought at least a measure of satisfaction. But the very fact that America has been out of reach of a concrete demonstration of German hatred has made more serious the conditions existing in the empire today with reference to America, which are those of an actual menace. And the form it takes is the widespread and highly popular agitation for the resumption of the rucksichtslose (ruthless) Lusitania type of U boat warfare.

Throughout Germany the agitation for this plan grows stronger day by day. The Chancellor is holding out against it, but how long he can restrain it no one can say. I left Germany convinced that only peace could prevent its resumption. And the same opinion is held by every German with whom I spoke, and it is held also by Ambassador Gerard. The possibility was so menacing that it formed the principal cause of the Ambassador's return at this time so that he might report to Washington. The *World* set this point out in detail in a wireless dispatch I sent on October 10 from the *Frederik VIII*, on which the Ambassador returned.

But while the plan of returning to the *Lusitania* type of submarine warfare is made more popular by the fact that it would be a blow at America, since America struck this weapon from German hands, it must not be thought that the advocates of the resumption view it merely as an offering to hat; they insist that it is an instrument of great military value, and they pretend to believe that its use will tend to shorten the war. However, the most ardent disciples of this plan can give no logical reasons for their belief, while those supporting the Chancellor in his opposition are able to demonstrate the soundness of their attitude. In normal circumstances this alignment of reason against unreason would be a guarantee against the success for the "rucksichtslose" advocates, but when a nation has its back against the wall, fighting for existence, reason gives way to fury, and fury stops at nothing.

If it be impossible to indict a nation, it appears to be equally difficult to hate a whole nation without centering the hatred upon some one point or man. In the case of Germany, President Wilson personifies America, and so the German hatred is centered on Wilson. Further, because President Wilson is represented by Ambassador Gerard, that official is loaded down with responsibility for all the shortcomings the Germans are able to perceive in our attitude toward them. It is a difficult thing for neutral to be neutral in Germany today. The best friends of Germany must admit that her demands on one's sentiments are rather harsh. In Berlin any one who is not outspokenly an advocate of German supremacy is gazed upon with coldness and suspicion....

America's failure to have effected a peace before now has

been more of a crime in German eyes than her own failure to have forced one through military conquests. That is another count in the indictment lodged against Wilson. That is another reason why Wilson's defeat on Election Day would be regarded as a gigantic German triumph. Every one I spoke to in Germany believes this. It would be treated as a victory, not because the Germans feel there is certainty that Hughes is the man the Germans want, but because there is certainty that Wilson is the man the Germans don't want.

In my three months abroad, and in all my intercourse with representatives of the various strata that make up life in Germany—soldiers, sailors, laborers, politicians, clergymen, professors, newspaper men, business men, farmers—I did not hear one voice raised for Wilson except that of Maximilian Harden, the famous journalist, whose series on "If I Were Mr. Wilson" touched and pleased the President deeply but met scant favor in Germany. Not even Dr. Helfferich, Secretary of State for the Interior, and a vital factor in keeping the peace between the two countries, can see in the President's utterances any friendliness toward Germany. He, in common with the others, seeks to differentiate between the President and the American public, which is believed wishes a greater friendliness to Germany and German methods than Wilson has shown.

There are those in Germany who doubt that this fancied sentiment would actually be reflected by Hughes were he to be elected. One prominent banker with whom I spoke said that it would be too much to expect that the son of a Welsh Baptist minister would be apt to do much for the Germans. But his half-formed fear is nothing to the resentment against Wilson, and so German encouragement to the opposition to his re-election goes on.

7

FLOYD GIBBONS

REPORTING IN HARM'S WAY

On February 26, 1917, after spending six hours in a lifeboat, Chicago *Tribune* correspondent Floyd Gibbons clambered onto the docks of Queenstown, England, rushed to the cable office, and typed out what he thought was going to be a terrible story.

"I couldn't write it," he told his colleague George Seldes; "so I began by a note to the editor apologizing for my condition. I began by describing myself: I'm here in Queenstown, soaked, frozen, ice on my face, ice in my hair, dripping water on the floor; I can hardly move my fingers to write the story; I was torpedoed on the *Laconia*....What do you think they did? Some damn fool didn't realize it was a note to the editor, so they started it off that way."

The lead, the story, and the reporter became famous. Gibbons had defied death one more time and come out with one of the most memorable stories of World War I. Newspapers throughout the world reprinted the story about the cruise liner sunk by a German U-boat. The story shocked Americans and provided one of the overt acts needed to draw the United States into World War I.

Not a bad scoop for a reporter who only five years before had walked into the *Tribune* offices out of work and penniless. That day, Gibbons looked like he had slept in a boxcar. A day or two of stubble covered his face, and his clothes hung from him in dirty, wrinkled bunches. The Socialist paper for which he had worked had failed, and he needed a job. His old boss, now a copy editor at the *Tribune*, put in a good word, and the paper hired him.

A cash advance paid for a bath and a new suit, a gray one with loud checks. Although the pants were a size too small, the outfit fit Gibbons' character. Bold and brash, he was a throwback to a bygone era, perhaps the last of the great journalistic adventurers. During his twenty-seven years of reporting, he covered nine wars, usually from the front lines. World War II would have been the tenth if ill health had not restricted him to his Pennsylvania farm, where he died in 1939.

Born in Washington, D.C., July 16, 1886, he was the eldest of five children. A good Catholic, he boasted of his shanty-Irish origins. Reared in Minneapolis, Minnesota, he sold newspapers as a boy to help support his family. He later attended Georgetown University but was kicked out in his fourth year for pulling pranks. While shoveling coal in Lucca, North Dakota, he started helping the editor at a local weekly and became hooked on newspaper work. In 1907 he went to work for the Minneapolis *Daily News* but didn't last long. He bounced to the Milwaukee *Free Press* as a police reporter and then back to Minneapolis—this time as a reporter for the *Tribune*. He soon owned the police beat, writing colorful, dramatic stories and regularly scooping the competition. He refused to let anything stop him from getting a story. He would steal "pictures from the homes of suicides and murderers," Seldes said, "or pennies from the eyes of the dead if for some reason they were needed for a story." His unorthodox approach produced entertaining copy from even the most monotonous assignments.

It was on the big assignments, however, that he demonstrated his true talent. In 1910 a farmer opposed a lumber company's effort to gain control over a dam on his property. The company was in collusion with the local sheriff. Then working for the Minneapolis *Tribune*, Gibbons had scooped the twenty-five other reporters covering the story so many times that "Red" Schwartz of the rival Minneapolis *Journal* hired a lumberman to hold the lone telephone wire that the journalists shared until Schwartz could file his story. But before Schwartz could send his story, Gibbons cut the phone wire with a hatchet. He then hurried to the telegraph office to score another scoop. He was jailed on a felony charge for cutting the wire, and his newspaper paid $500 to get him out.

Two years later, he joined the Chicago *Tribune*, which employed a talented staff under editor Walter Howey. Howey's dramatic sense and zealous loyalty to newspapering were caricatured by Ben Hecht and Charles MacArthur in *The Front Page*. Although the managing editor, E.S. Beck, emphasized the human interest to the point of melodrama, he also felt responsible to his readers to provide accurate, fair, dependable, and readable stories.

Gibbons had the same commitment. He covered the murder of a local gangster whose girlfriend was taken into custody but not charged. After Gibbons and several other reporters watched the police mildly grill her, he persuaded the police matron to let him interview the girlfriend. At the office, he wrote his story and turned it in too late for the first edition. The night editor read the story and then bawled out Gibbons for missing the news of the girl's confession that had come across a local wire service. Gibbons swore the girl hadn't confessed, but the editor refused to listen. A half hour after the news of the confession was plastered across the front page, the wire service ordered the story "killed." Before quitting the wire service, a reporter had concocted the story to spite his editor. The night editor's stature diminished while Gibbons rose in prominence.

At the *Tribune*, Gibbons fine-tuned his dramatic style and turned out one scoop after another. How did he do it? A colleague, Burton Rascoe, claimed Gibbons had an "air" about him. His six-foot frame and authoritative voice gave him a forceful, intimidating presence. Those physical features, combined with enthusiasm and boldness, helped him overcome obstacles that thwarted other reporters. He also understood his readers, writing the types of stories they wanted to read. His writing had a personal flair that made readers feel as if they, too, had just been rescued from the *Laconia* or survived one of Gibbons' other adventures.

In 1916 Gibbons headed for Mexico to find Pancho Villa, who was raiding American bordertowns. The bandit revolutionary threatened to kill the next American journalist to come south of the border, and Gibbons called his bluff. He found Villa and interviewed him. Villa provided Gibbons with a special car on his personal train. Gibbons witnessed three of Villa's biggest battles and reported on the weaknesses of National Guard action against him. Later, Gibbons returned to Mexico to follow Gen. Pershing's punitive expedition. "Floyd Gibbons and R. Dunn were the only two news persons permitted to go with the Pershing expedition," explained Dr. R.H. Ellis, a physician from El Paso, Texas, who served as Villa's medical chief of staff. "Villa was acquainted with Gibbons, one of the best journalists to cover the revolution. I had many associations with Gibbons and know that he is level-headed and non-drinking." Gibbons' criticism of the inefficient American military mobilization along the border sparked controversy throughout the United States.

In 1917 the *Tribune* assigned Gibbons to cover World War I in Europe. It booked passage for him from New York on the *Frederick VIII*, the same ship on which the German ambassador was traveling. The ambassador's presence assured the liner's safe passage through waters infested with German U-boats. Gibbons, however, wanted to ride on a ship vulnerable to submarine attack. He chose the *Laconia*, an 18,000-ton passenger ship whose scheduled sea route would take it through the submarine zone. The *Tribune* equipped Gibbons with a special life preserver, a fresh-water bottle, electric flashlights, and a flask of brandy.

As Gibbons had hoped, a German submarine torpedoed the ship—although he seemed disappointed because the muffled explosion failed to match his imagination of how great it would be. Seldes claimed Gibbons was not "too regretful when the freezing waves and the freezing winds engulfed the old man [in the lifeboat that Gibbons had boarded] and knocked him into the sea, and then [an] old woman, and took her down also, adding death to his story." Gibbons, however, refuted Seldes' claim by pointing to factual inaccuracies in the latter's account.

In London, Gibbons worked to find ways to file his stories without government censors deleting information. Sometimes, he found the trick was easy. After watching Pershing's arrival in Britain, he filed the story without naming the port because British censors refused to allow him to state the location of the landing. So Gibbons started his dispatch, "PERSHING LANDED AT BRITISH PORT TODAY AND WAS GREETED BY LORD MAYOR OF LIVERPOOL."

Gibbons followed the American expeditionary force to France, where all the firsts—such as the first American killed, wounded, and honored—topped the early news. The Army herded most of the reporters around in a press pool, which often missed the front by several miles.

On one fruitless expedition to witness American artillery fire its first shell, the correspondents halted miles from their destination. As they waited, they saw a battery of American artillery pass with one of their own riding on the caisson: "Hey, there's Gibbons!" yelled correspondent Damon Runyon. "How the hell did he get there?" Gibbons and Raymond Carroll were the only reporters to see the first shot fired by American artillery. Gibbons picked up the shell case and refused to give it up until convinced that it should be presented to President Woodrow Wilson. For their ingenuity, the reporters were arrested and held for forty-eight hours. Thus, their "beat" appeared two days after their colleagues had cabled their stories.

In 1918, German troops broke through Allied lines and stood poised to march on Paris. The Second Division of Marines had set up positions in a wheat field at Belleau Woods near Château Thierry. Most of the press corps stayed at the end of the wheat field while the Marines went ahead. Not Gibbons. He advanced in front of most of the Marines, flanked by his friend, Lt. Oscar Hartzell, who had been a New York *Times* reporter before the war. A sniper with a machine gun opened fire. Three bullets struck Gibbons. One wounded him in the arm, another struck him in the shoulder, and the last tore through his helmut and knocked out his eye. "I caught [the eye] in my hands as I fell," he recalled.

Hartzell pulled Gibbons back to a narrow road where his colleagues carried him to an ambulance driven by a correspondent's brother. The reporters persuaded the driver to disregard regulations and take Gibbons to the American hospital in Neuilly. Doctors operated on Gibbons less than two hours after he had been shot. After he recovered, he rejoined the press corps, wearing a patch over his eye and his arm in a black sling. The French Government honored him with the Croix de Guerre. "Some of his enemies thought he was trying to look romantic," a fellow reporter said about the patch, "but the fact was the eye socket was gone too and he could not hold a glass eye in his head."

Later, writing for *American Magazine*, Gibbons explained his motivation for placing himself in the line of fire:

"Just how does it feel to be shot, on the field of battle? Just what is the exact sensation when a bullet burns its way through your flesh?

"I always wanted to know. As a reporter I 'covered' scores of shooting cases, but I could never learn from the victims what the precise feeling was as the piece of lead struck. But now I know! For three German bullets, which violated my person, completely satisfied my curiosity."

In those two paragraphs Gibbons revealed two critical ingredients in the makeup of a great reporter. First, he wanted to know the sensation felt by the people he wrote about. He probed for those feelings and perceptions that would allow him to re-create the event for the reader. Second, he sought to experience personally the stories he covered. Part of his approach stemmed from his adventurous spirit and his obsessive drive to get the news. It also grew out of a curiosity and enthusiasm for whatever subject he happened to write about.

That characteristic is evident in Gibbons' writing. His style was not fancy, but it was truly readable and colorful in its ability to tell a good story. Gibbons' account of how he got his wound, for example, contains all the elements he made famous—drama, adventure, courage, and lunacy.

Five minutes before five o'clock the order for the advance across the field reached our pit. It was brought there by a second lieutenant, a platoon commander.

"What are you doing here?" he asked, looking at the green brassard and red "C" [for correspondent] on my left arm.

"Looking for the big story," I said.

"If I were you, I'd be about forty miles south of this place," said the lieutenant; "but if you want to see the fun, stick around. We are going forward in five minutes."

...And then we went over. There are really no heroics about it. There is no bugle call, no sword waving, no dramatic enunciation of catch commands, no theatricalism— it's just plain get up and go over. And it is done just the same as one would walk across a peaceful wheat field out in Iowa.

As he had done in the *Laconia* story, Gibbons contrasted his expectations with the real thing. He told the story in much the same way he might have related it to a group of friends back in the States. First, he described the crackle and rattle of enemy machine gun fire. "Our men advanced in open order, ten and twelve feet between men," he said. "Sometimes a squad would run forward fifty feet, and drop. And as its members flattened on the ground for safety, another squad would rise from the ground and make another rush." Shouts signaled "work was being done with bayonets," and the silencing of the machine guns meant the "wood had been won." Gibbons and Hartzell joined up with Maj. Berry, the commanding officer, who allowed the pair to go forward with him. While walking through an open field, Berry was hit by machine gun fire. Gibbons crawled to help him, pushing "forward by digging in with my toes and elbows so as to make as little movement in the oats as possible. I was not mistaken about the intensity of fire that swept the field. It was terrific."

Then the moment Gibbons had anticipated happened. "The lighted end of a cigarette touched me in the fleshy part of my upper left arm. That was all," he recalled. He felt no discomfort other than the burning touch where the bullet had entered. So he continued to crawl forward. "Then the second one hit," he said. "It nicked the top of my left shoulder. And again came the burning sensation, only this time the area affected seemed larger." Still, he had use of his arms, and headed forward to the major. "Then there came a crash. It sounded to me as if someone had dropped a glass bottle into a porcelain bathtub. A barrel of whitewash tipped over, and it seemed that everything in the world turned white....I remember this distinctly, because my years of newspaper training had been but one direction—to sense and remember. So it was that, even without knowing it, I was making mental notes on every impression my senses registered."

In those words—"sense and remember"—Gibbons shared a key to good journalistic writing. Mental note taking rivals physical note taking in that it helps re-create a picture for the reader's mind.

After the war, Gibbons continued to set the example. In 1921, he chronicled the human suffering caused by famine in the Soviet Union without sensationalizing it. The three other correspondents who were traveling with him were distraught over what they saw. Gibbons, however, was intent on transmitting his story back to American newspapers. Accustomed to working in disaster areas, he found the nearest telegraph office, wrote his story, and told the one surviving telegraph operator, "Send that on to Riga." Since the operator had no other telegrams to send, he tapped out Gibbons' thousands of English words, none of which were intelligible to him. Meanwhile, the three other correspondents filed their stories after returning to Moscow. By the time they arrived, Gibbons' first story was three days old.

Gibbons turned over the Russian job to another reporter and set off for a safari to Timbuktu to fulfill a childhood dream and taunt an editor who had once said that's where Gibbons belonged. Gibbons filed a story with that town's dateline and sent a postcard to his old editor. *Tribune* owner Katherine McCormick never forgave him the $25,000 expense of the trip. In 1926 the paper dropped him from its staff.

Gibbons went into radio, where his rapid-fire, clear voice made him famous. He returned to print journalism as an International News Service correspondent covering the Sino-Japanese War, the Spanish Civil War, and Italy's invasion of Ethiopia. His stories received wide attention in the United States, but the physical struggles to get them ruined his health.

He died September 24, 1939. In his obituary, the New York *Times* wrote that Gibbons "seemed to have devoted his life to the search of thrills," but that he differed from most other highly publicized personalities in that "he actually lived up to his publicity."

●◆

"NOTHING WAS LEFT BUT THE MURKY MOURNING OF THE NIGHT"

In 1917 the Chicago *Tribune* wanted more than just the watered-down, censored accounts flowing in from England about World War I. The paper assigned Gibbons to cover the war and booked passage for him on a German liner, the safest mode of transportation through waters infested with

German U-boats. But Gibbons had other ideas. He wanted to know what it was like to be on a ship attacked by a German submarine. He picked the *Laconia*, an 18,000-ton ship of the Cunard line traveling through the submarine zone. He wasn't disappointed.

GERMAN U-BOAT SINKS LACONIA
Floyd Gibbons
Chicago *Tribune*
February 26, 1917

Queenstown, February 26 (Via London)—I have serious doubts whether this is a real story. I am not entirely certain that it is not all a dream and that in a few minutes I will wake up back in stateroom B 19 on the promenade deck of the Cunarder *Laconia* and hear my cockney steward informing me with an abundance of "and sirs" that it is a fine morning.

It is now a little over thirty hours since I stood on the slanting decks of the big liner, listened to the lowering of the lifeboats, heard the hiss of escaping steam and the roar of ascending rockets as they tore lurid rents in the black sky and cast their red glare over the roaring sea.

I am writing this within thirty minutes after stepping on the dock here in Queenstown from the British mine sweeper which picked up our open lifeboat after an eventful six hours of drifting and darkness and baling and pulling on the oars and of straining aching eyes toward the empty, meaningless horizon in search of help. But, dream or fact, here it is:

The Cunard liner *Laconia,* 18,000 tons' burden, carrying seventy-three passengers—men, women, and children—of whom six were American citizens—manned by a mixed crew of 216, bound from New York to Liverpool, and loaded with foodstuffs, cotton, and raw material, was torpedoed without warning by a German submarine last night off the Irish coast. The vessel sank in about forty minutes.

Two American citizens, mother and daughter, listed from Chicago and former residents there, are among the dead. They were Mrs. Mary E. Hoy and Miss Elizabeth Hoy. I have talked with a seaman who was in the same lifeboat with the two Chicago women, and he has told me that

FLOYD GIBBONS

he saw their lifeless bodies washed out of the sinking boat.

The American survivors are Mrs. F.E. Harris of Philadelphia, who was the last woman to leave the *Laconia*; the Reverend Father Wareing of St. Joseph's Seminary, Baltimore; Arthur T. Kirby of New York; and myself.

A former Chicago woman, now the wife of a British subject, was among the survivors. She is Mrs. Henry George Boston, the daughter of Granger Farwell of Lake Forest.

After leaving New York, passengers and crew had had three drills with the lifeboats. All were supplied with life belts and assigned to places in the twelve big lifeboats poised over the side from the davits of the top deck.

Submarines had been a chief part of the conversation during the entire trip, but the subject had been treated lightly, although all ordered precautions were strictly in force.

After the first explanatory drill on the second day out from New York, from which we sailed on Saturday, February 17, the "abandon ship" signal, five quick blasts on the whistle, had summoned us twice to our life belts and heavy wraps (with a flask and a flashlight) and to a roll call in front of our assigned boats on the top deck.

On Sunday we knew generally we were in the danger zone, though we did not know definitely where we were—or at least the passengers did not.

In the afternoon, during a short chat with Captain W.R.D. Irvine, the ship's commander, I had mentioned that I would like to see a chart and note our position on the ocean. He replied, "Oh, would you?" with a smiling, rising inflection that meant "It is jolly well none of your business."

Prior to this my cheery early-morning steward had told us that we would make Liverpool by Monday night, and I used this information in another question to the Captain.

"When do we land?" I asked.

"I don't know," replied Captain Irvine; but my steward told me later it would be Tuesday, after dinner.

The first cabin passengers were gathered in the lounge Sunday evening, with the exception of the bridge friends in the smoke room.

Poor Butterfly was dying wearily on the talking machine [phonograph], and several couples were dancing.

About the tables in the smoke room the conversation was limited to the announcement of bids and orders to the stewards. Before the fireplace was a little gathering which had been dubbed the Hyde Park corner—an allusion I don't quite fully understand. This group had about exhausted available discussion when I projected a new bone of contention.

"What do you say are our chances of being torpedoed?" I asked.

"Well," drawled the deliberative Mr. Henry Chetham, a London solicitor, "I should say four thousand to one."

Lucien J. Jerome, of the British diplomatic service, returning with an Ecuadorian valet from South America, interjected: "Considering the zone and the class of this ship, I should put it down at two hundred and fifty to one that we don't meet a sub."

At this moment the ship gave a sudden lurch sideways and forward. There was a muffled noise like the slamming of some large door at a good distance away. The slightness of the shock and the meekness of the report compared with my imagination were disappointing. Every man in the room was on his feet in an instant.

"We're hit!" shouted Mr. Chetham.

"That's what we've been waiting for," said Mr. Jerome.

"What a lousy torpedo!" said Mr. Kirby in typical New Yorkese. "It must have been a fizzer."

I looked at my watch. It was 10:30 P.M.

Then came the five blasts on the whistle. We rushed down the corridor leading from the smoke room at the stern to the lounge, which was amidships. We were running, but there was no panic. The occupants of the lounge were just leaving by the forward doors as we entered.

It was dark on the landing leading down to the promenade deck, where the first-class staterooms were located. My pocket flashlight, built like a fountain pen, came in handy on the landing.

We reached the promenade deck. I rushed into my stateroom, B 19, grabbed my overcoat and the water bottle and special life preserver with which the Tribune had equipped me before sailing. Then I made my way to the upper deck on that same dark landing.

I saw the chief steward opening an electric switch box in the wall and turning on the switch. Instantly the boat decks were illuminated. That illumination saved lives.

The torpedo had hit us well astern on the starboard side

and had missed the engines and the dynamos. I had not noticed the deck lights before. Throughout the voyage our decks had remained dark at night and all cabin portholes were clamped down and all windows covered with opaque paint.

The illumination of the upper deck, on which I stood, made the darkness of the water, sixty feet below, appear all the blacker when I peered over the edge at my station boat, No. 10.

Already the boat was loading up and men and boys were busy with the ropes. I started to help near a davit that seemed to be giving trouble, but was stoutly ordered to get out of the way and get into the boat.

We were on the portside, practically opposite the engine well. Up and down the deck passengers and crew were donning life belts, throwing on overcoats, and taking positions in the boats. There were a number of women, but only one appeared hysterical—little Miss Titsie Siklosl, a French-Polish actress, who was being cared for by her manager, Cedric P. Ivatt, appearing on the passenger list as from New York.

Steam began to hiss somewhere from the giant gray funnels that towered above. Suddenly there was a roaring swish as a rocket soared upward from the captain's bridge, leaving a comet's tail of fire. I watched it as it described a graceful arc in the black void overhead, and then, with an audible pop, it burst in a flare of brilliant colors.

There was a tilt to the deck. It was listing to starboard at just the angle that would make it necessary to reach for support to enable one to stand upright. In the meantime electric floodlights—large white enameled funnels containing clusters of bulbs—had been suspended from the promenade deck and illuminated the dark water that rose and fell on the slanting side of the ship.

"Lower away!" Someone gave the order, and we started down with a jerk towards the seemingly hungry rising and falling swells.

Then we stopped with another jerk and remained suspended in mid-air while the men at the bow and the stern swore and tussled with the lowering ropes. The stern of the lifeboat was down, the bow up, leaving us at an angle of about forty-five degrees. We clung to the seats to save ourselves from falling out.

"Who's got a knife, a knife, a knife!" shouted a sweating seaman in the bow.

"Great God, give him a knife!" bawled a half-dressed, jibbering Negro stoker, who wrung his hands in the stern.

A hatchet was thrust into my hand, and I forwarded it to the bow. There was a flash of sparks as it crashed down on the holding pulley. One strand of the rope parted and down plunged the bow, too quick for the stern man. We came to a jerky stop with the stern in the air and the bow down, but the stern managed to lower away until the dangerous angle was eliminated.

Then both tried to lower together. The list of the ship's side became greater, but, instead of our boat sliding down it like a toboggan, the taffrail caught and was held. As the lowering continued, the other side dropped down, and we found ourselves clinging on at a new angle and looking straight down on the water.

Many feet and hands pushed the boat from the side of the ship, and we sagged down again, this time smacking squarely on the pillowy top of a rising swell. It felt more solid than mid-air, at least. But we were far from being off. The pulleys stuck twice in their fastenings, bow and stern, and the one ax passed forward and back, and with it my flashlight, as the entangling ropes that held us to the sinking *Laconia* were cut away.

Some shout from that confusion of sound caused me to look up, and I really did so with the fear that one of the nearby boats was being lowered upon us.

A man was jumping, as I presumed, with the intention of landing in the boat, and I prepared to avoid the impact, but he passed beyond us and plunged into the water three feet from the edge of the boat. He bobbed to the surface immediately.

"It's Duggan," shouted a man next to me.

I flashed a light on the ruddy, smiling face and water-plastered hair of the little Canadian, our fellow saloon passenger. We pulled him over the side. He spluttered out a mouthful of water and the first words he said were:

"I wonder if there is anything to that lighting three cigarettes on the same match? I was up above trying to loosen the rope to this boat. I loosened it and then got tangled up in it. The boat went down, but I was jerked up. I jumped for it."

His first reference concerned our deliberate tempting of

fates early in the day when he, Kirby, and I lighted three cigarettes from the same match and Duggan told us he had done the same thing many a time.

As we pulled away from the side of the ship, its receding terrace of lights stretched upward. The ship was slowly turning over. We were opposite that part occupied by the engine rooms. There was a tangle of oars, spars, and rigging on the seat and considerable confusion before four of the big sweeps could be manned on either side of the boat.

The jibbering, bulletheaded Negro was pulling directly behind me, and I turned to quiet him as his frantic reaches with his oar were hitting me in the back. In the dull light from the upper decks I looked into his slanting face, eyes all whites and lips moving convulsively. Besides being frightened, the man was freezing in the thin cotton shirt that composed his entire upper covering. He would work feverishly to get warm.

"Get away from her; get away from her," he kept repeating. "When the water hits her hot boilers, she'll blow up, and there's just tons and tons of shrapnel in the hold!"

His excitement spread to other members of the crew in the boat. The ship's baker, designated by his pantry headgear, became a competing alarmist, and a white fireman, whose blasphemy was nothing short of profound, added to the confusion by cursing everyone.

It was the giveaway of nerve tension. It was bedlam and nightmare.

Seeking to establish some authority in our boat, I made my way to the stern and there found an old, white-haired sea captain, a second cabin passenger, with whom I had talked before. He was bound for Nova Scotia with codfish. His sailing schooner, the *Secret*, had broken in two, but he and his crew had been taken off by a tramp and taken back to New York.

He had sailed from there on the *Ryndam*, which, after almost crossing the Atlantic, had turned back. His name is Captain Dear.

"The rudder's gone, but I can steer with an oar," he said. "I will take charge, but my voice is gone. You'll have to shout the orders."

There was only one way to get the attention of the crew, and that was by an overpowering blast of profanity. I did my best and was rewarded by silence while I made the announcement that in the absence of the ship's officer assigned to the boat, Captain Dear would take charge.

We rested on our oars, with all eyes on the still lighted *Laconia*. The torpedo had struck at 10:30 P.M., according to our ship's time. It was thirty minutes afterward that another dull thud, which was accompanied by a noticeable drop in the hulk, told its story of the second torpedo that the submarine had dispatched through the engine room and the boat's vitals from a distance of two hundred yards.

We watched silently during the next minute, as the tiers of lights dimmed slowly from white to yellow, then to red, and nothing was left but the murky mourning of the night, which hung over all like a pall.

A mean, cheese-colored crescent of a moon revealed one horn above a rag bundle of clouds in the distance. A rim of blackness settled around our little world, relieved only by general leering stars in the zenith, and where the *Laconia's* lights had shone there remained only the dim outline of a blacker hulk standing out above the water like a jagged headland, silhouetted against an overcast sky.

The ship sank rapidly at the stern until at last its nose stood straight up in the air. Then it slid silently down and out of sight like a piece of disappearing scenery in a panorama spectacle.

Boat No. 3 stood closest to the ship and rocked about in a perilous sea of clashing spars and wreckage. As the boat's crew steadied its head into the wind, a black hulk, glistening wet and standing about eight feet above the surface of the water, approached slowly and came to a stop opposite the boat and not six feet from the side of it.

"What ship was dot?" The correct words in throaty English with the German accent came from the dark hulk, according to Chief Steward Ballyn's statement to me later.

"The *Laconia*," Ballyn answered.

"Vot?"

"The *Laconia*, Cunard line," responded the steward.

"Vot does she weigh?" was the next question from the submarine.

"Eighteen thousand tons."

"Any passengers?"

"Seventy-three," replied Ballyn, "men, women, and

children, some of them in this boat. She had over two hundred in the crew."

"Did she carry cargo?"

"Yes."

"Vell, you'll be all right. The patrol will pick you up soon," and without further sound, save for the almost silent fixing of the conning-tower lid, the submarine moved off.

●◆

"NO LIVING SOUL IN SIGHT, NO BARKING DOG, NO PLAYING CHILDREN"

Throughout the summer of 1921 news of widespread famine trickled out of Russia. Gibbons wanted the "inside Russia" story and wanted it first. Other correspondents flocked to the border; but the Russian ambassador, Litvinov, refused entry into the famine area. Gibbons stormed into Litvinov's office and said he had hired a plane and was going to have it land in Red Square unless he received permission to enter the country. The bluff worked. Litvinov accompanied Gibbons on the next train into the Soviet Union. Walter Duranty, who would spend nearly two decades covering the Soviet Union for the New York *Times*, marveled at Gibbons' bravado. He said Gibbons "fully deserved his success because he had accomplished the feat of bluffing the redoubtable Litvinov stone-cold...a noble piece of work." The New York *Times* grudgingly carried the story from the Chicago *Tribune* reporter.

WAITING FOR DEATH IN RUSSIAN VILLAGE
Floyd Gibbons
New York *Times*
August 27, 1921

MORDOVEKAIA, BORDOVODA, STATE OF SAMARA (fifteen miles inland and 120 miles by wagon from the nearest railroad station). Aug. 27.—Here is a village of living death. We first saw it from the distance of a mile when our careening droskies emerged from a silent pine wood and plunged hub deep into sand and chuck-holes in the snake-like Russian road winding across a rolling plain of bare, blackened fields over which hungry crows flapped and cawed.

Against the sunless gray sky was a double line of thatched roofs separated by a broad, unbroken village street 200 feet wide and unadorned with either paving or sidewalks. The thatch was gone from a number of the roofs. There was no living soul in sight, no barking dog, no playing children—no sign of life was apparent. Coming up the middle of the street we looked into the windows of log huts on either side, but not a single face peeped out. Our two panting horses were the only animals in the scene, over which hung a terrible silence.

"Which house?" my interpreter asked the secretary of the Governor of the State, who was accompanying us.

"Any one. They are all the same. One is as bad as another," replied the Secretary.

We drew up in front of the nearest, passed through a small door made of hewn planks, and stepped into a low-ceilinged room with a flooring of loose boards. On some cleanly scrubbed planks in the center of the room was a brightly washed brick oven, reaching almost to the ceiling. In one corner was the family ikon and a collection of brightly colored pictures of saints in gilded frames.

There was a woman in the room. She saw us as we entered and rose from a stool before the oven. Her head was covered with a white kerchief tied under the chin. Her face was wrinkled and gaunt, but her eyes were piercing. She wore a man's flannel shirt and a much-patched but clean skirt made of a material resembling flour sacking. Her stockingless feet were encased in home-made cloth slippers, which were much worn. A rapid exchange of Russian between the interpreter and the woman was followed by the latter's translation of her reply.

"Why do you see no one in the village?" the woman repeated. "Because all are too weak to move about except in case of absolute necessity. I have not tasted real black bread since Easter. Where is my husband? He died three weeks ago—there in the bed in the corner. He was so thin—then came vomiting. The doctor forbade all else to touch him. I washed and buried him—I and my children."

Our eyes followed the final wave of her hand toward the ceiling over the edge of which appeared four pairs of eyes— four white faces—four small mouths, munching listlessly on sunflower seeds. The false ceiling located over the oven was getting the full benefit of the heat rising therefrom. In spite of the lack of ventilation the drying socks and cloths on the oven door smelled clean—no dirt was apparent.

"We shall all follow him soon," she continued. "We sit and wait and grow weaker every day. We have hunted long for food—there is no more. We have eaten grass, straw, weeds, the bark of trees and roots, and we still eat these things that we never would have fed to our cattle—but there is no food in them. Here is our bread."

She produced a damp black chunk of sour-smelling punk from which protruded wisps of straw and green and yellow chunks of fiber.

"It is made from melon rinds dried in the oven and then ground," she explained. "It fills, but it does not feed. The children do not know, but I do. Each day they grow thinner. Every morning I see them more wasted. They ask me for bread, and this is all that I have to give them, but not much longer."

Her chin quivered as she summoned her strength to support her peasant pride that forbade weeping.

We visited other huts in the long, silent street which once was a village containing 250 families of 1,000 souls. Now it is reduced almost one-third by starvation, cholera, typhus and flight. Some families still maintained a skeleton cow or horse which they refused to devour for food because "it would not be Christian" to destroy animals necessary for the next harvest, which none of these villagers are likely to live to see.

The news of the arrival of strangers brought several dozen villagers to their windows and doors, among them the village doctor.

"There is nothing that I can do," he said. "They ask for medicine. It is not medicine that they need, but food, and there is no food. These fields are bare for nine miles. Some of the people go out into the fields and die of exhaustion. They never come back. We never hear of them again. It saves us the painful exertion of burial. I do not belong here. I am a medical professor at Samara.

"The Soviet mobilized me and sent me here to care for these people; but I have nothing to feed them, and I know of no way that anything can be sent here. I have been ordered to remain, so I expect to die with them, and I do not think that my death is more than a month away. I am old, and it does not matter; but it is the children that seem to die first. They drop over in the street. We old ones just live on; gnawing our way to death and dreaming of it at night. God pity us!"

8

ALEXANDER WOOLLCOTT

Capturing Humanity Amid War

There is nothing like the glitter, the glamor, the glory, and the glitz of gleaming Broadway. Nothing, that is, except the mud, the mustard gas, the mourning, and the monotony of a miserable war. To Alexander Woollcott, war seemed the greater of the two.

Born in 1887, Woollcott was an important Broadway critic for the New York *Times* by the time World War I started. He wished fervently, however, to serve in Europe. He got his chance, first in the hospital detail, measuring corpses for burial and emptying bedpans. With the birth of the newspaper *The Stars and Stripes*, he was asked to join its staff as a correspondent. He agreed reluctantly, afraid he would be writing for a propaganda sheet.

Woollcott's stories from the battle lines instead turned out to be some of the most heartfelt, moving pieces of war reporting ever written. After years of being stagestruck, Woollcott at last found himself a character in one of the largest productions of humanity. Forgetting that he had a prejudice against propaganda, he critiqued his fellow performers lovingly, patriotically, and admiringly.

He did not underestimate his own role in the play, either. "*The Stars and Stripes*...[was] that irreverent, homespun, and highly unmilitary weekly which was such a characteristically American contribution to the defeat of Germany and to the art of war," he said. It was "the first newspaper to be successfully used as a weapon in modern war." With pride he recalled that military commanders were "not above taking an occasional cue" from *The Stars and Stripes* and that 250,000 copies were sent home to the United States every week. Best of all, it inspired the soldiers and helped them understand the colossal struggle in which they were essential bit players. "It was no uncommon thing," Woollcott said, "...for the correspondent of *The Stars and Stripes* to see in some tattered regiment that had just dropped back a little way for breath, slum, and replacements, groups of men poring over *The Stars and Stripes* account of the battle in which, a few hours before, they themselves had been pretty desperately engaged."

No wonder the soldiers loved Woollcott's work. He told his war stories with a brother's compassion and a patriot's fervor. His deep admiration and love for his subject showed in every word. The troops he saw and loved were tireless, dedicated to the end—or even after the end. He told, for instance, of Captain Frances M. Leahy, who was struck by a German shell that "plowed up the earth" and then hit Leahy, tearing a hole in his chest.

"Good-by, boys," [Leahy] said, and his head sagged forward.

Then it was as if, somewhere in the universe, a Commander Invisible had called "Attention!" Captain Leahy raised his head. With clearing voice, he spoke the name of the officer to whom it would be his duty to turn over the battalion in the event of his being called away.

"Lieutenant Hansen," he said, "the command is 'Forward.' See the boys through."

Then he died.

Woollcott drew his portraits of the war with great feeling and deep emotion. He looked for and wrote about nobility, dedication, bravery, determination, and loyalty. His stories were calculated, as if by a master playwright, to tug at the heartstrings and burn into the memory. Far from reciting mere facts about battles, he delved into the men's emotions and tried to reproduce them on paper. He wanted his readers to feel exactly what the soldiers felt. He achieved that by vivid use of the language.

Bright, correct language was so important to him that as a child he exasperated his beloved older sister Julie about it.

She had to tell him, "Don't you talk to me about nouns, Aleck Woollcott. I don't know what a noun is and I don't want to!" Many years later as an adult, Woollcott was still carrying on his crusade for just the right word. He once teased his friend Ira Gershwin mercilessly for misusing a word. "[I'm] hoping you fry in hell," Woollcott joked.

One of Woollcott's favorite devices was repetition. Over and over again, he'd drive home an idea through repetitive, distinct description. He used repetition, for instance, to describe the jumbled confusion of tired troops as they rambled toward the next confrontation:

It was late Wednesday, just before sundown, that we knew we were going into an attack. The day before—that was Tuesday, the sixteenth, wasn't it?—we had suddenly pulled up stakes, piled into trucks, and started off for somewhere, we didn't know where.

We were going along roads we didn't know, through a countryside we'd never seen before. The boys were all singing and kidding, because they thought, most of them, that they were going to a rest area. They wanted to do nothing in the world except sleep for about a week. Lord knows, they'd earned it....

I don't think I can ever tell you what the roads were like that Wednesday night. It seemed to us as if all the soldiers from all the nations in the world were moving, moving, moving—somewhere. French lancers, French of many a uniform, Jasbos and doughboys, doughboys, doughboys— horses snorting, drivers coaxing, cursing; doughboys laughing—tanks, ammunition trains, ambulances, supply trains, mules, horses, water carts, wheels, wheels, guns, guns, guns—all creeping along in the mud and the dark and the rain—all creeping over little, rotten, twisting, country roads that climbed hills and dipped down into valleys, roads all cut up by shell-fire, roads that hadn't been mended since Joan of Arc advanced along them.

Although Woollcott was expert at writing from his own point of view, a quality he learned as a drama critic, his war reports often were more strictly told in the third person. He stood aside as an admiring observer of the men who served so selflessly. And those men, he realized, contributed all the emotion and color a story could need. He simply became the men's vehicle for telling their stories. The soldiers were the actors, and Woollcott was their reviewer. Thus, without involving himself in the stories, he watched and described the scenes. Occasionally he analyzed them. His observant style reflected the true liveliness and zest of the men themselves, thus providing movingly animated accounts of life on the front as seen by the common soldiers. That quality can be seen, for instance, in his tale of a 16-year-old machine gunner, Private First Class Albert E. Scott, which is reprinted in this anthology. Accustomed to dealing with stage characters, Woollcott described Scotty in great detail, assessing his character by his actions and not by mere words.

That type of characterization, peppered with actions that described the subject far more clearly than mere statistics could, was the hallmark of Woollcott's war reporting. He described, for instance, the heroism of the runners who carried messages to outlying posts. Several went at a time in case the others were gruesomely halted by German shells. He told of partners Al Boysen and Billy Shupp, rushing a message across a battlefield. Boysen was following Shupp, when Boysen "saw his friend struck and tossed into the air in a geyser of earth. He himself was wounded, painfully wounded, in the leg, but he was not done for, and a few moments later the battalion adjutant caught him as he pitched, weak and white-faced, into the dugout.

"'They've killed Shupp, sir,' he blurted, 'and they've wounded me.'"

Woollcott described the next scene in painful detail. Boysen repeated his message twice and then turned around "as if to start out again—out into the storm." His buddies stopped him.

"'Where 'm I going?' he cried, the hysterical note mastering his voice. 'Where 'm I going? I'm going to get my buddy.'

"Then he fainted."

Woollcott's approach was essentially to report clearly and matter-of-factly, either through his own eyes or through someone else's. He did not try to impose artificial sentimentality on the stories. The sentiment came from the action of the men, who were dedicated to their cause.

Woollcott especially admired the men at the front, perhaps because he himself was such a bad soldier. A fellow soldier on the troop ship transporting his company to Europe described him, overweight and nearsighted, as a "pregnant mermaid." A New York *World-Telegram* reporter described his odd "uniform" during an attack. "Aleck had a frying pan strapped around his waist, and an old gray shawl across his shoulders," the reporter said. "Whenever it was necessary to duck from a burst of shellfire, Aleck would place the shawl carefully in the middle of the road and sit on it." Furthermore, the reporter said, Woollcott was so impassioned about a drama review he had read that he argued with another war correspondent about dramatic criticism as shells burst around them. Flat on their bellies, they bickered on.

The incident was indicative of Woollcott's outlook toward the war. Despite the seriousness of war, soldiers had other interests, nonmilitary interests outside of guns and shellfire and battles. Knowing this, Woollcott wrote and staged a play, his only success as a playwright, for the men in France. Otherwise, he wrote stories about offbeat topics that had great appeal because anyone, even folks back home, could understand them. He looked beyond the obvious stories of battles and troop movements and politics of surrender to find the human angle that his readers would love. For instance, Woollcott, like other soldiers in conquered Germany, began to see the power and prestige of very ordinary things. "With a musette bag full of soap," he told his readers, "a soldier could travel like a king from one end of Germany to the other. One of those dinky little pieces of issue soap, like those we used to see on Pullman trains, will buy anything." Dinky slivers of soap, he reported, had bought a pumpkin (which the owner refused to sell for mere money), a goose, and handsome souvenirs. "Soap boxes are now under triple guard, and the billeted officer who leaves his soap on his washstand is like the butterfly society woman back home who was forever leaving her jewelry around where some one could pick it up." Woollcott's best-loved report from the front was, in fact, about a nonmilitary subject, a plain old mongrel dog, whom the soldiers had adopted and named "Verdun Belle." That story is reprinted below.

Among other nonmilitary subjects, he wrote about New York stage performers who wound up in the Army. They were put to work performing as well as soldiering, slogging out life in the mud when they would have enjoyed warm baths and prissy treatment in New York. Woollcott observed wryly that the Army was "the great chastener of temperament." He noted, "The ingenue, the props, the first bass, the low comedian, the second violin, and the librettist must all lend their muscles to the task of carrying the piano down a flight of 173 German steps to have it ready for the grand overture. And when the audience has retired to its dugouts and the lights are out, the whole company lies down and goes to sleep on the floor of the theater."

Although Woollcott returned to journalism after World War I as a widely respected drama critic, and although he became a much-loved radio personality, he considered his World War I reporting to be the best of all he wrote. As Walter Winchell later recalled, two of Woollcott's associates realized that their buddy had disappeared when the Armistice ending World War I was announced.

"Where was Aleck while we were celebrating?" one of them asked.

"Probably in a corner, crying his eyes out," the other replied.

◆

A MARINE'S LOVE FOR A MONGREL DOG

Verdun, France, in World War I was the grim site of trench warfare. Such warfare saw the first use of the machine gun, mustard gas, the hand grenade, the anonymous enemy. Traditional combat gave way to a faceless kind of fighting. War seemed to have made a great leap into the technological and robot-like era of modern fighting. It was not the kind of fighting that the World War I soldiers' fathers and grandfathers could recall.

Despite the new and impersonal face of warfare, the soldiers in the trenches managed to retain a sense of humanity. In the case of Verdun Belle, the humanity of the men showed in their affection for a plain old dog. In telling the story, Woollcott painted a vivid picture of the love of a Marine for his dog. Without saying it in so many words, the story told of human kindness triumphing in the hardship of battle.

By departing from the obvious military subject matter, Woollcott turned out one of the best stories of the war—any war. By describing the men's actions, he showed that they were still human in the middle of one of the most awful conflicts humanity had ever known.

VERDUN BELLE
Alexander Woollcott
The Stars and Stripes
June 14, 1918

This is the story of Verdun Belle, a trench dog who adopted a young leatherneck, of how she followed him to the edge of the battle around Château-Thierry, and was waiting for him when they carried him out. It is a true story.

Belle is a setter bitch, shabby white, with great splotches of chocolate brown in her coat. Her ears are brown and silken. Her ancestry is dubious. She is undersize and would not stand a chance among the haughtier breeds they show in splendor at Madison Square Garden back home. But the marines think there never was a dog like her since the world began.

No one in the regiment knows whence she came, nor why. When she joined the outfit in a sector near Verdun, she singled out one of the privates as her very own and attached herself to him for the duration of the war. The young marine would talk long and earnestly to her, and everyone swore that Belle could "compree" English.

She used to curl up at his feet when he slept, or follow silently to keep him company at the listening post. She would sit hopefully in front of him whenever he settled down with his laden mess kit, which the cooks always heaped extra-high in honor of Belle.

Belle was as used to war as the most weather-beaten *poilu*. The tremble of the ground did not disturb her, and the whining whir of the shells overhead only made her twitch and wrinkle her nose in her sleep. She was trench-broken. You could have put a plate of savory pork chops on the parapet, and nothing would have induced her to go up after them.

She weathered many a gas attack. Her master contrived

a protection for her by cutting down and twisting a French gas mask. At first this sack over her nose irritated her tremendously, but once, when she was trying to claw it off with her forepaws, she got a whiff of the poisoned air. Then a great light dawned on Belle, and after that, at the first *alerte*, she would race for her mask. You could not have taken it from her until her master's pat on her back told her everything was all right.

In the middle of May, Belle presented a proud but not particularly astonished regiment with nine confused and wiggling puppies, black and white or, like their mother, brown and white, and possessed of incredible appetites. Seven of these were alive and kicking when, not so very many days ago, the order came for the regiment to pull up stakes and speed across France to help stem the German tide north of the troubled Marne.

In the rush and hubbub of marching orders, Belle and her brood were forgotten by everyone but the young marine. It never once entered his head to leave her or her pups behind. Somewhere he found a market basket and tumbled the litter into that. He could carry the pups, he explained, and the mother dog would trot at his heels.

Now the amount of hardware a marine is expected to carry on the march is carefully calculated to the maximum strength of the average soldier, yet this leatherneck found extra muscle somewhere for his precious basket. If it came to the worst, he thought, he could jettison his pack. It was not very clear in his mind what he would do with his charges during a battle, but he trusted to luck and Verdun Belle.

For forty kilometers he carried his burden along the parched French highway. No one wanted to kid him out of it, nor could have if they would. When there followed a long advance by camion, he yielded his place to the basket of wriggling pups, while he himself hung on the tailboard.

But then there was more hiking, and the basket proved too much. It seemed that the battle line was somewhere far off. Solemnly, the young marine killed four of the puppies, discarded the basket, and slipped the other three into his shirt.

Thus he trudged on his way, carrying those three, pouched in the forest green, as a kangaroo carries its young, while the mother dog trotted trustingly behind.

One night he found that one of the black and white pups was dead. The road, by this time, was black with hurrying troops, lumbering lorries jostling the line of advancing ambulances, dust-gray columns of soldiers moving on as far ahead and as far behind as the eye could see. Passing silently in the other direction was the desolate procession of refugees from the invaded countryside. Now and then a herd of cows or a little cluster of fugitives from some desolated village, trundling their most cherished possessions in wheelbarrows and baby-carts, would cause an eddy in the traffic.

Somewhere in this congestion and confusion, Belle was lost. In the morning there was no sign of her, and the young marine did not know what to do. He begged a cup of milk from an old Frenchwoman, and with the eye-dropper from his kit he tried to feed the two pups. It did not work very well. Faintly, the veering wind brought down the valley from far ahead the sound of the cannon. Soon he would be in the thick of it, and there was no Belle to care for the pups.

Two ambulances of a field hospital were passing in the unending caravan. A lieutenant who looked human was in the front seat of one of them, a sergeant beside him. The leatherneck ran up to them, blurted out his story, gazed at them imploringly, and thrust the puppies into their hands.

"Take good care of them," he said. "I don't suppose I'll ever see them again."

And he was gone. A little later in the day, that field hospital was pitching its tents and setting up its kitchens and tables in a deserted farm. Amid all the hurry of preparation for the big job ahead, they found time to worry about those pups. The problem was food. Corned willy was tried and found wanting.

Finally, the first sergeant hunted up a farm-bred private, and the two of them spent that evening chasing four nervous and distrustful cows around a pasture, trying vainly to capture enough milk to provide subsistence for the new additions to the personnel.

Next morning the problem was still unsolved. But it was solved that evening.

For that evening a fresh contingent of marines trooped by the farm, and in their wake—tired, anxious, but undiscouraged—was Verdun Belle. Ten kilometers back, two days before, she had lost her master and, until she should find him again, she evidently had thought that any marine was better than none.

The troops did not halt at the farm, but Belle did. At the gate she stopped dead in her tracks, drew in her lolling tongue, sniffed inquiringly the evening air, and like a flash—a white streak along the drive—she raced to the distant tree, where, on a pile of discarded dressings in the shade, the pups were sleeping.

All the corps men stopped work and stood around and marveled. For the onlooker it was such a family reunion as warms the heart. For the worried mess sergeant it was a great relief. For the pups it was a mess call, clear and unmistakable.

So, with renewed faith in her heart and only one worry left in her mind, Verdun Belle and her puppies settled down on detached service with this field hospital. When, next day, the reach of the artillery made it advisable that it should move down the valley to the shelter of a fine hillside château, you may be sure that room was made in the first ambulance for the three casuals.

This was the Château of the Guardian Angel, which stands on the right of the Paris-Metz road, just north of La Ferté as you hike toward Château-Thierry.

In a grove of trees beside the house the tents of the personnel were pitched, and the cots of the expected patients ranged side by side. The wounded came—came hour after hour in steady streams, and the boys of the hospital worked on them night and day. They could not possibly keep track of all the cases, but there was one who did. Always a mistress of the art of keeping out from underfoot, very quietly Belle hung around and investigated each ambulance that turned in front of the main road and backed up with its load of pain to the door of the receiving room.

Then one evening they lifted out a young marine, listless in the half stupor of shell shock. To the busy workers he was just Case Number Such-and-Such, but there was no need to tell anyone who saw the wild jubilance of the dog that Belle had found her own again at last.

The first consciousness he had of his new surroundings was the feel of her rough pink tongue licking the dust from his face. And those who passed that way on Sunday last found two cots shoved together in the kindly shade of a spreading tree. On one the mother dog lay contented with her puppies. Fast asleep on the other, his arm thrown out so that one grimy hand could clutch one silken ear, lay the young marine.

Before long they would have to ship him on to the evacuation hospital, on from there to the base hospital, on and on and on. It was not very clear to anyone how another separation could be prevented. It was a perplexing question, but they knew in their hearts they could safely leave the answer to someone else. They could leave it to Verdun Belle.

●◆

THE HEROISM OF A BOY SOLDIER

It was glamorous to go to Europe during World War I. Young Americans, far too young to fight, lied about their ages and slipped through to fight in a man's world.

PFC Albert E. Scott, age 16, was not the only underage boy to find his way into battle. He was not the only youth whose schooling went unfinished and whose mother worried constantly back home in the States. Of course, Scotty was not the only kid to show great courage.

Woollcott saw a universal spark of youth in Scotty's story. He saw characteristics of both the man and the little boy as he gave his tribute to Scotty—and to all underage kids who joined up with youthful exuberance and resolve to whip the enemy.

SCOTTY
Alexander Woollcott
The Stars and Stripes
August 2, 1918

Private First Class Albert E. Scott died last week on the field of honor.

He was the youngest man in his regiment, and his colonel thinks he was the youngest man in all the A.E.F.

In the One Hundred and First they are talking these days of all the good pals they lost in the fierce, unforgettable chase they gave the Germans in the great retreat from the Marne. But most of all—a little oftener and a bit more fondly— they talk of Scotty.

"He was a good kid," they say, "and he died on his gun."

Scotty was only fifteen and still going to high school back in Brookline when war came to America and he held up his right hand. Though he stood no more than five feet six, though his fair hair was curly and very boyish, though his mother probably wondered how even an overworked recruiting officer could ever have mistaken him for a grown-up, he was husky enough to pass for the eighteen years he boldly claimed.

Afterwards, there was some worried suggestion that he'd better stay home with his folks, but there were so many men in the outfit who knew the family, so many officers his father knew, above all he himself was so pleadingly eager to go, that when one fine day in September, the regiment sailed away, Scotty, barrack bag, rifle, mess kit, and all were stowed away in the hold with the rest.

In all his soldiering, Scotty never appeared on sick report, was never late at formations, never hid from dirty details. It was only once in a while that the older heads in the company were reminded how very young he was.

They could not help thinking of it when they found that the birthday he was celebrating one bleak November day in the monotonous training area somewhere in France was only his sixteenth. Nor when they realized he never knew the pride of using that shiny razor which had been thoughtlessly doled out to him, along with his housewife [sewing kit] and shoe brush in the camp back home. Nor when Christmas came and brought with it for Scotty some kid games from his Down East aunts, who had forgotten it was a soldier they had in France.

On such occasions the company commander was worried over his responsibility, and one day he formally appointed the supply sergeant as Scotty's guardian. The sergeant saw to it that he wrote home regularly, went to mass every Sunday, and gave every *buvette* a wide, wide path. Not that he needed watching, for, as the supply sergeant said, there never was a better kid than Scotty.

It is true that once he was absent for some unaccountable hours in the major's automobile. That was why they reduced him to a buck private. But they restored him to his original rank the first day they saw him with a sho-sho gun.

The French officers, who came to instruct in the use of that light automatic machine-gun which fires eighteen shots in a twinkling, found it was the youngster of the regiment who mastered it first and who, before many weeks had passed, became the best shot of them all. He was such a wonderful gunner that older soldiers were proud to be his feeders, because they knew their gun would do the most damage with Scotty at the sights.

And cool. He was always a quiet one, but under shellfire he became deadly quiet and cool as a cucumber. They found that out at Seicheprey in April, when a shell struck the edge of the parapet, throwing the gun into the trench and burying it, the boy, and his feeders in an avalanche of dirt. Scotty wriggled out, extricated his beloved sho-sho, took it in his arms, and with never a word to any one, marched fifteen feet along the trench, set the gun up again and went on firing.

But his great chance came when, on that historic 18th of July, his regiment got the order for which, through many a month of dreams, it had longed—the order to advance. It went eighteen kilometers without stopping, chasing the Boche [German soldiers] up hill and down dale, fighting its way through patch after patch of inviting woods that would prove treacherous with hidden machine-guns.

Scotty would have told you that he belonged to what the general proudly called his iron battalion, and that in that battalion, the men of his company—Company H—were known as the Indians. They got that name from the wild warwhoops with which they went rip-roaring into battle—strange, unintelligible savage cries that were echoes, perhaps, of the ones that sounded long ago around the huts and stockades of primitive America.

But the men of Company H had another character. They were good Catholics, most of them. No one knows where they got the idea or who first suggested it, but had you been watching at dawn on the morning of the 18th, you would have found that when they went over the top, each one of the Indians wore something that is no part of issue regulations, looped around the felt shoulder strap of his blouse. It was a rosary.

In the first days of that battle, the movement was so swift that more than once a small German rearguard and an advance Yank Platoon would meet in the forest and fight out then and there a complete and separate battle all their own. So it was with the Indians one afternoon, as they were making their way past the bitterly won town of Epieds.

At a crossroad they saw troops approaching them in a column of squads. The officer in charge caught them in the focus of his field-glasses. They were Boches—coming on. The Yanks waited, itching to open fire, but biding their time. Suddenly, the Boches deserted the road and came at them through the forest.

The lieutenant placed his men along a roadside ditch. He placed Scotty and his sho-sho beside a tree and squarely opposite a narrow woodland path that opened across the way. He could see straight down that path, and the Boches were bound either to come along it or to cross it.

"See that path, Scotty," said the lieutenant. "That's your target. Not one of them must cross it."

"Yes, sir," said Scotty, and dropped beside his gun.

Then, from the high branches of many a tree and from many a shelter, the German fire opened, and the Yank fire answered.

A gray figure darted suddenly into the leafy path. He fell.

Another appeared. He fell.

There was perhaps ten minutes of that, and what was left of the German party was withdrawing when a handful of soldiers scampered along the road. They were Germans, but they shouted as they ran, "Don't shoot, we're Americans!"

For a moment, just for the space that a breath is held, Scotty thrust his head up to see. From his perch in some tree, a sniper shot him in the forehead. Another bullet found his heart. He fell forward, dead, on his gun.

They had killed him, but the number of their dead that was counted was thirty.

"Thirty," the Indians will tell you, "and he died on his gun."

9

DAMON RUNYON

KING OF SENSATIONAL REPORTING

Damon Runyon did not finish high school. His background was the streets, the saloons, and the brothels of Pueblo, Colorado. Yet his writing style was so effective that other writers picked it up and then gave it his name. His newspaper stories were collected into books, and the books made into movies.

"Runyonese" was the language he used, and "Runyonesque" was how people described his style. A colorful blend of detail, metaphor, present tense, and vernacular mixed into a unique style of writing and reporting. Runyon loved his hobos, gangsters, and sports heroes, and he imagined that most of his readers loved them, too. He was right. He was one of the most widely read reporters of the '20s and '30s—covering everything from murder trials to society bashes to boxing matches and giving every event his special touch.

It was the era of sensationalism, and Runyon was the King of Sensational Reporting. He knew his readers. "He understood the prejudices, fears, and interests of the audience for whom he wrote," Patricia Ward D'Itri explained in the biography *Damon Runyon.* "They wanted to know about such external badges of status as the participants' clothing and automobiles. His careful eye for detail and his subjective reactions pandered to the readers' interest in sensationalism. Runyon served as Everyman's eyewitness in the courtroom."

When he covered the famous Snyder-Gray murder trial

of 1927, the lead on one of the stories could have been the start of a mystery novel. With the story, written for the International News Service, Runyon came into his own as a trial reporter. The lead read:

> A chilly-looking blonde with frosty eyes and one of those marble, you-bet-you-will chins, and an inert, scare-drunk fellow that you couldn't miss among any hundred men as a dead setup for a blonde, or the shell game, or maybe a gold brick.
>
> Mrs. Ruth Snyder and Henry Judd Gray are on trial in the huge weather-beaten old courthouse of Queens County in Long Island City, just across the river from the roar of New York, for what might be called for want of a better name, The Dumbbell Murder. It was so dumb.

The trial was forever after known as "The Dumbbell Murder" or "The Trial of the Eternal Blonde." Gray and Mrs. Snyder both confessed to killing Mr. Snyder with a window sash weight as he slept, and then each tried to place the blame on the other. Said Runyon: "It was stupid beyond imagination, and so brutal that the thought of it probably makes many a peaceful, home-loving Long Islander of the Albert Snyder type shiver in his pajamas as he prepares for bed."

Runyon described The Eternal Blonde:

> Mrs. Snyder, the woman who has been called a Jezebel, a lineal descendant of the Borgia outfit, and a lot of other names, came in for the morning session of court stepping along briskly in her patent-leather pumps, with little short steps.
>
> She is not bad-looking. I have seen much worse. She is thirty-three and looks just about that, though you cannot tell much about blondes. She has a good figure, slim and trim, with narrow shoulders. She is of medium height, and I thought she carried her clothes off rather smartly. She wore a black dress and a black silk coat with a collar of black fur. Some of the girl reporters said it was dyed ermine; others pronounced it rabbit.

Yes, Runyon showed his prejudice toward blondes and probably reflected the prejudices of most of America toward blondes. He said Mrs. Snyder was especially good at leading astray men of Gray's type with her "blue-green eyes...as chilly looking as an ice cream cone."

He ended with this recommendation: "...hereafter no blonde shall be permitted to purchase a window sash weight without a prescription and that all male suburbanites should cancel their life insurance forthwith and try all the doors before going to bed."

The description of Mrs. Snyder contrasted with this one of Gray:

[A] spindly fellow in physical build, [Gray] entered the courtroom with quick, jerky little steps behind an officer, and sat down between his attorneys, Samuel L. Miller and William. L. Millard. His back was to Mrs. Snyder, who sat about ten feet distant. Her eyes were on a level with the back of his narrow head.

Gray was neatly dressed in a dark suit, with a white starched collar and subdued tie. He has always been a bit on the dressy side, it is said. He wears big, horn-rimmed spectacles, and his eyes have a startled expression. You couldn't find a meeker, milder-looking fellow in seven states, this man who is charged with one of the most horrible crimes in history....

Both Mrs. Snyder and Gray were found guilty and were electrocuted. The New York *Daily News* sneaked in a photographer at the execution of Mrs. Snyder. The photograph it published of her as she was jolted by electricity is one of the most shocking and controversial in newspaper history. How well Runyon fit into the era!

And how well he fit into writing for the sensational Hearst paper, the New York *American*, which in 1911 hired him from the *Rocky Mountain News* in Denver. Hired to write baseball stories, he and Grantland Rice and other sports writers of the day changed the style of sports reporting. Before, sports events were written in a straight-forward style. Said Edwin P. Hoyt in his biography of Runyon, *A Gentleman of Broadway*: "...his readers were delighted with his joyful approach to every aspect of [baseball] ....Damon did add breadth and color to sports writing. He was a dude, there was no doubt about it."

Runyon's technique was to arrive early at the playing field, race track, or boxing ring and walk around. He observed the fans and the players, soaking up the color. While typing his story, he occasionally would rip out the page, crumple it, and throw it in the direction of the trash can. Once he got into the flow of the story, he would peck two-finger style rapidly to the end. Normally he was the last reporter to leave the scene.

His stories may not have had the score until the fourth or fifth paragraph, but what came before the score could dazzle the reader. The following one, written during his first year with the New York *American*, about Christy Mathewson and the Giants and their defeat of the Cincinnati Reds was typical. It read:

Mathewson pitched against Cincinnati yesterday.
Another way of putting it is that Cincinnati lost a game of baseball.
The first statement means the same as the second.

That same year, he wrote of another event, a horse show in Madison Square Garden. As the story demonstrated, he always managed to take a different look at an event than might be otherwise expected. Instead of reporting on the horses' abilities and chances of winning the show, he turned in a poem called "Mr. Deeters of Cheyenne." It began:

Son, call that man in the hard-boiled bib and order us one more snort;
My name is Deeters, if I failed to say; I'm a well known Cheyenne sport.
Does I know the hawse? Well, son, I does; I savvies a hawse right well—
For I win the buster belt one year ago on a critter they call O'Hell.

Although Runyon often began his stories with verse, poetry was not especially important to him. Many sports reporters of the day began or ended their stories with poetry. Even though Runyon published two volumes of poetry, short stories and reporting were his real loves. In 1914 he began a daily column, "The Mornin's Mornin." He covered World

War I for the Hearst newspapers in 1916, was syndicated with King Features and International News Service in 1919, and wrote two biographical series of columns about boxer Jack Dempsey in 1919 and 1921.

While doing all this, he also published several magazine short stories, in which appeared many of the characters he met while writing for newspapers. He wrote most of the stories in the "slanguage" of the underworld who inhabited Broadway—using such devices as present tense and rhyming language. Critics accused him of inventing the language, but recently linguists have come to defend him, saying he correctly described the language of the people of the streets.

Later, his Broadway stories would be placed in the collection *Guys and Dolls*. Other collections—*Blue Plate Special* (1934), *Money From Home* (1935), *Take It Easy* (1938), and *Runyon a la Carte* (1944)—contained more Broadway stories. In the 1930s, he began writing columns about a mythical father and columns narrated by a fictional character named Joe Turp. These columns were anthologized in 1939 and 1940.

It is difficult to sever Runyon's heyday of the 1920s and '30s from his beginnings. His early life in an unstable family had a major influence on his later writing. He was born Alfred Damon Runyan in Manhattan, Kansas, in 1880, the only son and the oldest of four children. His father, Al Runyan, was a newspaperman of sorts, having inherited a printing shop from his father. Al had a fierce temper and suffered from addictions to drinking and gambling. He tried to start at least two newspapers of his own, but failed each time, mainly because he couldn't get along with his partners.

When Damon was seven years old, the family moved to Pueblo, Colorado, hoping to ease Mrs. Runyan's illness. She died the following year, however, and Damon's sisters went to live with relatives in Kansas. He lived with his father, who worked for the Pueblo *Colorado Advertiser*, in a shack in Pueblo's red-light district. The elder Runyan was not a good father, to say the least. Damon ran the streets of Pueblo while his father worked or gambled in Pueblo's saloons. At fifteen, Damon had two stories published in his father's paper.

When he reached eighteen, he left home and joined the

military. While he was serving during the Spanish-American War, the spelling of his last name was changed to Runyon. Like his father, he loved to make up stories. He claimed he taught English to Chinese immigrants in the Philippines and that he was wounded in the Philippine insurrection. Neither account has been substantiated.

After the war, he worked for several small Colorado papers, fired from one after another because he would disappear for days at a time—usually so drunk as to be unconscious. One job was with the Denver *Post*. Josiah Ward, whom Runyon tagged as "the granddaddy of all city editors," disliked Runyon's use of the vernacular. His philosophy of reporting, Runyon said, was "work at it." Ward once told his reporter, "Come, come, Runyon. Kindly eliminate this aroma of new-mown hay, this note of good evening neighbor...." In 1906, the *Post* sent Runyon to work in San Francisco, a short-lived assignment. *Post* editors did not appreciate his West Coast writing any more than they had his Colorado work.

Later that year, however, the *Rocky Mountain News*, the *Post's* arch-rival, hired him. Finally, someone was willing to take a chance on him, and it was with the *Rocky Mountain News* that he grew as a reporter and a writer. He and Frank "Doc Bird" Finch, a caricaturist, began a partnership that reached many readers. They would cover an event together, Finch drawing cartoons and Runyon writing commentary. Their fame grew with their coverage of such events as the Cheyenne, Wyoming, Frontier Days and Fourth of July celebrations. Their partnership was, however, short-lived, ending when Runyon disappeared in the middle of an assignment. In 1908, Finch was hired away to the Denver *Post*; he died of alcoholism.

Finch was one of the few true friends Runyon had. Runyon, according to biographer Hoyt, "lacked the gregariousness, the human kindness that was Doc Bird's finest quality." A "reporter with a sour disposition," he smoked endlessly, and "his moods could be black and unpleasant."

Despite the personality flaws, Runyon's writing in Denver in 1909 and 1910 was among his best. It forecast what he would achieve later in New York. "The self-consciousness of an earlier period," Hoyt said, "had disappeared. He did not drop g's or use the vernacular in newspaper writing," although that style would reappear from time to time. Also, a maturer and, presumably, wiser Runyon began to collect characters for his fiction.

Runyon's early loose style can be detected in this excerpt from a story about a boxing match at the Denver Athletic Club:

> Two small-sized human torpedo boats, in the form of Freddie Weeks of Cripple Creek, Colorado, and Frank Carney of Newcastle, Pennsylvania, lay broadside in the ring at the DAC last night and for thirty minutes engaged in a duel that was about the most rapid fire occurrence which has been seen in Denver in some time.

Although Runyon continued to write as casually as he pleased, he sometimes did produce serious pieces, as illustrated by the following story about a football game between the Colorado School of Mines and the University of Colorado at Boulder. It was one of the last of the "Me and Mr. Finch" series, and its lead was a foreshadowing of the later great leads Runyon was to put on his stories at the New York *American*:

> Like a soft smoke, the dusk drifted across the field, and forms were taking on phantom shapes yesterday afternoon when the shrill note of the referee's whistle signalled taps for the greatest football battle ever fought in Colorado, and the Silver and Blue of the School of Mines shot upward, triumphant, with the Silver and Gold of Old Colorado trailing.

Readers loved his style. From 1908-1910, he was the *Rocky Mountain News'* star reporter. He covered not only sports, but also society gatherings, trials, politics, and even religion. In 1909, he wrote a series exposing Colorado land speculators, and he covered a visit by evangelist Billy Sunday. He was at his best, though, covering criminal trials, where the drama of the courtroom setting and the high stakes riding on the outcome provided just the right material for his style. The following lead, from a story on the trial of a fraudulent clairvoyant, was typical:

"Money, money, money—all around and about you I see money; nothing but money; you should never work again," is the clairvoyantly conjured picture presented to weary women, worn from endless labor, by Mrs. W. W. Wheeler to run their tiny hoard of money into her own pocket, if the extraordinary stories related in West Side Criminal Court yesterday by wet-eyed victims are true.

Later, Runyon would use similar courtroom details to give readers the memorable stories on the Snyder-Gray murder trial.

Runyon quit drinking in 1911 as a promise to his bride, society writer Ellen Egan. He would not, however, give up smoking, and he died of throat cancer in 1946. He wrote for newspapers literally until the day he died. His last story was about the death of Franklin Roosevelt, written from the perspective of a father talking to his son.

◆

GAWKY COWPUNCHER KNOCKS OUT FAT CHAMP

In the two stories reprinted here, Runyon made especially effective use of detail, along with alliteration and internal rhyme. The stories can also serve as models for the use of transition from one thought to the next. Often Runyon was criticized for being disorganized in his presentation, but one can also see a method to the madness. The first story describes the heavyweight fight in which Jess Willard knocked out the aging champion, Jack Johnson.

THE HAVANA AFFAIR
Damon Runyon
New York *Journal-American*
April 16, 1915

HAVANA, April 5—Tonight, Jess Willard, a gawky, green-looking Kansas farmer cowpuncher, is champion heavyweight of the world, with all the world before him, while Jack Johnson, late lord of the pugilistic realm, is just a portly middle-aged colored man, browsing on the memory of one of the greatest battles ever made by a fighter of his years.

One ferocious right-hand smash to the pit of Johnson's fat stomach, that crumpled the body of the Negro in grinding pain at the opening of the twenty-sixth round, followed less than a minute and a half later by a terrific right-hand clip to the jaw, are blows that made new history for American sport on alien soil this afternoon.

With alien tongues drowning the sound of American voices in the weird demonstration that followed, Johnson fell and was counted out by referee Jack Welch in Willard's corner.

For twenty-five rounds, the Negro had battled bitterly and bravely against this gigantic young white opponent, waging a warfare of such gameness and craft as to finally arouse the admiration of even the sporting men at the ringside who have been waiting since 1910 for this day.

And, while the finish was obvious, no one looked for it so soon. Only the round before, someone in the crowd remarked that Johnson had quit laughing. Johnson turned, winked his eye and lifted his bruised and bloody lips in the ghost of his famous old "golden smile," then stumbled out of his corner for the twenty-sixth round.

Willard met him with that lifting smash in a neutral corner, the blow driving through the Negro's guard. Johnson was badly hurt and dropped both hands completely, but quickly pushed them up again before him. The memory of that murderous smash was ever uppermost in his mind during the next eighty seconds as he shuffled wearily around the ring, and it was probably a repetition of that wallop that he was trying to avoid when he was knocked out.

He backed over into Willard's corner, where Willard feinted as if to again whip his right into the paunchy cushion across the black man's middle. Johnson once more lowered his guard, trying to get away, and the next instant the massive gloved right fist of the Kansan crashed into the black jay.

Johnson dropped flat on his back, without scarcely staggering. Even referee Jack Welch seemed stunned with surprise when the big black toppled over, but he quickly began counting over the dark form that lay with face upturned to the sun of a dying afternoon; and just as the withered hand of the old referee toiled on the finish of a champion, the crowd made a wild rush for the ring, with the Americans in the van.

Johnson did not seem to be totally unconscious, recovering soon after his seconds had gathered him up. He stood a minute in the center of the ring with a white towel wrapped around his black face, blinking his eyes at the sun and listening to the roar about him; then he went to his corner.

Meantime, Willard would have been lost in the great swarm in his corner but for his great height. The big farmer grinned amiably while frenzied men reached for his hand. The Cuban soldiers had to pile into the ring with drawn sabres to rescue both fighters from the crush.

When Jack Curley went over to Johnson's corner to cut the gloves off his hands, the Negro looked up, smiled feebly, and said, "Let me keep these."

"How do you feel?" asked Curley.

"All right," said Johnson. "Everything is all right; the best man won."

Later, Johnson told Tom Flanagan he was glad he lost. He said;

"Now all my troubles will be over. They will let me alone."

Johnson knew he was gone sooner than anybody else. In the rest between the twenty-first and twenty-second rounds, he sent for H.H. Frazee and asked him to find Curley. Soon afterwards, he told Flanagan he was getting weak and could not last much longer.

"I want you to get my wife out of here," he said.

Flanagan told him to on a few rounds and see how he felt. Between the twenty-fifth and twenty-sixth, Curley was found.

Johnson repeated his request to him. Curley went to the box occupied by Mrs. Johnson, back of Willard's corner, and told her what Jack said. He offered to take her out. Mrs. Johnson agreed to go.

The twenty-sixth round had started when she arose. As she moved past Willard's corner, the knockout came. Her husband dropped before her eyes.

She exclaimed, "Oh, my God," then disappeared in the mad crush of 18,000 people suddenly gone mad.

Something approaching a race riot followed. Thousands of people began parading the race track, yelling "Viva La Blanca" [Long Live the White Person], while the blacks drew off in little groups. The Cuban cavalry, which had finished fighting their way to Willard, drew up in close formation to quell any real trouble, but the people finally dispersed.

When autos were coming in from the track with first news, thousands of men and women, and even children, lined the streets roaring approval. The chauffeur who drove the first car to leave the track flew along, handling the car with one hand and the other holding up a picture of Willard, while even the traffic policemen gave him a cheer.

Tonight the town buzzes with elation over the victory. While Americans join with the Cubans in rejoicing, they do not hesitate to give Johnson full praise for his fight.

Prominent ring followers were not ashamed to be seen shaking the hand of the old black, during the jam about his corner at the finish. He fought a masterly battle and wonder is he was able to last as long as he did, for the result has been regarded here as an almost foregone conclusion for days.

Without taking anything from Willard's victory, few believe he would have had the slightest chance with Johnson a few years back.

It was a battle of one lone black man against the whole world, so to speak. Fat, ill-conditioned, harassed by anathemas from people in the crowd, with age obviously tugging throughout, Johnson nevertheless fought along with marvelous craft against this crude but amazingly powerful young opponent.

Willard was a big surprise. It is true, Johnson has gone far back, but Willard outboxed him and outroughed him all the way. His abnormal height gave him some advantage over Johnson, but his strength was his main asset. He fought carefully, as he said he would, with Tom Jones whispering instructions in his ear between rounds.

While still far from being a finished fighter perhaps, he was anything but as awkward as some expected to see him.

Johnson did not talk as much to Willard as used to be his custom with other opponents. He had little to say to the crowd. Whenever he spoke to Jess, it was good-naturedly. Jess answered in monosyllables. Only once did Jack answer a remark from the crowd with any heat; but the old "golden smile" rarely broke across his countenance. He frequently nodded to acquaintances in the crowd between rounds, but his whole attitude indicated depression.

Johnson said tonight he is going back to Paris. He expects his interest in the pictures will bring him an income.

The gate receipts today approximated $160,000.

While the twentieth round was being fought, Jack Curley took compassion on the frenzied throngs at the gates and admitted them at a dollar per head, but the dollar went to "Curley" Brown as admission to the races which followed the fight.

Each left the track at once and returned to town. Willard was only slightly marked, while Johnson showed no bruises of the battle.

Probably never before has there been a heavyweight championship battle where advance opinion was so general as on the result of this one. That stout stomach of Johnson's was largely responsible, but even before, it was apparent the Negro could not get into condition.

The member of the syndicate which controls Willard had been sending telegrams to friends in the States urging them to bet on the white man. Despite this feeling, there was not much betting. Even today, most of the wagers were small. Pari-mutuel machines at the track paid 5 to 6 on Willard. After the tenth round, Willard was a strong favorite. One man bet 8 to 1 Willard would win inside of twenty-five rounds.

Willard's own description of the finish is about as has been recorded. He says Johnson seemed to be in deadly fear of another stomach punch from the time he got a blow at the opening of the last relief, and that he intended to keep pounding away at that point until he saw the opening for the jaw.

The fight promoters are talking of a special train to take Willard back to New York, but Jess is still most happy in the company of two friends from Kansas.

Jess suffered his greatest surprise today immediately after the fight, when two Cubans rushed up and kissed him with resounding smacks on the cheeks.

The ring was erected right under the finish wire in the home stretch of Curley Brown's race track, which is located in a pleasant valley surrounded by gently rising little hills and topped by waving palms.

Some of the cheaper seats were as far away from the ring as the quarter pole. The higher priced chairs were set on the ground right up against the platform on which the ring was pitched.

Beginning as early as 11 o'clock, the roads leading to the track were filled with racing motors that left only white streaks of dust behind. There are no specified motor laws in Cuba, so the drivers made it a grand race. Despite the frequent patrols of mounted police, there were numerous accidents.

◆

THAT "HANDY GUY NAMED SANDE" COASTS TO DERBY WIN

The race track was one of Runyon's favorite hangouts. His easy familiarity with horse racing shows in the following story about the 1930 Kentucky Derby, with its track lingo, descriptions of spectators, and race-day atmosphere. Its quality lies in its ability to transport readers to the scene, as if they had viewed the whole event themselves.

HANDY SANDE
Damon Runyon
New York *American*
May 17, 1930.

I

Say, have they turned the pages
Back to the past once more?
Back to the racin' ages
An' a Derby out of the yore?
Say, don't tell me I'm daffy,
Ain't that the same ol' grin?
Why it's that handy
Guy named Sande,
Bootin' a winner in!

II

Say, don't tell me I'm batty!
Say, don't tell me I'm blind!
Look at that seat so natty!
Look how he drives from behind!
Gone is the white band under his chin—
Still he's that handy
Guy named Sande,
Bootin' a winner in!

III

Maybe he ain't no chicken,
Maybe he's gettin' along,
But the ol' bean's goin' strong.
Roll back the years! Yea, roll 'em!
Say, but I'm young agin',
Watchin' that handy
Guy named Sande,
Bootin' a winner in!

Why, it wasn't even close!

Gallant Fox, pride of the East, with the old master mind of the horsemen sitting in his saddle as easily as if he were in a rocking chair on a shady veranda, galloped off with the $50,000 Kentucky Derby this afternoon. He won by two lengths, going away.

Gallant Knight, owned by B.B. Jones, of Virginia, who races under the name of the Audley Farm, was second, and Ned O., belonging to G.W. Foreman, of Maryland, was third. Gone Away, another Easterner, was fourth. He belongs to William Ziegler, Jr., the baking powder king. The time was 2:07 3-5, which is a bit slow for the mile and a quarter of the Derby.

To William Woodward, owner of Gallant Fox, and President of the Harriman banks, of New York, who breeds horses in Maryland as a personal hobby, was presented the gold trophy that goes with the stake, by none other than Lord Derby of England, for whose family the English Derby, the Kentucky Derby and all other turf derbies are named.

When Gallant Fox came trotting back to the judges' stand with Sande bobbing on his back, the crowd of 60,000 let go a terrific roar. The demonstration was more for Sande than for the horse. The racing public loves the great jockey, whose victory today made his third Kentucky Derby. He won on Zev and again on Flying Ebony.

The field of fifteen horses was at the barrier not over two minutes when Starter Bill Hamilton yelled "Come on," and they shot out of the starting stalls like a big bundle of bright color.

Tannery, the hope of Kentucky, was first to break, but going past the stand the first time Hal Price Headley's filly Alcibiades was in front. High Foot, the Chicagoan, was second and Buckeye Poet, one of the Bradleys, was third. Sande lay about fifth with "The Fox." He began moving up as they rounded the first turn, the red hood on Gallant Fox's head slowly but surely shoving forward, with the red cap on Sande's head so far up on the withers of "The Fox" that it seemed almost a part of the blazing hood.

Not until he reached the back side, however, did Sande really set out for Alcibiades, the only filly in the race. About midway down the back stretch, Gallant Fox took the lead, and suddenly out of nowhere came his celebrated rival, Crack Brigade. The boys are commencing to call Crack Brigade "The Fox's" sparring partner. He finished second to the Woodward horse in the Wood Memorial, and also the Preakness and the Kentucky Derby.

Crack Brigade's challenge was brief. Gallant Fox just naturally raced the ears off "Doc" Cassidy's steed going down the back stretch, and going into the far turn to the stretch, "The Fox" commenced to move away. He was galloping along easily, and the race was in little doubt. As they turned into the stretch, Sande urged "The Fox" gently, and daylight showed between him and the next horse.

During the run down the stretch, Gallant Knight showed clear of the bunch back of Gallant Fox, and began making something of a bid, enough to encourage the crowd to cheer for him. But Sande just let out a link, and Gallant Fox moved off and on under the wire two lengths in front. Gallant Knight was an easy second. Ned O. had a scramble for third.

A great horse and a great rider was the combination that was too much for the best the West and the South could offer against the East today. Gallant Fox, whose daddy is Sir Galahad III, old rival of Epinard, the French horse across the pond, may be one of the best horses the American turf has had in years.

Sande's face was wrinkled with smiles as he trotted his mount to the stand. The great jockey came back this season to some of his greatest triumphs, after a year in retirement. He was getting too heavy to ride, he thought, so he bought some horses and began racing his own stable, riding only occasionally. He lost $75,000 before he realized it was no game for him, and during the winter he sold his horses, and went back into training. He was on Gallant Fox when the Woodward horse, which is trained by Jim Fitzsimmons, won the Wood Memorial and Preakness.

The smiles on Sande's face came and went in waves as he listened to the cheers of the crowd. They hung a floral horse-shoe on Gallant Fox, and handed a bunch of roses to Sande. The horse has a curious trick of nodding his red-hooded head at a crowd after a race as if taking bows. He nodded quite briskly in the gathering dusk of a late Kentucky afternoon day, apparently accepting the plaudits of the mob as the right of his new kingship of the horses of his time.

As the horses, blanketed from head to hocks, were led across the infield, a big crowd rushed for the paddock to watch the saddling. This is a ceremony that seems to intrigue strangely many racegoers. Also, they figure they may pick up a tip there. The Three D's declared to win the Broadway Limited, if possible, and put P. Walls, their crack jockey, on the steed that went for a price as a yearling that made it famous.

There was plenty of delay between the fourth and fifth races to permit the public to sock it into the windows, but even so, many were shut out when the long line of silky-skinned steeds came stringing out of the paddock, and went teetering along the soft earthen path in what is called the post parade.

In his glass-enclosed cage in front of the grandstand, Lord Derby was seen to manifest considerable interest in the different horses. He inspected Gallant Fox closely. This is one of the finest-looking horses that ever peeked through a bridle, though some horse experts think he has too much leg, or something to that effect.

Crack Brigade is also a magnificent-looking colt. From the network of amplifiers on the lawn came the voices of the radio announcers quite distinct above the hum of the crowd.

The grandstand spectators sought their seats in some confusion. The air was very moist, and you couldn't call the track fast. Nor was it so very slow. It was what the experts pronounced dull. The Churchill Downs track is peculiar in that it is never fast in moist atmosphere, even if it isn't actually raining.

In many respects, the Derby is the classiest sports event of all, in personnel of the crowd. It draws heavily on what we are pleased to call society, and on the business and political spheres, not to mention the turf. However, it doesn't pull much from Broadway, which deems it too far away. Only a few of the real hot sports from the big white line were detected in the mob, and they looked lonesome.

Wall Street was well represented, however. The bankers and the brokers go for the Derby in a large way. They like to load up special cars with their pals, and bring their own licker [sic]. The local licker isn't so forte. Kentucky is still strong in its traditions as the home of fine horses and beautiful women, but the good whiskey that it used to brag about is a distant memory.

From the blue grass region of Kentucky came big delegations today, most of them talking of Tannery, though a lot of them wagered on Colonel E.R. Bradley's entry just from force of habit. The white, green hoops-and-cap of the Idle Hour farm is far away the most popular set of colors in this part of the world. Colonel Bradley is the home boy of Ol' Kaintuck. Of course when you come right down to it, most horses trace back to Kentucky in breeding, but once a nag falls into Eastern ownership, it is no longer regarded as a Kentucky horse.

The Kentuckians were more subdued today than usual about the Derby, for the reason that they didn't have a standout entry as in other years. When Kentucky has something like Bubbling Over going in the big heat, the citizens make plenty of noise about it. Today they listened to the Easterners rave about Gallant Fox; they heard the Chicagoans gabble of High Foot and said nothing. They slipped quietly to the mutuel windows and bet on the Bradleys just the same. The Kentuckian is a sentimental soul when it comes to horses.

I have often read windy dissertations as to the general significance of the Kentucky Derby. Loyal Southerners like to see it as a survival of the sporting spirit of the old, old

South, and always give it a background of rebel yells. They love to picture Churchill Downs as the meeting place and the reunion premises of the scions of the confederacy.

The only trouble with that etching now is that the sidewalks of New York and the Chicago loop have commenced to move into Kentucky of late years, and when you go looking for a Kentucky Kunnel you are apt to bump into John Curry, Tammany Leader, or Palmer House Ryan, from Chi.

I mean to say the atmosphere of the sweet magnolia bloom, and the aroma of the mint julep that may have clung to Derby Day in other times, have gotten mixed up with cosmopolitan odors. The Derby hat of the effete East has largely supplanted the wide-brimmed black dicer that tradition tells us is typical of the old "Sooth."

I fear that unless the Southerners make a more determined stand, the New Yorkers and the Chicagoans will be claiming the Derby as their very own in a few years. Incidentally, Pittsburgh, Cleveland and Philadelphia are joining in the invasion. I saw special trains from these cities parked in the railroad yards, and passengers were walking around the streets of Louisville with a proprietorial air.

10

WILLIAM BOLITHO

THE MAGICIAN OF JOURNALISM

The New York City taxi driver may have struggled to pronounce the South African writer's name, but he didn't have any trouble describing William Bolitho's work.

"I read him more than any other columnist," the cabbie said, "because I always know there's something there, but, boy, on plenty mornings I couldn't tell you what he was talking about."

Fellow journalist Heywood Broun wondered if Bolitho had been kidnapped from another planet. "The gulf set between his column and the want-ad readers of a New York morning newspaper is quite as wide as the expanse of ether which lies between the Earth and Mars." Nonetheless, thousands in England and the United States read Bolitho's work religiously in the 1920s. Bolitho wrote most of his stories from his home in Paris, but spent 1929 in New York writing a column three times a week for the *World*. With Herbert Bayard Swope as editor, the *World* had one of the best writing staffs ever assembled on one newspaper. Many prominent journalists believed Bolitho was the best writer on the paper. Others, however, placed Bolitho's work outside the realm of journalism because his style didn't fit the general newspaper mold. Instead of recording the facts of an event, he dissected it into its constituents, spending more time explaining why something occurred than regurgitating an account of what happened.

His writing style was unorthodox. At times his prose flowed like poetry, painting vivid images, but within the same story or even the same sentence, the words might tumble out in a jumbled disarray of structure patched together with semicolons. Alexander Woollcott, his contemporary, said readers of Bolitho would gain much food for thought and emerge from the experience "with the slightly dishevelled feeling of having been tossed in a blanket."

Bolitho's hypnotic style made reading his stories an adventure worth taking. As Broun said when Bolitho died in 1930, "Bolitho's best was far and away beyond the topmost reach of any newspaper competitor." A reviewer for the New York *Times* described Bolitho's work in 1924 as "journalism tinctured with magic. He writes with the interpretive power of the imaginative historian."

Bolitho's literary triumphs elicit even more astonishment when contrasted to his tragic childhood. He was born William Bolitho Ryall in Cape Town in 1890 to Dutch-English parents. His father was an impoverished Plymouth Brother preacher, and his mother "a nagging harried woman." The family fought on the side of the Dutch colonists in the Boer War, and the British retaliated by burning the Ryall home. Forced out on the streets, Bolitho sold newspapers, worked as a mason's helper, and participated in building the Cape Town Cathedral.

As a child, he believed his situation was hopeless, and he could see, he later wrote, only "a miserable and obscure life in front of me." He recognized education, however, as the way to put poverty behind him. When he started school, the one-time street urchin had already studied the Elizabethan dramatists and taught himself to read Cicero and Racine. Woollcott attributed Bolitho's unique writing style to his "scarred," poverty-stricken youth when he "fiercely tore his learning from books hard to come by." Having never heard the speech of educated men, the youth developed the "uneasy and ungainly prose of the self-taught," Woollcott said. Bolitho used the term "autodidact" (rather than the simpler "self-taught") to describe himself. Once his formal education began, Bolitho excelled. At South African University, he became an honor student in metaphysics and Hebrew, and even played rugger football for the university team.

He was invited to be a candidate for the Moslem priesthood, but his thirst for adventure led him elsewhere. Wanting to fight in World War I, he made his way to England working in the stokehole of a British ship. He enlisted in the British army, fought in some of the war's fiercest battles, and rose to the rank of lieutenant. While stationed on the Somme in France, he was one of sixteen men buried in a trench when a German shell exploded nearby. A passing Tommie pulled him out by the legs. He was the only survivor, but he had a broken neck and other injuries.

The war tortured and almost broke him, but it also opened the door to journalism. While recovering from his injuries, he made contacts in the hospital that led to an assignment as an assistant to Eric Maclagen. An intelligence officer, Maclagen acted as liaison to the French press corps at the Peace Conference in Paris. A short time later, Maclagen recommended Bolitho to the Manchester *Guardian*. The newspaper accepted the suggestion and hired Bolitho as its Paris correspondent.

George Slocombe, then the "dean of British foreign correspondents," described Bolitho as a thin young man of medium height. He had "sleek red hair, a mottled complexion, darting and brilliant blue eyes, and a mouth always twisted in a self-deprecatory if sardonic grin."

In 1923 the New York *World* hired Bolitho as its European correspondent; and his vivid word pictures, brilliant and varied vocabulary, and interpretive approach grabbed the attention of American readers. During his first year with the *World*, he wrote about world-famous actress Sarah Bernhardt's final days and death. The account bordered on literature as Bolitho wrapped Bernhardt's story around the metaphor of the last performance of the famous actress. The story is included in this anthology.

A month after writing the Bernhardt story, Bolitho traveled to the tiny Parish Church of Les Saintes-Maries-de-la-Mer in southern France. He was covering the yearly migration of the gypsies to see the Three Holy Maries shrine located in the church. In his story for the London *Outlook,* he reported on what the gypsies did at the chapel in Camargue and tried to unravel the mystery behind why they did it. The cadence of his prose illuminated the scene at the gypsie camp:

On the twenty-third day of May, as we reckon it, they arrive, in their families, clans, and tribes; with their homes, their wives, their children, and their vermin; their horses for sale and horses to keep; their basket-ware, their cook-pots and the whole of the baggage of their lives—thousands thick, and block the dunes with their camps.

Having set the scene vividly, Bolitho then shared his insight into gypsie culture:

These are tight-lipped folk. The "business of Egypt" was never yet blabbed. They have kept the secret of this pil-grimage so long from others that they have themselves clean forgotten its meaning. Only the ritual remains and the unbroken tradition of the journey to Carmargue. But, as long as the brown church stands high and dry, like the hull of a wreck, the Gitanos will keep this rendezvous.

Bolitho wrote with a passion, publishing four books, one of which, *Twelve Against the Gods*, became extremely popular in the United States. His first, *Leviathan*, published in 1924, included journalistic essays about the ballet, the mob, and even the sound of a saxophone. His account of the experience of hearing a saxophone for the first time seduces as much as it entertains, helping the reader vicariously feel what Bolitho felt when he listened in awe to the music:

The band begins softly, as if considerate for the general hush. The leader stands away from his chair, which he will not use while playing; for mimicry and grimaces are a part of what he is paid for; and his audience expects that he should himself plainly feel the intoxication of his own music....
Then suddenly I hear the real note of the saxophone, un-forgettable, high and clear, as if from a heart of brass, the new thing, the thing we have come to hear. To me, it has quite passed out of humanity, this famous upper register, but it is still near enough for me to understand; piercing musical, the cry of a faun that is beautiful and hurt. The leader tips his instrument into the air; he blows with all his force, but his cheeks remain pale....He is the priest possessed with a half-human god, endlessly sorrowful, yet utterly unsentimental, incapable of regret, with no past, no memory, no future, no hope. The sound pricks the dancers,

parts their lips, puts spring into their march. These unexpressive, unethical, unthinking men have discovered their unethical, unsentimental reaction to our age.

The critics praised *Leviathan* as both conservative and revolutionary. Bolitho's prose, according to *Current Opinion*, moved from dull to wildly erratic. The magazine compared his style to that of the English writer Thomas Carlyle. Yet to some American writers, Bolitho's style seemed alien to the sometimes barren journalistic landscape of the day. Walter Lippmann, a prominent columnist, called Bolitho the "ideal writer from Mars. He sees with an unprejudiced eye, therefore, apparently with an oblique eye, as if the object had never been observed before and yet with the wrinkled sophistication of the old habitue who has been through it all many times before."

Bolitho's next book, *Italy Under Mussolini*, condemned fascism and its brutality. The text came from a series of stories written for the *World* in December 1925. It established Bolitho's reputation as a political observer with definite opinions about government leaders and governments. He decried fascism, especially because it buried, suppressed, or censored the press. In an article for *Survey* magazine, he shared his views about press freedom:

> The politics of the newspaper must be the politics of millions: that is, exempt, and I dare to say above, the expedients and bargains of any political party. A rare genius like Pulitzer may dare to say what his public will agree with tomorrow, but the date must not be set much further forward; woe to him who lags or overshoots. By suppressing (censoring) the newspapers under the same law and doctrine as they suppressed their rivals, Mussolini and Lenin cannot hide the greater sacrilege of which they were guilty. Newspapers are not and cannot be mere organs of a party but the eyes and ears of average humanity, which is democracy.

In 1926 he published his third book, *Murder For Profit*, which included an account of the trial of the French mass murderer Henri Landru. Bolitho described the deviance of the "monstrous criminal" by using different, sometimes sinister words. Instead of writing that Landru was bald, Bolitho described his "naked cranium" and "skull." Landru's nose was "as thin and transparent at the ridge as a sheet of greased paper." With a brief depiction of Landru's comings and goings at the trial, Bolitho shed light on the dark, haunting interior lurking beneath the murderer's unremarkable exterior:

> We saw his full face but rarely: when he entered, stumbling and blinking through the side door that ended the stone stairs from the prison yard every morning; and sometimes when he turned to the roaring arena to protest. Then we caught a glimpse of his cavernous eyes, which never lost their abstraction even when he was shouting. Usually his manner was chosen and finicky, but after a few minutes in this style he would drop back into his Paris twang. When Fernande Segret was giving her evidence, he closed his eyes; once when the rough Attorney General, coming to the matter of Therese Marchadier's pet dogs, which were found strangled with a waxed thread under an oleander clump at Gambais, rushed at him the question: "Is that how you killed all your victims, Landru?"—he seemed scared, and shook.

While some reviewers panned Bolitho's books, most echoed John Carter of the New York *Times*, who referred to him as "that strangely elliptical writer whose vigor and obliquity combined enable him to pierce the heart of a subject without destroying its life."

Many of the world's artists and writers made pilgrimages to visit Bolitho and his wife, Sybil, at his Avignon home in France. Young Ernest Hemingway was greatly influenced by his journalistic style and his knowledge of politics and government leaders. American playwright Noel Coward said the first thing that struck him about Bolitho was his intensity. "It was not an obvious intensity," he explained. "In fact, his manner was on the whole singularly detached. He looked, if anything, a little irritated, as if the close proximity of so many people irked him and made him feel uneasy." Coward noted that Bolitho whacked his nose with his finger when he wanted to emphasize a point. Time seemed unimportant at the Bolithos', and Coward recalled sitting for hours arguing, discussing, and shouting back and forth with Bolitho. "He talked with fire and grace and beauty, and with apparently a profound knowledge of every subject under the sun." Coward said Bolitho had the richest and most loving mind of any person he ever met:

Those all too brief ten days I spent in his company turned me inside out, stimulated the best of my ambitions, readjusted several of my uneasy values, and banished many meretricious ones, I hope, forever, and I went back to London strongly elated and bursting with gratitude to him for the strange new pride I found in myself.

Walter Duranty, a foreign correspondent for the New York *Times*, also traveled to Avignon. "Of all the people I have met in the last twenty years," he wrote in 1935, "...I think William Bolitho had the finest intellect. He taught me nearly all about the newspaper business that is worth knowing. I have never met anyone who could see further through a brick wall than he could, or who was better, to use the newspaper phrase, at 'doping out the inside facts of any situation.'"

Bolitho's insight and unique, poetic prose drew admiration from some of the great writers of the 1920s. Old-school journalists, on the other hand, refused to call Bolitho a newspaperman for the same reasons others praised him. Heywood Broun said "the graybeards" of the press detested frills and wanted the bare bones of the news. "They feel that it is the part of newspapermen to behave like members of the Light Brigade and refuse to reason why." Bolitho was far more interested in explaining events. Sometimes, however, he was much like the eager shortstop, Broun opined, covering a wide territory, yet hurting his team "by throwing the ball before it has reached his hands." In other words, Bolitho began some of his analyses prematurely.

Despite Bolitho's faults and despite the fact that he died young—at the age of 39, a victim of misdiagnosed appendicitis—Broun still believed he was the "most brilliant journalist of our time." Broun wrote, "It was as the leader of journalistic exploration, deep into the human heart and mind, that Bolitho made his mark. If the standard which he set can even be approximated, it may well be that seekers after education will not turn to some five-foot shelf or scrapbook, but find their road to knowledge in the living daily record of things which lie about them."

◦◦

"HOW UNPUNCTUAL IS DEATH"

Not long after he joined the staff of the New York *World* as a European correspondent, Bolitho wrote a classic piece of journalism describing the passing of Sarah Bernhardt. Considered one of the greatest actresses of all time, Bernhardt performed throughout the world to large, admiring audiences. In chronicling her final moments of life, Bolitho did more than just report the event; he peered into her personality—revealing her eccentricities as well as her grandeur.

Using a barrage of literary devices, including alliteration, simile, and metaphor, the story moved beyond an ordinary description of the event. With his descriptive prose, Bolitho helped the reader feel the emotions of a front-row spectator. He used details that drew pictures in his readers' minds and created sounds in their ears.

SARAH BERNHARDT'S LAST SCENE
William Bolitho
New York *World*
April 3, 1923

The air was steady and bright, the day they buried Sarah Bernhardt. The crowd heard the wheel creakings as she passed and smelled the loads of costly roses like heavy incense in their faces. Even those at the back, who could see nothing, had this satisfaction: they grumbled less than is usual at so great a show. From the pavement we saw people in the window balconies and on the roofs. Something of our emotion must have reached them, for they nudged each other and seemed to smile.

Sarah Bernhardt was always her own stage manager. She planned to make her last appearance on the mortal stage the best of all her parts. All her life she meditated on it. Once in a dream, she saw herself buried abroad, far from Paris; this would have ruined all. Ever afterwards she carried with her on all her travels, a rosewood coffin, lined with white satin; packed in an unwieldy case. She was sure at least of this. Like the simplest woman of her city, she trusted no foreigners in such essential matters.

Everyone sees death differently; some as a black ghost; some as a hope; or a bankruptcy, or a dreamless relief. Sarah thought of it as a supreme tragedy to be played in triumph. That is as good a way as another. She was an actress in the inward places of her heart. Though she had worked for seventy years, and had tasted all joys, and known all possible sorrows, she forgot her fatigue when she thought of the stage set for her final performance. Now everything had been set out as she had directed: the huge, battered case, that had lumbered behind her on all her travels, was waiting in the hall for its final journey, next to the mound of trunks that never would serve her any more. The priest was beside her bed; the moment was near. Before she let herself sink, she went over methodically, meticulously, the setting she had made for her great Exit. Service in the dark, little church of Saint Francois de Slaes, that tiny hiding place for peace in the worldly Plaine Monceau. The long route allegorical of her life, down the stately Boulevard Malesherbes, through the midday crowd of the rich Rue Royale, across the glorious Place de la Concorde; through the long Reu de Rivoli, from the palaces at one end to the narrow streets where working housewives would be doing their morning shopping; a moment's pause beside her own theater; then slowly on, to the city of the Dead, Pere Lachaise, there to lie forever in the past, beside Rachel and her elders.

She could hear from not far below in the street, the reporters, her last critics, discussing the decision of the Hotel de Ville to bury her in state. And workgirls, on their way to the factory, asking how she did. The last House was full, waiting impatiently for her. At noon she felt this, and said, half impatiently, as if it were an actor who was late, "*Comme mon agonie set longue!*" How unpunctual is Death. Nothing remained now to do but to play that supreme role for which she had so well prepared. It would not be tiring. Some light through the shutter slats, of a spring sun, comforted her. By an unexpected chance, the season would help her out.

And with her last breath she said, "Je veux des fleurs, beau-coup de fleurs," The last touch; more flowers than she had ever had for a gala night.

Three blows of the sexton's staff on the stone pavement of the aisle; signal in France for the raising of the curtain; given as she had appointed as her coffin came through the door.

All the first-night crowd were there; all that had a name in fashion, riches, art; following her funeral procession, co-actors in her greatest production. There were flowers she had asked: more than she had dreamed of. They filled the place before the porch; waist-high; weighed down seven coaches. All the details of her strange fancy had been car-ried out. It was a stage play; a playing to the gallery. Small critics may mistake her, and regret; or stupidly blame. Her death was a pageant she had planned; for she was an actress, not merely in her trade, but in her soul. Her art was not sep-arate from her; nor to be put off at the end. Her whole life, loves, miseries, was a well-constructed play, a romantic legend of the sort she most admired. The Paris streets were her last gallery; crushed on a five-mile route to see Sarah play her fifth act.

Her life and death were as single-purposed as a saint; and with the same ruling purpose: to give all to her fellows. Flattery and the rewards of her profession, she felt no more than a billionaire thinks of new gains on the curb; and money was not more in her thoughts than is the need for his daily bread to a monk. What she had, she gave freely, the last morsel; to her family, to a countless crowd of parasites she pitied and protected; to her companions, to the public. She wished they might have pleasure in her going.

But in this last part, played before a vaster gallery than ever she had in life, she had to ask our indulgence. The en-chantments of her voice were mute forever; her graces and gestures were taken from her. And in spite of the roses that banked over and covered it, as she the greatest actress of our times passed, in a narrow black coffin drawn by black, sil-ver-spangled horses, the stage illusion was at last stripped from her, and we knew that we were looking at the funeral of a poor, old woman, going to the rest she had well deserved. It was not the curtain she had planned; it was a greater one; and Sarah's last scene touched emotions that she never had in the days of her fresh glories.

◆

"AN UNCONTROLLABLE, BOUNDLESS HORDE"

The following story demonstrates Bolitho's capacity to recognize and capture the essential nature of an event. It is a
graphic account of French premier Edouard Herriot's return
to Paris after the acceptance of the Dawes Report. The report,
which had been approved at a London conference, was believed to have removed the question of German reparations
for World War I from the sphere of political controversy
and, ecstatic Frenchmen thought, the threat of another war
from Europe. Rather than focusing on the formal political
issues involved, Bolitho concentrated his attention on the reactions of the Paris crowd to Herriot's return. He was alert
enough to international relations, however, that he saw the
paradox in the Allies' attempt to keep peace by appeasement.
In the crowd scene, therefore, he contrasted the joy of most of
the people with a "shrill...whistle of protest."

HOW HERRIOT CAME HOME
William Bolitho
(London) *Outlook*
August 30, 1924

When it saw M. Herriot standing in the doorway of his
compartment, the inconstant crowd at the Gare St. Lazare
rushed the detective cordon, like a mob ready for murder.
The faces of his Ministers smiling out of the train windows
paled and ducked back for an instant. But M. Herriot,
braver or better diviner, abandoned the brass handrail and
lifted his hand, palm upward, with a large sweep that meant
conquest and joy and a rosy, prosperous triumph.

Three months ago Paris was for war and Poincaréism.
Now at M. Herriot's wave the Parisians were yelling,
formidably, *"Vive la Paix!"* The vanguard—the hatless,
breathless first fringe, with flowing fancy ties and desperate

notebooks that even a hand-to-hand crowd cannot wrench from them—are the journalists. In lunatic imitation of a band of schoolboys round a master who has some vitally interesting lesson to impart, they ring M. Herriot round, knowing that to forget the least banality he may utter will mean their ruin. The young, the cubs at their first big story, fight unashamed for the nearest place. The old hands, red-faced, panting, indignant, and despairing, use their weight, and pass the fragments of speech they can catch to the confreres of their own age in camaraderie.

The rest of the ear-splitting mass that is struggling for inches of forward room down the platform, down the complete length of the immense Hall of Lost Footsteps, now covers the cobbled courtyards a quarter of a mile apart and every street that gives into them. It is an uncontrollable, boundless horde, yelling for Herriot, for Peace, for excitement, most of all for a better sight of what is going on in the centre of their dark multitude. Outside the interlocked ring of journalists are twenty thousand Radical fanatics, army-haters, election victors who have come from the suburbs and the city to make Herriot's arrival a success, whatever he may have brought in that bulged wallet, of worn brown leather, that hooks on the doorhinge and impedes his descent for a moment on to the platform. They are fanatics for their party, for their chief, in this furnace of enthusiasm. The party whips, the party organization has brought them to wait and cheer. They cheer as they would vote, for Herriot, for continuance of their party in power, for sweets of office, for destruction of their foes, decisively, plumping for Peace. *Vi, Vah, La...*

Round this kernel, there is an enormous shapeless rind of the Public—women, newsboys, bourgeois, typists, Communists, business men, white-haired Pacifists, enthusiasts, indifferent; in the main good Paris people who were glad before they came that peace was made and the Ruhr expedition over. Now in the infection of resonant enthusiasm inside, which is shaking the sooty steel girders and rattling the dirty glass of the vast hall, by contagion of numbers, by mere contact with that new cry, which for ten years has never been heard in Paris, "Long Live Peace," they have been set on fire. A brown scuffling knot appears in the station entrance, MM. Herriot and Clementel; and hot-faced journalists are forced, in spite of their resistance, away from the telephone booths where they want to go. The whole courtyard salutes them: "Herriot, Herriot, *Vive la Paix!*"

The train had been late. When it arrived it was past six. It is the hour when hundreds of thousands of working Parisians catch the trains to the outer suburbs. The whole of the St. Lazare contingent had been caught in the first flood of Peace greeters. Their wives and allotments were waiting, but there was no protesting. For whole minutes together the composite impatient mob as one man, with a voice like a cyclone, acclaimed the new gods, Herriot and Peace.

But in the pauses one heard another sound, shrill, hateful, that cuts like a wire whip—the whistle of protest. Sharper than any other sound, in a theatre, when a poor singer has missed her note, is this Paris whistle, bitter as Hell. It ripped the monotony of the shouting. M. Herriot, on the steps, hears it, lifts up his broad, gratified face, changing his look. He can do more than make peace; he can fight—this good-humored, honest-tempered man. He stares down, searching the enemy, challenging, with a half-frown. The police, who have pushed next to him through the routed reporters, follow his look—severe men as broad-backed as their supreme chief, not fellows to trifle. A girl who is standing in a niche among the cement pillars staring, quiet, catches their eye. "Move away," says the nearest Sûreté man, in that tone they have. She had not whistled, I am sure, but she had not applauded. A face and allure like the Berton girl—thin, delicate, disquieting. "What's up with you? I'm doing nothing," she answered, in the accent of the Barrier. The detective motioned with his hand. She had the habit of obeying: in a moment she was lost in the vague masses behind.

The rest, hearing the thing that had changed the scene, paused a little, as if puzzled and at a loss, then began again, a degree louder. The acclamation rose irresistible, drowning, while it lasted, all other sounds. From the station to his car and [for a distance as] its smooth back disappeared by degrees, held up by the outliers of the crowd, or by the flow of the traffic that had now again begun in the lower streets, that cheer pursued him. Paris had given the man who gave up the Ruhr a bigger reception even than President Wilson had in 1919—the most magnificent applause from his fellow creatures any man ever had in our times before, I suppose. Leave it at that. M. Herriot's reception made all that Poincaré or the war men had received before small, tepid affairs. But in the intervals, when the crowd, hoarse and tired, slackened its cry, there was always—piercing, hateful, reckless—that shrill counter-music from the hidden corners of the whistling dissenters, monosyllabic, indisputable, punctuating with menace the chorus of "*Vive la Paix!*"

11

GRANTLAND RICE

Most college graduates whose majors are Greek and Latin would appear destined for a life of academia. In Grantland Rice's case, sports—and not the study of languages—was to become his life. Although he majored in the classical languages, "As for English," he said, "I honestly can't recall having studied it." His father suggested that since Grantland hadn't studied anything practical, he might as well go into journalism.

To Rice, language was alive and was meant to be used in creative, unusual ways. He changed the language of sports reporting and is revered for his work during the "Golden Age of Sport," the 1920s.

Language was poetry to Rice, whether he was writing poems or writing about golf or football. He was serious about the craft of writing, even though most people would not think the subject of sports was a serious topic—but sports was life to Rice.

"Sports," he said, "has its triumphs and its tragedies, its great joys and heavy sorrows with more spectacular effect than most dramas may ever know....The drama of sport is a big part of the drama of life, and the scope of this drama is endless." Reporting sports was serious work to Rice. To him, sports events were examples of personal heroic struggles, and he brought to his readers the drama of life.

He was the "dean"—or, as some called him, the "master"—of modern sports writing. He injected into his stories and columns a bit of humor, a touch of realism, and a creativity that had been absent from sports reporting previously. Before 1911 when he started at the New York *Evening Mail*, sports normally was written as just another colorless hard news story. Rice brought what one critic called "tart description" to sports stories.

"There is more action and movement in sportswriting than there is in writing news," Rice said. "...In a nutshell, the sports fan of today is a different person....There is no stringing that estimable gentleman along....It doesn't take the public long to get wise to a sloppy writer, and such a writer cannot last long."

In the '20s, Rice was the most prominent of a brilliant new generation of sportswriters. "Self-labeled the 'Gee Whizzers,' their enthusiasm for sport may have even exceeded that of the fans," wrote Benjamin G. Rader in *American Sports*. "...Rice and his colleagues released future sportswriters from the obligation to report sports as 'hard' news. The sports page itself became a source of entertainment."

In the foreword to Rice's autobiography, *The Tumult and the Shouting*, Bruce Barton noted that previously sports was considered fit for "boys and for fools" and not for grown, responsible adults. "This austere tradition Grant helped mightily to break down. He was the evangelist of fun, the bringer of good news about games. He was forever seeking out young men of athletic talent, lending them a hand and building them up, and sharing them with the rest of us as our heroes. He made the playing fields respectable. Never by preaching or propaganda, but by the sheer contagion of his joy in living, he made us want to play. And in so doing he made us a people of better health and happiness in peace: of greater strength in adversity."

Rice came by his enthusiasm for sports early in life. Born in Tennessee in 1880, he attended Tennessee Military Institute and the Nashville Military Institute before going to Vanderbilt University. At Vanderbilt, he was an outstanding shortstop but declined an offer to play professional baseball. He also played football but was too small to excel. He worked for newspapers in Atlanta, Cleveland, and Nashville before going to New York. While at the *Daily Mail*, he began a column, "The Sportlight," which he continued to write until his death. In 1914, he moved to the New

York *Daily Tribune* and later to the *Herald Tribune*. In 1920 he was an editor of *American Golfer* and succeeded Walter Camp as the judge for *Collier's* All-American Football Teams. Besides baseball and football, he also reported on boxing and horse racing. However, his personal passion was for golf. In 1930, the North America Newspaper Alliance syndicated the "Sportlight" column, and Rice became the most widely read columnist in the country.

A friend and fellow sports reporter, Frank Graham, said that Rice "had a simple design for living." He would wake up early and after eating breakfast would go back to bed to read papers and magazines. Then after noon, he would set out for the race track or the boxing arena or the football field to cover an event.

In 1921, Rice began another career—broadcasting. He announced the first radio broadcast of a World Series, between the New York Giants and the New York Yankees. He later combined his announcing skills with cinema and began producing a series of one-reeler shorts entitled "The Sportlight." They continued well into the 1950s and covered the unusual aspects of sports—salmon fishing, quail shooting, big game hunting, and so on. He won the 1943 Oscar for one entitled "Amphibious Fighters." He disparaged television but admitted that it would contribute to America's love of sports.

Rice's greatest thrill was the 1932 World Series when Babe Ruth pointed to the right-field fence in Wrigley Field and then hit the pitch out of the park. Rice was there. In 1948, after The Babe's death, he wrote the poem "Game Called." It read:

Game called by darkness—let the curtain fall,
No more remembered thunder sweeps the field.
No more the ancient echoes hear the call
To one who wore so well both sword and shield.
The Big Guy's left us with the night to face,
And there is no one who can take his place.
Game called—and silence settles on the plain....
The Big Guy's gone—by land or sky or foam
May the Great Umpire call him "safe at home."

Poetry often preceded or followed Rice's stories. Al-

though some of it was drivel, much of it was good, and a few
lines are immortal. For example, Rice wrote,

> For when the One Great Scorer comes
> To write against your name
> He marks—not that you won or lost —
> But how you played the game.

Rice didn't write poetry only about sports. During World
War I, he wrote for *The Stars and Stripes*. He once told a
friend that the only problem he had with the war was that
"cooties" (lice) kept disturbing his poetry.

In *Not Under Oath*, fellow sportswriter John Kieran
wrote, "The 'Old Master' of the sports writing clan was a poet
at heart and deep student of world history. He was also about
as fine a gentleman as I ever had the luck to meet. Our paths
crossed briefly in France during World War I, and I like to
remember him as a soldier-poet and author of these lines":

> All wars are planned by older men,
> In council rooms apart,
> Who call for greater armament
> And map the battle chart.
>
> But out along the shattered field
> Where golden dreams turn gray,
> How very young the faces were
> Where all the dead men lay.
>
> Portly and solemn, in their pride,
> The elders cast their vote
> For this or that, or something else,
> That sounds the martial note.
>
> But where their sightless eyes stare out
> Beyond life's vanished joys,
> I've noticed nearly all the dead
> Were hardly more than boys.

Irvin S. Cobb said in the foreword to a collection of Rice's
verse entitled *Songs of the Stalwart*, "Grantland Rice is a
sweet and kindly human being who has a habit of saying

things in a sweet and kindly way. Sometimes he says them in verse, which is still better....Some of these days, they are going to nominate a successor to the late James Whitcomb Riley as our most typical writer of homely, gentle American verse. I have my candidate already picked out. His name is Grantland Rice."

Rice carried his poetry writing style into his prose. His description of ballgames has been called overdone by critics, but it had a poetic quality. In *The Realm of Sport*, Herbert Warren Wind observed that Rice was an "unabashed romantic where sports were concerned....[H]e usually managed to provide his stories with a soaring 'lead' and a flock of high-flying, bright-plumed metaphors even when he was battling the pressure of a deadline." His famous 1924 story on the Notre Dame-Army football game demonstrated that style. Comparing the Fighting Irish backfield to the four horsemen of the apocalypse may be a bit much, but Rice carried this theme throughout the account, conjuring up images of battles, thunderstorms, and cyclones. Indeed, the game was a real tribulation to the thoroughly defeated Army team. How much more imaginative to express that in poetic terms than in just simply saying Army suffered a humiliating loss. The story is reprinted in this anthology.

The nicknames he gave to sports greats and the poetry appealed to his readers, making his work easy to remember. "Granny," as Rice was known to his close friends, named Jack Dempsey "The Manassa Mauler." Red Grange was "The Galloping Ghost of the Gridiron." The most descriptive was the "Four Horsemen." Rice had such a talent for coining quotable lines that coaches recited him to inspire their players.

Rice said that poetry meant more to him than sports, and the combination of sports and poetry was perfect. "Nothing else is needed," he explained, "where brain and brawn, heart and ligament are concerned. Rhythm, the main factor in both, is one of the main factors in life itself. For without rhythm, there is a sudden snarl or tangle."

His personality also showed in his work. Said Paul Gallico, another sports writer: "The personality of Grantland Rice shone throughout his columns—that of a sweet, gentle man with something endearingly childlike in him, who passionately loved his work and his world." Parents and preachers admired his ethical, homespun view of the world. Herbert Wind said Rice was "as kind and chivalrous in his relations with his friends and colleagues as with his heroes."

Rice died in 1954, one day after suffering a stroke while typing a story in his newspaper office. Bruce Barton, who had written the foreward to Rice's autobiography, said, "People felt better in his presence. He made us all feel better—made us feel that somehow we could do more, be more. This was his gift to his friends." That was his gift to his readers, too.

Barton quoted this poem by Rice:

Only the brave know what the hunted are—
The battered—and the shattered—and the lost —
Who know the meaning of each deep, red scar,
For which they paid the heartache and the cost.
Who've left the depths against unmeasured odds
To ask no quarter from the ruling gods.

Born—live—and die—cradle along to the grave.
The march is on—by bugle and by drum —
Where only those who beat life are the brave —
Who laugh at fate and face what is to come,
Knowing how swiftly all the years go by,
Where dawn and sunset blend in one brief sky.

◆

"THE MOST DRAMATIC MOMENT" IN BASEBALL HISTORY

After his famous account of the Notre Dame-Army football game, Rice ranked as his next best newspaper story his saga of the final game of the 1924 World Series. Chosen from Rice's lifetime of writing, it appeared, coincidentally, just eight days before the football story. Rice may have liked it so much not mainly as an example of his writing, but because the event itself was filled with high drama. The story recounted the Washington Senators' victory built around the theme of Walter Johnson, the aging star of former years,

taking the mound in the final innings and performing with
the overwhelming talent that he had possessed in his ancient
prime. As darkness symbolically crowded in, almost ending the game, Destiny crowned the old hero. It was the stuff
of legend.

SENATORS WIN TITLE, 4 TO 3
Grantland Rice
New York *Herald Tribune*
October 11, 1924

WASHINGTON, Oct. 10.—Destiny, waiting for the final curtain, stepped from the wings to-day and handed the
king his crown.

In the most dramatic moment of baseball's sixty years of
history, the wall-eyed goddess known as Fate, after waiting
eighteen years, led Walter Johnson to the pot of shining gold
that waits at the rainbow's end.

For it was Johnson, the old Johnson, brought back from
other years with his blazing fast ball singing across the plate
for the last four rounds, that stopped the Giants' attack, from
the ninth inning through the twelfth, and gave Washington's fighting ball club its world series victory by the score of
4 to 3, in the seventh game of a memorable struggle.

Washington won just at the edge of darkness, and it was
Johnson's great right arm that turned the trick. As Earl
McNeely singled and Muddy Ruel galloped over the plate
with the winning run in the twelfth, 38,000 people rushed onto
the field with a roar of triumph never heard before; and for
more than thirty minutes, packed in one vast serried mass
around the bench, they paid Johnson and his mates a tribute
that no one present will ever forget. It was something beyond
all belief, beyond all imagining. Its crashing echoes are
still singing out across the stands, across the city, on into the
gathering twilight of early autumn shadows. There was
never a ball game like this before, never a game with as
many thrills and heart throbs strung together in the making
of drama that came near tearing away the soul, to leave it
limp and sagging, drawn and twisted out of shape.

Washington, facing the last of the eighth inning, was a
beaten team, with the dream about closed out. And then like a

heavy blast from hidden explosives, a rally started that tied the score, the two most important tallies of baseball lore sweeping over the plate as Bucky Harris's infield blow skirted the ground and suddenly leaped upward over Lindstrom's glove.

It was this single from the great young leader that gave Johnson his third and final chance. For, as the Giants came to bat in the ninth, with the score knotted at 3 and 3, there came once more the old familiar figure, slouching across the infield sod to his ancient home in the box. Here once more was the mighty moment; and as 38,000 stood and cheered, roared and raved, Johnson began to set the old-time fast one singing on its way. With only one out in the ninth inning, Frank Frisch struck a triple to deep center, but in the face of this emergency "Old Barney" turned back to something lost from his vanished youth, and as Kelly tried in vain to bring Frisch home, the tall Giant suddenly found himself facing the Johnson of a decade ago—blinding, baffling speed that struck him out and closed down on the rally with the snap of death.

Johnson was on his way, and neither Destiny nor the Giants could head him off. He had suffered two annihilations, but his mighty moment had come, and he was calling back stuff from a dozen years ago. To show that he was headed for another triumph and that young blood was coursing through his veins again, he came to the eleventh and struck out Frisch and Kelly. It was the first time in four years of world series play that any pitcher had struck out the keen-eyed Frisch. But the Fordham Flash to-day was facing the Johnson that used to be, the Johnson that nailed them all, the high and low alike, with a fast ball that few could see and fewer still could hit.

All this while the drama of the day was gathering intensity from round to round. Washington missed a great chance in the eleventh after Goslin had doubled, but the end was now near at hand. The human heart couldn't hold out many moments longer. The strain was too great for any team or any crowd to stand. Thirty-eight thousand pulses were jumping in a dozen different directions at the same moment as nervous systems were going to certain destruction.

For four innings now Johnson had faced [Giant pitchers]

Nehf, Bentley and McQuillan; and two of these had been conquerors. He was on the verge of getting his complete revenge in one sudden swirl of action. Still cool, serene and steady with the old right arm coming through with its easy and endless rhythm, Johnson again rolled back the Giant charge in the twelfth. In these four innings he had fanned five men, and most of them were struck down when a hit meant sudden death.

The long, gray afternoon shadows had now crept almost across the field. There was grave doubt that even another inning could have been played when fate in the shape of a catcher's mask intervened. With one man out and Bentley pitching, Ruel lifted a high foul back of the plate. Hank Gowdy, one of the most reliable of all who play, started for the ball, but in dancing beneath it his feet became entangled in the mask; and before he could regain his balance, the ball dropped safely to earth through his hands.

This was the spot which destiny picked as the place to hand "Old Barney" the long delayed crown, for Ruel on the next swing doubled to left. Johnson was safe on Jackson's error at short, and with only one out McNeely decided to follow the Harris attack. He slashed one along the ground to third; and as Lindstrom came in for the ball, for the second time in the game the ball suddenly bounded high over his head as Ruel crossed with the run that brought world series glory to Washington's game and crippled club.

The hit that tied it up and the hit that won were almost identical, perfect duplicates, as each reared itself from the lowly sod as if lifted by a watchful and guiding fate that had decided in advance that Washington must win. In the wake of this hit, the ravings and the roarings again came near dislodging the giant rafters of the big stands, for this was the hit that meant Johnson's triumph, the hit that meant Washington's victory.

No club from the sixty years of play ever came from behind as often to break down the ramparts and get to the top. But Washington had the habit; and even when crippled and almost beaten, Harris and his mates refused to waver for a moment as they formed again with what remnants were left to lead another counter charge. It was a home run by Harris that gave Washington its first score, and it was the manager's single that gave Johnson his chance to follow the old dream to the end of the route.

While Barnes held the winners to one hit for six innings, he weakened at last, and McGraw threw in Nehf, McQuillan and Bentley in a vain effort to save a waning cause. Washington, needing two games to win on Wednesday night, had won them both by one of the gamest exhibitions in the long span of all competitive sport.

Another perfect day with another spread of blue sky and yellow sun, the seventh in succession, helped to bring about the second $1,000,000 world series, the first being last year. This made the fourth $1,000,000 program in American sport, Dempsey-Carpentier, Dempsey-Firpo and two world series, with the former fight on top by nearly a million iron men.

The gathering around the Presidential box just before the first salvo was fired indicated the day's first excitement. When the camera-men reached the scene in the scurrying groups, they discovered the President and Mrs. Coolidge, Secretary Slemp, Judge Landis, John J. McGraw, Bucky Harris and Clark Griffith all set for the last official pose of the long war's final day. With the ball park packed to the ultimate elbow, the crowd outside was even larger, as endless lines extended back around corners and alongside streets almost blocking traffic. Inside it was a quieter and more tense gathering than the day before, with a part of the pre-game chatter stilled.

It was not until Warren Harvey Ogden, "The Sheik of Swarthmore," struck out Fred Lindstrom to start the game that rolling waves of sound indicated the amount of suppressed excitement.

After Ogden had walked Frisch, he gave way to Mogridge with a string of left-handed hitters up....

Great plays began to sparkle early like diamonds shining in the sun. In the second inning Hack Wilson slapped one along the ground at a whistling clip almost over second base. Here was a budding hit, if we ever saw one. But Bluege, who is remarkably fast, cut over and by an almost impossible effort knocked the ball down with his glove, scooped it up with the right and nailed his man at first from short center by a cannon ball throw.

In the third inning Joe Judge started one toward right center with a rising inflection. It was on its way to gold and glory when Frank Frisch broke the high jump record and cut off a budding triple. After three innings and a half of brilliant pitching, the first big crash came in the fourth. Here, with one out, came Bucky Harris reaching for another laurel sprig. His line drive over Hack Wilson carried into the stands, although Hack almost broke his massive spine in trying to pull down the drive. His impact with the low, green barricade sounded like a barrel of crockery being pushed down the cellar stairs.

Just a moment later the same Hack, having recovered his breath, came racing in for a low, rakish hit by Rice. He dived for the ball and dug it up six inches from the turf, skating along for many feet upon his broad and powerful system, stomach down. Here was another hit totally ruined by fancy fielding.

The sixth was replete with loud noises and much strategy. It was here that the stout Washington defense cracked wide open. Mogridge started the trouble by passing Pep Young. Kelly laced a long single to center, sending Young scurrying around to third. Here McGraw sent in Meusel to hit for Terry, and Harris countered by removing Mogridge, the southpaw, and sending Marberry to the rifle pit. Meusel lifted a long sacrifice to Sam Rice, scoring Young. Wilson followed with a lusty hit, sending Kelly to third. Here the run-getting should have ended.

Jackson tapped one sharply to Judge at first; and Judge, attempting to hurry the play for the plate, first fumbled the ball and lost his bearings completely as Kelly scored, Jackson reached first and Wilson moved to second on a simple chance. Gowdy tapped one along the ground toward Bluege, and this brilliant infielder let the ball trickle between his feet to left field as Wilson came over with the third run. It was a pitiful infield collapse after a day of superb support up to this moth-eaten spot. The infield cave-in gave the Giants two extra runs and a tidy lead.

The eighth was the most dramatic spot of the entire series. It was full of throbs, thrills and noises. With one out, Nemo Leibold, batting for Taylor, doubled down the left field line. This started the racket with a howl and a roar. Ruel then drew his first hit of the series, an infield blow that Kelly knocked down but couldn't field. With the clamor increasing at every moment, Tate, batting for Marberry, walked, filling the bases, with only one out. There was a brief lull as

McNelly flied out. The vocal spasm broke loose with renewed fury when Harris rapped one sharply toward Lindstrom, and the ball, after skirting the ground, suddenly
bounded high over Lindstrom's head for the single that
scored Leibold and Ruel and tied it up. Harris had driven in
all three runs, and the gathering paid its noisiest acclaim.

It was Art Nehf who checked Washington's assault, and
it was Walter Johnson who hurried in to face the Giants in
the ninth with his third shot at destiny.

For a moment in the ninth he rocked and reeled on the
edge of the precipice. With one out, Frisch tripled to deep
center. But after Johnson had purposely passed Pep Young,
he struck out Kelly and then led Meusel to an infield out that
left Frisch stranded far from home.

Washington came within a span of winning in the
ninth. With one gone, Joe Judge laced a single to center.
Bluege tapped to Kelly at first, and Kelly whipped the ball at
high speed to Jackson, the ball bounding away from Jackson's glove as Judge raced to third. A man on third and first
and only one out—what a chance. But Miller rammed one
sharply to Jackson at short, and a crushing double play
wiped out Washington's chance with Judge almost home.

Groh, batting for McQuillan, opened the ninth with a
clean hit. He limped to first and gave way to Southworth.
Lindstrom sacrificed, but Johnson, calling on all he had,
struck out Frisch and Kelly in a row, Frisch fanning for the
first time in four years of world series play.

It was Johnson's day at last.

●❖

"FOUR HORSEMEN" RIDE OUT OF THE WEST

The following story is Rice's masterpiece and probably the
best known sports story ever written. No lead for a news
story has been quoted more often. Although critics have
panned the story for being flowery, it is full of imagery and
captures the reader.

Rice played on the theme of the horsemen after observing
the members of Notre Dame's backfield playing against
Army in 1923. He was on the sidelines, watching the game
on his knees. Two of the four backs ran off the field and

jumped over Rice. "It's worse than a cavalry charge," he said to a friend. "They're like a wild horse stampede." In 1924 Rice revived the image and used it in the famous piece.

It is ironic that the Notre Dame backfield—Harry Stuhldreher, Jim Crowley, Don Miller, and Elmer Layden— became so famous. They were incredibly small—Layden at 164 pounds was the heaviest; Stuhldreher, the quarterback, weighed 154 and was the smallest. Rice played on their size in his story and on the theme of succeeding despite the odds. To Rice, courage was primary, in sports and in life. It was a theme he used in all of his work.

Several years after the story appeared, Miller told Rice that he had immortalized the four men as no achievement of their own could have done. Few reporters can say that their writing made legends of anybody.

NOTRE DAME'S CYCLONE
BEATS ARMY, 13 TO 7
Grantland Rice
New York *Herald Tribune*
October 19, 1924

Outlined against a blue-gray October sky, the Four Horsemen rode again. In dramatic lore they are known as Famine, Pestilence, Destruction and Death. These are only aliases. Their real names are Stuhldreher, Miller, Crowley and Layden. They formed the crest of the South Bend cyclone before which another fighting Army football team was swept over the precipice at the Polo Grounds yesterday afternoon as 55,000 spectators peered down on the bewildering panorama spread on the green plain below.

A cyclone can't be snared. It may be surrounded, but somewhere it breaks through to keep on going. When the cyclone starts from South Bend, where the candle lights still gleam through the Indiana sycamores, those in the way must take to storm cellars at top speed. Yesterday the cyclone struck again as Notre Dame beat the Army, 13 to 7, with a set of backfield stars that ripped and crashed through a strong Army defense with more speed and power than the warring cadets could meet.

Notre Dame won its ninth game in twelve Army starts

through the driving power of one of the greatest backfields that ever churned up the turf of any gridiron in any football age. Brilliant backfields may come and go, but in [Harry] Stuhldreher, [Don] Miller, [Jim] Crowley and [Elmer] Layden, covered by a fast and charging line, Notre Dame can take its place in front of the field.

[Army] Coach [John J.] McEwan sent one of his finest teams into action, an aggressive organization that fought to the last play around the first rim of darkness, but when [Notre Dame Coach Knute] Rockne rushed his Four Horsemen to the track they rode down everything in sight. It was in vain that 1400 gray-clad cadets pleaded for the Army line to hold. The Army line was giving all it had, but when a tank tears in with the speed of a motorcycle, what chance has flesh and blood to hold? The Army had its share of stars in action, such stars as Garbisch, Farwick, Wilson, Wood, Ellinger and many others, but they were up against four whirlwind backs who picked up at top speed from the first step as they swept through scant openings to slip on by the secondary defense. The Army had great backs in Wilson and Wood, but the Army had no such quartet, who seemed to carry the mixed blood of the tiger and the antelope.

Rockne's light and tottering line was just about as tottering as the Rock of Gibraltar. It was something more than a match for the Army's great set of forwards, who had earned their fame before. Yet it was not until the second period that the first big thrill of the afternoon set the great crowd into a cheering whirl and brought about the wild flutter of flags that are thrown to the wind in exciting moments. At the game's start Rockne sent in almost entirely a second string cast. The Army got the jump and began to play most of the football. It was the Army attack that made three first downs before Notre Dame had caught its stride. The South Bend cyclone opened like a zephyr.

And then, in the wake of a sudden cheer, out rushed Stuhldreher, Miller, Crowley and Layden, the four star backs who helped to beat Army a year ago. Things were to be a trifle different now. After a short opening flurry in the second period, Wood, of the Army, kicked out of bounds on Notre Dame's 20-yard line. There was no sign of a tornado starting. But it happened to be at just this spot that Stuhldreher decided to put on his attack and begin the long and dusty hike.

On the first play the fleet Crowley peeled off fifteen yards, and the cloud from the west was now beginning to show signs of lightning and thunder. The fleet, powerful Layden got six yards more, and then Miller added ten. A forward pass from Stuhldreher to Crowley added twelve yards, and a moment later Miller ran twenty yards around Army's right wing. He was on his way to glory when Wilson, hurtling across the right of way, nailed him on the 10-yard line and threw him out of bounds. Crowley, Miller and Layden—Miller, Layden and Crowley—one or another, ripping and crashing through, as the Army defense threw everything it had in the way to stop this wild charge that had now come seventy yards. Crowley and Layden added five yards more; and then, on a split play, Layden went ten yards across the line as if he had just been fired from the black mouth of a howitzer.

In that second period Notre Dame made eight first downs to the Army's none, which shows the unwavering power of the Western attack that hammered relentlessly and remorselessly without easing up for a second's breath. The Western line was going its full share, led by the crippled Walsh with a broken hand.

But there always was a Miller or Crowley or Layden, directed through the right spot by the cool and crafty judgment of Stuhldreher, who picked his plays with the finest possible generalship. The South Bend cyclone had now roared eighty-five yards to a touchdown through one of the strongest defensive teams in the game. The cyclone had struck with too much speed and power to be stopped. It was the preponderance of Western speed that swept the Army back.

The next period was much like the second. The trouble began when the alert Layden intercepted an Army pass on the 48-yard line. Stuhldreher was ready for another march.

Once again the cheering cadets began to call for a rallying stand. They are never overwhelmed by any shadow of defeat as long as there is a minute of fighting left. But silence fell over the cadet sector for just a second as Crowley ran around the Army's right wing for 15 yards, where Wilson hauled him down on the 33-yard line. Walsh, the Western captain, was hurt in the play but soon resumed. Miller got 7 and Layden got 8 and then, with the ball on the Army's

20-yard line, the cadet defense rallied and threw Miller in his tracks. But the halt was only for the moment. On the next play Crowley swung out and around the Army's left wing, cut in and then crashed over the line for Notre Dame's second touchdown.

On two other occasions the Notre Dame attack almost scored. Yeomans saved one touchdown by intercepting a pass on his 5-yard line that he ran back 35 yards before he was nailed by two tacklers. It was a great play in the nick of time. On the next drive Miller and Layden in two hurricane dashes took the ball 42 yards to the Army's 14-yard line, where the still game Army defense stopped four plunges on the 9-yard line and took the ball.

Up to this point the Army had been outplayed by a crushing margin. Notre Dame had put under way four long marches, and two of these had yielded touchdowns. Even the stout and experienced Army line was meeting more than it could hold. Notre Dame's brilliant backs had been provided with the finest possible interference, usually led by Stuhldreher, who cut down tackler after tackler by diving at some rival's flying knees. Against this, each Army attack had been smothered almost before it got under way. Even the great Wilson, the star from Army, one of the great backfield runners of his day and time, rarely had a chance to make any headway through a massed wall of tacklers who were blocking every open route.

The sudden change came late in the third quarter, when Wilson, raging like a wild man, suddenly shot through a tackle opening to run 34 yards before he was finally collared and thrown with a jolt. A few minutes later Wood, one of the best of all the punters, kicked out of bounds on Notre Dame's 5-yard line. Here was the chance. Layden was forced to kick from behind his own goal. The punt soared up the field as Yeomans called for a free kick on the 35-yard line. As he caught the ball, he was nailed and spilled by a Western tackler, and the penalty gave the Army 15 yards, with the ball on Notre Dame's 20-yard line.

At this point Harding was rushed to quarterback in place of Yeomans, who had been one of the leading Army stars. On the first three plays the Army reached the 12-yard line, but it was fourth down, with two yards to go. Harding's next play was the feature of the game.

As the ball was passed, he faked a play to Wood, diving through the line, held the oval for just a half breath, then, tucking the same under his arm, swung out around Notre Dame's right end. The brilliant fake worked to perfection. The entire Notre Dame defense had charged forward in a surging mass to check the line attack; and Harding, with open territory, sailed on for a touchdown. He traveled those last 12 yards after the manner of fodder shot from guns. He was over the line before the Westerners knew what had taken place. It was a fine bit of strategy, brilliantly carried out by every member of the cast.

The cadet sector had a chance to rip open the chilly atmosphere at last, and most of the 55,000 present joined in the tribute to football art. But that was Army's last chance to score. From that point on it was seesaw, up and down, back and forth, with the rivals fighting bitterly for every inch of ground. It was harder now to make a foot than it had been to make ten yards. Even the all-star South Bend cast could no longer continue to romp for any set distances, as Army tacklers, inspired by the touchdown, charged harder and faster than they had charged before.

The Army brought a fine football team into action, but it was beaten by a faster and smoother team. Rockne's supposedly light, green line was about as heavy as Army's, and every whit as aggressive. What is even more important, it was faster on its feet, faster in getting around.

It was Western speed and perfect interference that once more brought about Army doom. The Army line couldn't get through fast enough to break up the attacking plays; and once started, the bewildering speed and power of the Western backs slashed along for 8, 10 and 15 yards on play after play. And always in front of these offensive drives could be found the whirling form of Stuhldreher, taking the first man out of the play as cleanly as though he had used a hand grenade at close range. This Notre Dame interference was a marvelous thing to look upon.

It formed quickly and came along in unbroken order, always at terrific speed, carried by backs who were as hard to drag down as African buffaloes. On receiving the kickoff, Notre Dame's interference formed something after the manner of the ancient flying wedge, and they drove back up the field with the runner covered from 25 and 30 yards at almost every chance. And when a back such as Harry Wilson finds few chances to get started, you can figure upon the defensive strength that is barricading the road. Wilson is one of the hardest backs in the game to suppress, but he found few chances yesterday to show his broken field ability. You can't run through a broken field until you get there.

One strong feature of the Army play was its headlong battle against heavy odds. Even when Notre Dame had scored two touchdowns and was well on its way to a third, the Army fought on with fine spirit until the touchdown chance came at last. And when the chance came, Coach McEwan had the play ready for the final march across the line. The Army has a better team than it had last year. So has Notre Dame. We doubt that any team in the country could have beaten Rockne's array yesterday afternoon, East or West. It was a great football team brilliantly directed, a team of speed, power and team play. The Army has no cause for gloom over its showing. It played first-class football against more speed than it could match.

Those who have tackled a cyclone can understand.

12

WALTER WINCHELL

THE GOSSIP WHO RESHAPED JOURNALISM

Walter Winchell was a gossip. A knowing-look, chat-over-the-back-fence, did-you-hear-the-latest, out-and-out gossip. His victims utterly despised him—and his fans utterly adored him. Few journalists have been so popular—and few, so deeply controversial.

Winchell probably would have guffawed with satisfaction to know that his reporting was still causing dissension and discussion decades after his death. He would thoroughly agree with those who claimed that he had reshaped the course of journalism. He would bitterly denounce detractors who said he was a pathetic, power-hungry liar.

Which one was Winchell? The reshaper of journalistic writing—or the reshaper of truth? No matter what they felt, both sides would have to agree that Winchell's controversial style trumpeted a loud, breezy, personal, uniquely Winchell tune. Some said he was too personal, venturing to give his own opinion too often in the news. Others hailed him as the man who gave journalism back to the people. He was credited—and discredited—for adding a personal touch to journalism. "Lots of things have happened to me," he said, "and believe me—I've happened to lots of things!" Those personal happenings permeated his distinctive brand of writing.

Winchell got into journalism out of desperation and by accident. He dropped out of school in the sixth grade and joined a vaudeville act. As a child performer, he was cute; but by the time he had matured and married his co-star, his act had fallen on hard times. He and wife Rita were getting

few bookings. His only success seemed to be in a popular
scandal sheet he wrote and tacked up at the stage door. The
"Newsense" contained gossipy tidbits about various stars.
Soon the *Vaudeville News*, a theater publication, had noticed
and hired Winchell, and his career in the media was born.
He divorced his wife, and before long he was the Broadway
columnist for the New York *Graphic*. At last Walter
Winchell was a hit. He soon moved to New York's *Daily
Mirror*, which considered him a hot property.

The public viewed his column as hot reading, too. The
column sizzled with all sorts of innuendos, news, and
folksy language. If Winchell, with his meager education,
couldn't think of just the right word, he'd make one up. He
didn't worry too much either about grammar or spelling. He
wrote gossip on paper as he would say gossip aloud. For instance, he told the public:

•One of the Vanderbilts is about to be Reno-vated
[divorced]....
•The A.K. Rowans of the Vaudeville Set are expecting a
baby-joy....
•Are the Jerome Astors of High Sassiety tossing it out the
window?...
•A blondiful sextress is asking for trouble. Fooling around
with married men. Are there any other men? Hehehheh.

The Winchell column, with no attachment to any journalistic rules, definitely departed from the usual serious
personality of newspapers. It did not speak of earth-shatter-
ing events. It did not speak in grave language. It had little
bearing on the readers' knowledge of public affairs.

Readers loved it. It was as though they had been starved
to hear the juicy details of celebrities' lives. They hungered
to read something a little more salty and a lot more bawdy
than standard newspaper fare. They craved the casual language and chit-chat style that Winchell served up.

He became popular fast. Everyone began quoting his
made-up language. A few of his slang words stuck. Expec-
tant parents were looking forward to "a blessed event" or "a
bundle from heaven." He coined the slang "makin'
whoopee" and popularized an otherwise unknown slang for
the FBI, "G-man." His slang for a film, "a flicker," became

part of the language. Other Winchellisms did not become permanent additions to the language, but they had their heyday. W. J. Funk, the lexicographer, said in 1933 that Winchell was one of the top 10 contributors to American slang.

No subject was safe from Winchell's prying pen. Even his own family and his own embarrassing confessions found their way into his articles. He had remarried, and spats with his new wife turned up in print. His words were italicized, while those of his wife, June, were in Roman type:

> *"Did you read the column that I did about you and..."*
>
> "Don't you mention that thing—do you hear?"
>
> *"What's the matter—what was wrong with it?"*
>
> "I said don't mention it to me! I threw it down three times—although it got me so curious, I had to pick it up each time and finish the darn thing. Don't put me in the paper— don't make me say things I didn't say. People will think I'm silly or something. Walda [the Winchells' daughter], come here. Be careful what you say in front of Daddy— he'll put it in the paper!"
>
> *"Oh, cut that out. Everything I said you said, you said! Maybe not in the same day—but you said those things. It's a good idea for a column, and I'm gonna do it every now and then—and what do you think about that? It's intimate, personal, inside stuff about us—and several people have written in to say they liked it. Get me some orange juice."*

Not surprisingly, those "Mr. and Mrs. Columnist at Home" articles did not last long. June Winchell protested vigorously. Although her husband was rapidly becoming popular as the man who gave the news a human touch, the inclusion of his family in that scheme was just too much.

While such gossipy pieces continued to be Winchell's trademark throughout his long career in both newspapers and radio, he gradually found topics to write about besides gossip. He wrote a few serious pieces about the harshness of stars' lives. While they did not omit gossipy details, they featured the emotions of the ex-performer Winchell. Having known disappointment on the stage himself, he could understand. Thus, in a new way, his personal touch began showing in his writing. For instance, he said of Broadway:

...[I]t is at once an enticement and a hell, a Circe's cavern of lascivious and soul-destroying delights, an unholy place where producers are the seducers of women, where stars without talent are made meretriciously overnight, where pure girls succumb to rich admirers for diamond brooches, furs, imported automobiles, apartments and other luxuries—a Babylon, a Sodom and a Gomorrah all within the confines of a garish district extending from just below Forty-second Street to Columbus Circle at Fifty-ninth.

Broadway wasn't Winchell's only interest. He hung out in the night spots of New York, usually staying out much or all of the night and getting to know the city's corrupt underworld. Chummy with gangsters, he saw that they found their way into his articles. Once he correctly hinted that a certain gangster would be shot dead that night—and Winchell was nearly rubbed out in turn. An underworld king had to persuade angered gangsters not to kill him. At one point, J. Edgar Hoover's G-men were working alongside the henchmen of one of Chicago's top gangsters to guard Winchell. Both liked him and wanted to keep him safe.

Winchell's friendship with gangsters led to one of journalism's most memorable stories. After a high price was put on the head of the notorious gangster Louis "Lepke" Buchalter, he decided to turn himself in—but not to the police. No. Lepke would surrender only to Walter Winchell. He reasoned that no one would shoot him for the $50,000 bounty if he were with such a famous newsman. Reprinted in this anthology, Winchell's account of the event was all Winchell. It featured his observant, conversational style, with touches of personal tidbits that gave a full, clear picture of just how the spy-quality capture came about. Winchell was as much a part of the story as Lepke was, and the newsman didn't hesitate to tell the story from his personal point of view. The story read like a thriller, with Winchell as the royal "we" in the piece.

As Winchell was developing an interest in crime reporting, he also was developing a deep concern over world events. Adolf Hitler had taken over in Germany. Winchell, unlike a number of well-known people, saw the Führer as a

nightmarish menace. He began decrying Hitler in his typical gossipy style. He picked up on the rumor that Hitler was
homosexual. Hitler, Winchell said, was one of "the yoo-hoo
boys of the swishy set." He even printed a bogus "telegram"
from the Führer:

Cable, March 26 [1933]. Berlin.
To Walter Winchell, care of the Paramount Theatre,
Bklyn:
What are you doing over the week-end? Would you like
to spend it with me? I think you're cute.
Love. Adolf Hitler.

Such obvious fiction was written to prove a point in a
Winchellian tattletale way.
Winchell grew increasingly serious about the threat
from the Nazis, whom he called Ratzis. He wrote powerfully:

The wounded in the ditches, the homeless in the fields and
the starving by the roadside...are silent witnesses....Peo-
ple will not bow before the swastika 2000 years from now,
but they will still kneel before the Cross. If a tomb cannot
hold a man's soul, a concentration camp cannot hold his
spirit. Men will follow a rosary where they cannot be
driven by a whip....The humble and lowly man who died
1900 years ago was big enough to be tolerant even of the in-
tolerant....His last prayer was for the men who tortured
and crucified Him—and for all dictators: "Forgive them,
Father, for they know not what they do."

Winchell kept up a prolonged attack on Nazi Germany.
Germany attacked back. It officially proclaimed him as an
enemy of Hitler. "It is a high and personal honor,"
Winchell retorted gleefully, "as this is the only way in
which your humble newsboy could hope to be classed with
men such as Maeterlinck, Einstein and Toscanini."
As the world war approached, a strong American faction
actively sought to keep the United States from going to war,
but Winchell typically tried to direct events from his point of
view—and toward a battle with Hitler. The Indianapolis
Times noted that "Walter Winchell continues to direct the

foreign policies of the United States—and, by heck, gets away with it, too."

Despite the fact that he was speaking from his own point of view, Winchell knew he was also speaking to "Mr. and Mrs. America," as he called his readers and listeners. He knew the basic, clearest, least formal language had appealed to his readers from the very start. So he deliberately used such language in his articles on the Nazis. He warned:

> Joe Goebbels boasts that if von Ribbentrop could separate fifteen nations, he, Goebbels, can divide 48 states ....Goebbels' job, this summer, is to produce rioting on American street corners. He has made a fine start. He has already divorced the President from the national hero [Charles Lindbergh, who was against American entry into the war], and they have got nearly all of us taking sides ....After arguments in the corner drugstore comes the fist-fight. After that weapons. Then foreign rulers send supplies and men to the side they want to win. Remember Spain? The foreign military master who comes to help— remains to conquer. The bed you have made for your nation turns out to be your grave. Everything is ashes and tastes like it. And what happens to you—and you—and you? Well, this is what happens. A few of you who are American Quislings and Lavals will be in temporary power. Some of you—such as me—will be shot. Many of you will be put into concentration camps, and the rest of you will be slaves.

It was hard to get more personal than that. Winchell expected his public to see clearly, in simple terms, how the threatening Ratzis would rule if left unchecked. He made his points clear by putting each individual reader grimly into the picture.

Another side of Winchell's colorful, clear wording showed in his constant praise of his hero, Franklin Roosevelt. The president liked Winchell. Roosevelt won him over by treating him with respect and occasionally tipping him off about news items. Perhaps Roosevelt was shrewd; Winchell, after all, could make or break show-biz careers with his approval or disapproval. Roosevelt might have figured the same formula applied to political careers. Thanks to his friendliness with Winchell, Roosevelt got his whole-hearted approval. The president was one of the few of Winchell's friends who didn't eventually wind up as an embarrassing bit of gossipy trivia in the Winchell column. Instead, Winchell presented Roosevelt's achievements as everyday, bread-and-butter results which everyday people could understand. "An American's Thanksgiving," he wrote, "would not be complete without a prayer for FDR. No American would be gobbling turkey today if we lacked his brilliant guidance. We would all be nibbling crumbs behind barbed wire, if we were lucky enough to escape with whole skins. Americans! Every time you can pray in peace—thank Roosevelt. Every time you can speak freely or read a free American newspaper—thank Roosevelt. Every time you gaze at your home which was mercifully saved from bombs—thank Roosevelt. Every time you look at a child that has a warm bed to sleep in and enough food to eat—thank Roosevelt."

Although Winchell never did give up his trademark gossip columns, eventually America tired of his writings and his radio broadcasts. He tried his hand at television but had lasting success only as the narrator of *The Untouchables*, the story of Elliott Ness' fight against mobs in the 1930s. Despite his failure on TV, the sixth-grade dropout had achieved much. In the late 1940s he was making the highest salary of anyone in the United States at $800,000 a year. Before his career ended, he had become the most read and most listened to journalist in history. Some people considered him to be the most influential and popular journalist ever.

Despite his popularity, he knew his snoopy, personal, gossipy attitude had been the bedrock of his success. Accordingly, he suggested a humorous epitaph for himself: "Here is Walter Winchell—with his ear to the ground—as usual."

●◆

WALTER WINCHELL ON BROADWAY

Winchell got his first "real" news assignment as one of the reporters covering the trial of Bruno Richard Hauptmann for the 1932 kidnaping and murder of Charles Lindbergh Jr., baby son of the famous aviator.

In "The Private Papers of a Cub Reporter," Winchell let his faithful fans know exactly what it was like to be a reporter covering the trial. His gossip-column approach shone through.

Winchell's readers were familiar with the names and situations in the trial, and he didn't bother them with repeated explanations of who those people were. Modern readers, however, may need to know that Violet Sharpe was a servant at the home of the Morrows, the kidnaped child's grandparents. The phrase "Hey! Doctor!" was used in the passing of ransom money. Col. Schwarzkopf was the police officer in charge of the investigation. Runyon, of course, was reporter Damon Runyon, profiled elsewhere in this book.

Note that Winchell didn't hesitate to give himself some glory in the trial. (The ellipses in the following story are Winchell's.)

THE PRIVATE PAPERS OF A CUB REPORTER
Walter Winchell
New York *Daily Mirror*
January 18, 1935

Flemington, N.J.: The excitement and tenseness of the Hauptmann Trial will make some of us ill before it is over....You can't eat regularly, if at all....You must devour your food hastily—or a little of it, anyway....For someone near you is certain to bring up an "angle" you haven't figured before, and you can't wait to jot it down for the wires....After going without slumber for 27 hours (to rearrange the schedule and get up in time the first day of the trial) we felt sure we'd get some sleep the following night....We left a call for 8 a.m., and went to bed at 1:15....But at 6:45 we wakened and couldn't get back to sleep—from thinking, thinking and thinking of this and that about the case....The average sleep any of us gets is about 5 hours—hardly enough....Maybe enough for such men as the late Thomas Edison, but he merely invented electric lights; he didn't have to worry about a 1100-word column for the next day or "a special piece" for the city desk.

When Justice Trenchard adjourns court around 12:30

noon—he instructs us all to be back by 1:45....It takes a long while to get out of the place and you rush to get some lunch, which you eat sparingly because "the nerves" have you by then—and you are impatient to get to the Postal Telly's typewriter and ticker with notes on the morning session....The Postal man assigned to this column eats wordage faster than you can think of the next paragraph, and the man in charge buys you a cold drink of pop and places carbon between paper so you won't lose time....The articles for the city desk are written and sent within 15 to 18 minutes, and you have a few moments in which to rush back through the crowd into the court, where you fight with some stranger who has your seat....The stranger, of course, usually is someone whose husband is a big shot there, or a kin of some Admiral or editor—so you mustn't get sassy....Poor Boake Carter of the radio....He always comes too tardy and has to stand, or he gets a break and sits with the judge, almost.

There is a gal reporter in Flemington whose name is Louise Van Slyke, they say....And she is an absolute "double" for the late Violet Sharpe, who killed herself during the investigation at the Morrow home....One day after Violet died, the girl reporter ankled into the Flemington police station and the cops almost swooned....They thought they had the "haan'ts" and that they were being hexed....I hear, too, that many alleged photos published there of Violet Sharpe were actually likenesses of Miss Van Slyke....I must ask Miss Van Slyke the next time I bump into her and knock her down....After you show people samples of Bruno's handwriting and samples of the writing in the ransom notes—they all are converted....Hauptmann may be acquitted of the murder and snatch raps by "that" jury....One thing is certain, though....He will never beat the extortion charge in the Bronx....It is impossible!....The moment I am breathlessly anticipating (and I hope Mr. Wilentz has thought to arrange it) is this one: when Hauptmann is asked to call out "Hey! Dok-tur!"....Bruno's thick accent will be difficult to mask.

The improbable tip forwarded to me and turned over to Mr. Reilly, the defense attorney, goes this way, in part: That one Italian and two others plotted the crime....They were rum-runners and knew that a ship-builder was in need of coin....They promoted the money to help him out of a difficulty and later asked him for a favor in return....They planned, the story goes, to snatch the Lindy baby—and then demand that the father himself come to arrange its release....When Lindy arrived, he was to be kidnapped, and the U.S. Government instructed to pay the ransom of several million dollars....It is a fantastic story, but so is the actual crime!...When Uncle Sam had paid the ransom, Lindbergh was to be deposited at some foreign port via a boat owned by the bootlegger. It was a seagoing yacht....Lindbergh was almost delivered to the kidnappers, but the seas were rough and high and all concerned were forced to return to port and try again another time....In the meantime, the deal was found and the plot crashed....Defense counsel now has the names of the men involved....I don't believe a word of it.

Impressions in Court: Col. Schwarzkopf has a contagious smile. There was a buzz that the new Governor would replace him. This isn't true. The new Governor, who will be inducted on the 15th, told me that the Colonel is one of the most popular men in New Jersey—and is loved by the natives in the rural sectors....Ellis Parker could not be Schwarzkopf's successor, as it was rumored he might be....To succeed to Schwarzkopf's job you must have had two years military training....Parker hasn't that qualification....Adela Rogers St. Johns' daily pieces rap Reilly, and Reilly is a good friend of her boss....Proving this: That newspapers do not allow friendships to interfere with their staff members, which is as it should be....Not all the good reporters are in New York—the out-of-town boys and girls are distinguishing themselves daily with their swelegant reporting....On Reilly's table are numerous folders and files, one of which is marked: "Walter Winchell file"....It contains everything written or broadcast by this department on the case.

There was a buzz in and out of court that Mr. Reilly intended putting this column on the stand....We learned, however, that the plot was suggested by a person named Runyon, said to be an-anything-for-a-laugh guy....Defense counsel stated that this Runyon fiend and some other historians had offered him a swell write-up if he obliged them, but even that tempting bribe didn't penetrate Mr. Reilly....For which a sigh of relief plus the promise of a good notice if he ever goes into vaudeville....For the benefit of Mr. Runyon (we hope we're spelling the name correctly) even though we are summoned to the stand, the New Jersey statutes would save us, we hear—and hope!...In New Jersey you do not have to go to jail for contempt for not revealing your source of information....And even if we have been misled, and the laws there have been altered, we won't reveal our sources. Unless the sources okay it.

Well, well. Looka who's here! Mr. Gregory F. Coleman, the Bronx "angle" editor, with whom we've swapped sass over this and that on the case...."Hello, Walter," he says affably enough, "how's things?"....To which he replied: "But I caught hell; the circulation manager of our paper was very sore at me for fighting with you so much. It seems that the circulation of the Mirrow, instead of our paper, reached a new high in the Bronx!"...In the court are various people who went to the trouble of belittling items that ran here about the case before the trial began....Naturally, when any of the predictions are confirmed in court, we feel lots better than Bruno does....When Wilentz on the first day yelled that the State had found Sig. Thayer, who belittled that "beat" [but then] sent over an apology....We nodded our forgiveness, but we didn't mean it.

◆

MOBSTER SURRENDERS TO WINCHELL

Louis "Lepke" Buchalter was the chief of Murder, Inc., his personal killing-for-hire racket in the New York area. Although he had been in hiding from the law for a couple of years, he grew frightened when the government put a $50,000 price on his head. He figured some of his acquaintances might kill him to collect the reward.

He decided that he would turn himself in to Winchell. He said he knew no one would have the nerve to shoot at him if there were a chance of shooting so famous a newsman as well.

Winchell's story of the surrender read like a spy novel. His personal description and details of people's actions put the reader right on the scene.

Unfortunately for Lepke, his plan to turn himself in was not as successful as he had hoped. He had expected to receive a light sentence for coming forward, but he was sentenced to the electric chair anyway.

WAITING FOR LEPKE
Walter Winchell
New York *Daily Mirror*
August 29, 1939

New York, August 25 (INS)—The surrender of public enemy "Lepke" Buchalter to the government last night took place while scores of pedestrians ambled by, and two police radio cars waited for the lights to change, near Twenty-eighth Street and Fifth Avenue.

The time was precisely 10:17 p.m., and the search for the most wanted fugitive in the nation was over. The surrender was negotiated by this reporter, whom G-man John Edgar Hoover authorized to guarantee "safe delivery."

After a series of telephone talks with persons unknown, and with the head of the FBI, Lepke appeared to drop out of the sky, without even a parachute. The time was 10:15. The scene was Madison Square between Twenty-third and Twenty-fourth Streets, where we had halted our car as per instructions.

The following two minutes were consumed traveling slowly north on Fourth Avenue and west on Twenty-seventh Street to Fifth Avenue, where the traffic lights were red—and to the next corner at Twenty-eight Street, where Mr. Hoover waited alone, unarmed and without handcuffs, in a government limousine. Hoover was disguised in dark sunglasses to keep him from being recognized by passersby.

The presence of two New York police cruisers, attached to the Fourteenth Precinct, so near the surrender scene startled Hoover as well as Lepke. The G-man later admitted he feared "a leak."

Lepke, who was calmer than this chauffeur, was on the verge of rushing out of our machine into Hoover's arms. The police cruisers, ironically, were the first observed by this reporter in two hours of motoring to complete the surrender.

Not until the final seconds was there a sign of uniformed law. But it was too late. The long arm of the government had reached out and claimed another enemy. The Federal Bureau of Investigation and the city of New York had saved

$50,000—the reward offered.

While pausing alongside one police car at the Twenty-seventh Street intersection for the lights, Lepke, who was wearing spectacles as part of his disguise, threw them to the corner pavement. They crashed noisily. Two passers-by, middle-aged men with graying temples, stopped and looked up at a building.

Apparently they thought a window had broken above. They never realized that the man for whom every cop in the land was searching was within touching distance.

After parking our car behind a machine which was parked behind Hoover's, we shut off the ignition and escorted Lepke into Hoover's car.

"Mr. Hoover," we said, "this is Lepke."

"How do you do?" said Mr. Hoover affably.

"Glad to meet you," replied Lepke. "Let's go."

"To the Federal Building at Foley Square," commanded Hoover. His colored pilot turned swiftly south.

Lepke was a little excited. He seemed anxious to talk—to talk to anybody new—after being in the shadows for over two years with so many hunted men.

"You did the smart thing by coming in, Lepke," comforted Hoover.

"I'm beginning to wonder if I did," Lepke answered. "I would like to see my wife and kids, please?"

Mr. Hoover arranged for them to visit him shortly after Lepke was booked, fingerprinted, and Kodaked. He had $1700 on him. He gave $1100 to the boy and $600 to the jailer—for "expenses."

When the government car reached Fourteenth Street, we got out and went to the first phone to notify our editor, who groaned:

"A fine thing! With a World War starting!"

The negotiations which led to Lepke's surrender began in this manner. On Saturday night, August 5 last, a voice on the phone said:

"Don't ask me who I am. I have something important to tell you. Lepke wants to come in. But he's heard so many different stories about what will happen to him. He can't trust anybody, he says. If he could find someone he can trust, he will give himself up to that person. The talk around town is that Lepke would be shot while supposedly escaping."

"Does he trust me?" we inquired.

"Do you really mean that?" said the voice anxiously.

"Sure," we assured. "I'll tell John Edgar Hoover about it, and I'm sure he will see to it that Lepke receives his constitutional rights and nobody will cross him."

"O.K., put it on the air tomorrow night if you can get that promise," and then he disconnected.

We wrote a brief radio paragraph which was addressed to Lepke, "if you are listening now," which said we would try to get him assurance of a safe delivery. The next afternoon, Sunday, we phoned Mr. Hoover and read him the paragraph.

"You are authorized to state," said Hoover, "that the FBI will guarantee it!"

Hoover and his assistant director, Clyde Tolson, came to the studio and witnessed our microphoning. They remained for the repeat broadcast to the coast an hour later—in case another phone call came in.

For two nights, voices contacted us by phone and said:

"You're doing very well. You'll hear more later. If he agrees to come in, he will do it through you. But he may change his mind. Good-by."

And then all the dickering abruptly stopped—until last Tuesday night. Then a person we had never seen before, or since, approached us at Fifty-third Street and Fifth Avenue and said: "Where can you be reached on a pay-station phone in an hour?"

We went to the nearest phone booth, where the stranger marked down the number and instructed: "This is about Lepke. This time it's important. Please be here in an hour."

He hastened away, hailed a passing cab, and taxied north.

When we so reported to Mr. Hoover, after what seemed to him like too much stalling, he was exasperated. For the first time in our seven years of knowing him, he barked at us:

"This is a lot of bunk, Walter. You are being made a fool of and so are we. If you contact those people again, tell them the time limit is up! I will instruct my agents to shoot Lepke on sight."

Promptly an hour later, right on the button, that pay-station phone tinkled. We didn't give the voice a chance to talk. "I just spoke to Hoover," we said breathlessly. "He's fed up. If Lepke doesn't surrender by four p.m. tomorrow, Hoover says no consideration of any kind will ever be given him. For every day he stays away it may mean an extra two years added to his sentence."

The voice interrupted: "He's coming in, but you simply have to wait until he can arrange things. He's willing to come in, but it can't be tomorrow. Maybe the next night. Where can you be reached tomorrow night at six?"

We gave him another phone number. He said he'd call—and the call came. But it didn't seem to be the same voice. This time the instructions included: "Drive up to Proctor's Theater in Yonkers."

How sure could we be that the "meet" was for the surrender of Lepke? We weren't sure at all. But we hoped to convince the G-men that we weren't being made any "goat-between"! And so we motored up to Yonkers, and before we reached Proctor's Theater a car loaded with strangers—faces we don't recall ever seeing before—slowly drew alongside. We heard a voice say, "That's him."

One of the men got out, holding his handkerchief to his face as though he intended to blow into it. He got into our car, sat alongside, and kept the kerchief to his face throughout the brief conversation.

"Go to the drugstore on the corner of Nineteenth Street and Eighth Avenue," he instructed. "There are some phone booths there. Get in one and appear busy. About nine p.m. somebody will come up to you and tell you where to notify the G-men to meet you."

At 8:55 p.m. we were in that drugstore. We ordered a coke. The boy behind the counter looked at us as though we seemed familiar. Perhaps we imagined it. At any rate, we didn't get a chance to appear busy in the phone booth. A face met ours as we turned to look through the open door. The stranger jerked his head as though to telegraph "Come here." We joined him outside and walked to our car slowly.

"Go back in there and tell Hoover to be at Twenty-eighth Street on Fifth Avenue between 10:10 and 10:20," he instructed.

We did so. When we returned to the car, the man was at the wheel. He drove slowly, to kill time, for more than an hour. Up and down Eighth Avenue, Ninth, Tenth, in and out of side streets, down to Fourteenth, back to Twenty-third, and east to Madison Square, where he stopped the car and said:

"Just wait here—and good luck."

And so saying he left hurriedly. We took the wheel, turned our eyes left, and noticed many people across the street lounging around. It was very humid. Our clothes were dripping. The butterflies started to romp inside of us.

Suddenly a figure approached our car in haste. Out of nowhere, it seems. He opened the door, got in, and said: "Hello. Thanks very much."

We released the brake and stepped on the gas. "We'll be with Mr. Hoover in a minute or two," we said. "He's waiting in his car at Twenty-eighth Street."

"Yes, I know," said Lepke. "I just passed him."

13

BOB CONSIDINE

THE CHUMMY GUY FROM NEXT DOOR

"Listen to this, buddy!"

Sports fans leaned closer in the smoky light, sloshing their drinks as they reached for salty pretzels. Bob Considine, that guy from next door, was about to tell one of his great sports sagas. No one wanted to miss it. When Bob asked the buddies to listen, they were rarely sorry. He began:

> Listen to this, buddy, for it comes from a guy whose palms are still wet, whose throat is still dry, and whose jaw is still agape from the utter shock of watching Joe Louis knock out Max Schmeling.
>
> It was...a shocking thing, that knockout—short, sharp, merciless, complete. Louis was like this:
>
> He was a big lean copper spring, tightened and retightened through weeks of training until he was one pregnant package of coiled venom....

That's the way fans felt when reading one of Considine's stories, as if the reporter were leaning over and telling it in person.

For years, Considine was the chummy guy any sports fan would like to invite over to watch the big game. He was the guy whom anyone would welcome at a party. He was the guy who loved to tell a great story, whether it was about ballgames or battles or anything else. He was the guy who strolled casually into America's living rooms via newspaper for more than three decades to chit-chat about, well, anything.

Considine burst onto the reporting scene in the 1920s, not quite with fanfare, but with the typical attitude of anyone who has ever been misrepresented in the newspaper.

Considine was a government clerk who happened to play tennis on the side, even winning some local tournaments. He was pretty proud. He couldn't wait to see his name in the paper.

But the Washington *Herald* couldn't seem to spell "Considine." When the paper printed that "Robert Constantine" had won a tennis tournament, Considine was annoyed. He set off for the offices of the newspaper to straighten out the people responsible. The sports editor wound up telling Considine that if he wanted to see tennis news in the paper, he'd have to write it himself.

And that's how Bob Considine, government clerk, became Bob Considine, reporter. The editor's comment got him to thinking, and then his girlfriend Millie promised she'd never marry a government clerk. That settled it. Considine became a reporter—even though Millie, a government clerk herself, made more money than he did.

It didn't take long for him to advance. He started by writing a tennis column, in which he reviewed his own tournament performance under a pseudonym. The ladies in his night school creative writing class figured him out, much to his chagrin; but he soon blossomed into his own byline. He got to cover high school sports and then even college sports. Eventually he covered professional sports, features, and news as well.

Mindful of his amateurish entry into newspaperdom, Considine maintained a subtle sense of humor in his stories. He was baldly honest, which gave his words a curmudgeonly kind of grin. In 1950, for instance, he took a look at the world of sports. It was a fine world. Nice place. Maybe too nice. He wrote:

There's nothing wrong with modern sports that a squirt of plasma and a box of male hormone lozenges couldn't almost cure. With that much attended to, the redemption could be completed by shooting a few dozen sports officials, promoters, umpires, referees, and, naturally, a brace of

Forest Hills net-cord judges. As for these Pooh Bahs of muscledom, the world would little note nor long remember—to coin a clumsy phrase—their passing, and the luster of sweaty horseplay would improve.

The American athletic scene does not need new blood as much as it needs simply blood....It needs red meat.... [T]he unbridled rise of dictatorial power among officials [has] bred most of the guts out of the sports scene. The public hungers for a chew-tobacco oaf with 20-20 vision and supernatural muscular control who, like his forebears, accepts the fact that he was placed on earth to raise hell with law, order and the record books.

Considine's frank observations delighted sports fans. Who hasn't wanted to shoot an umpire, shred a referee, or shriek at a line judge? Who doesn't blame the officials for spoiling all the fun? In fact, has there been a game yet which did not suffer from an official's nearsightedness? Probably not, as far as fans were concerned, and Considine knew it. He played on the public's feelings, not with a growl but a grin.

Such was Considine's deep, subtle humor. It was a quiet undercurrent running through many of his stories. It was never obvious, but it was rarely absent. It worked because it shared readers' own points of view.

No subject was safe from Considine's wry commentary. He even wrote of himself. His humorous look at his own (and other reporters') work described reporting not as high and mighty newsmen saw it, but how the public saw it. His "Newspaperman's Prayer" read:

Dear God, may I be fair. Circumstances and dumb luck have placed in my thumby paws a degree of authority which I may not fully comprehend. Let me not profane it.

...When the customers write in to accuse me of being a bum, let me consider carefully the possibility or probability that I am...and try to do better. Let me work harder, try harder, and recall with proper humility that history produced some notably abler reporters, including four journeymen named Matthew, Mark, Luke, and John.

Let my stomach rebel at plucking meat from publicity handouts and let me not be miffed when someone says,

"You had a pretty good piece last week but I can't remember what it was."

Even when he was angry or disgusted, Considine retained a salty sense of humor. Writing the obituary in 1958 for the International News Service, which he had joined fifteen years earlier, he answered a critic in *Time* magazine:

The men and women who sat in our silenced newsrooms and read that farewell nose-thumbing felt more than anger. Many of them were seasoned at their trade when you, in all probability, were making your first little jabs at a typewriter....

Someday, son, venture out of doors and ask a couple of good men [at United Press and Associated Press]...what kind of time they used to have when they had even an undermanned team of INS reporters competing against them on a big, fast-moving story. Someday, son, if you improve, you'll be good enough to change the ribbons on their beat-up mills.

Considine was sorry, of course, that his beloved INS was closing; but he couldn't resist the wryly humorous jab at the *Time* writer. "It made some of us feel a little better," he recalled later. "But not much."

Considine's quietly entertaining copy was brimming over with his colorful, conversational tone. He wrote things on paper the way he'd say them in person. Describing the Louis-Schmeling fight, for instance, he noted that a trainer had thrown "the white towel of surrender" into the ring. "The referee snatched it off the floor and flung it backwards," Considine commented. "It hit the ropes and hung there, limp as Schmeling."

Such vivid, colorful language was not the language of a dry statistician or a boring analyst. It was the voice of a guy next door spinning a good yarn. It compared athletes with things people knew and understood. Baseball player Ted Williams, Considine said, "is even badder than the be-curled little girl" of nursery rhyme fame. The game of professional tennis attracted "pinheads and bird brains," according to Considine. The baseball dugout was a "damp, arthritic cave," and sports hero Leo Durocher "now sees

[Baseball Commissioner] Happy Chandler under every bed —a Happy Chandler with drops of distilled venom dropping off his fangs, ready to pounce on him with another fine or suspension."

While Considine spoke the language of everyone, he did not fall into the trap of revising spellings and monkeying with grammar to sound as if he were speaking in the vernacular.

Instead, he managed to achieve the casual, everyday voice with brilliance and clarity, with accurate grammar and correct spelling, thus making his work readable and understandable long after the jargon of the era had been replaced by the next set of colloquialisms.

If Considine had to quote the slang of the day, he did so with grace and humor:

[The pinch hitter] mounts the two or three steps and is exposed to the crowd. He is dimly aware of a faint round of applause (never enough), but the only thing he hears distinctly is a guy in the forty-eighth row of the distant bleachers who bawls, "Back in your cage, y' baboon!"

Our baboon, I mean our hero, makes a little show of selecting a couple of bats from the rack near the dugout, and then he walks that long last mile toward the plate.

Considine's clever use of everyday language could sparkle, as when he detailed the attempts of the Kentucky Derby to lure Bill Corum to be its director. The Derby's officials "asked Bill to fly to Louisville to talk things over. But Corum said to hell with it," Considine recounted. "Or rather, to heck with it. For Bill is a mild-spoken man."

Considine loved adjectives and good description, and he used both well. He saw no virtue in the notion that newswriting had to be slim and adjective-free. He attached as many adjectives and adverbs as possible to describe just the right shade of character or just the right degree of action. He described Schmeling hitting Louis with "a lethal little left hook."

Schmeling, in return, was pummelled and came away "dazed and sick." The man "looked drunkenly toward his corner" when he was struck again. Schmeling went down, "hurt and giddy," and looked "like a comical stew-bum doing his morning exercises."

In other stories, a new baseball player came in with "fresh muscles." Pitcher Floyd Bevens was "wild as a drunken dervish, to be sure." A fly ball "hit the wall in right field a few excruciating inches above the clutching paws of Yankee right fielder Tommy Heinrich." Considine said baseball managers were "often ruthless but never dull," but were being replaced by "slick Broadway chiseler types."

He praised a fellow sportswriter for his "sincerely rapturous copy." That same fellow was "an almost puzzling combination of carefree spendthrift and good businessman." Old-time boxers, Considine said descriptively, would have gone into the ring "with a busted paw or octave of sprung ribs."

Considine's descriptions never went over readers' heads, never sounded lofty or difficult. He worked hard to achieve the right tone. He believed one of reporting's greatest sins was to write "down" to people. "Let me write from the shoulder, and always with the assumption that those who read know more than I," he said.

Indeed, he did assume that his readers possessed a good range of information about the world. He set some of his stories in current events and political contexts. He also mentioned events from the past. When the history of a subject was obscure, he felt obliged to educate his readers about it, rather than merely report the immediate part of the news. He wrote of tennis:

> The game is an offshoot of ball-and-wall games dating back to the Egypt and Persia of 500 B.C. In 1874, Major Walter Wingfield patented "a new and improved portable court for playing the ancient game of tennis." His court was hour-glass shaped, like the torsos of the ladies of the day, and he named the sport "Sphairistike." A semibankrupt croquet club at Wimbledon—"The All England Croquet Club"—believed it might fill its coffers and attract new members by introducing the novelty. As an economy measure, it marked the boundaries of the courts on the grass. "Sphairistike" became "Lawn Tennis," and none too soon. The hardy British commoner, who couldn't make the social grade, was already calling the game "Sticky."

Besides providing detailed histories of sports and other topics, Considine frequently used historical comparisons. He expected that his readers understood such comparisons, and the metaphors and similes had the additional advantage of giving his stories a vivid and often humorous color. Continuing with his tennis story, for instance, he used several American Revolution metaphors to explain Americans' feelings about tennis.

The occasion was the first tennis tournament between British and American teams. "The British, amused by the challenge from a slovenly colony, sent over a team headed by their renowned singles champion, Arthur W. Gore," Considine wrote. "The Americans easily won the three full matches that were played, with a resultant burst of national pride hardly matched since the surrender of Cornwallis." Such historical references helped make the point clear in a readable way.

He liberally used literary allusions to the Bible and Homer's *Odyssey*, and he assumed that his readers would know what he meant. Most of them likely did. He did not choose obscure references that would befuddle. He instead wanted to make a point. He wondered, for example, how much more effective Christ and Moses and Socrates would have been than modern communicators are if they had had the same technological advantages. He referred to "Homeric" decisions by coaches. He twisted great quotes to suit his needs. His goal was to make a point more clearly. In his critique of modern sports, for instance, he had written that the world would "little note nor long remember" the deeds of sports officials. The greatness of the quote helped emphasize, ironically, the lack of greatness in sports officials.

In other cases, events came about in historic context, and Considine was eager to explain them. After World War II, he said, there were few decent boxers:

The educational aspects of the GI Bill of Rights probably had something to do with the present dearth. The young, tough doughboy of World War I had no such boon. He drifted toward or into boxing as the surest means by which he could realize two dreams now provided by the Government for the asking: an education and a down payment on a home. It is the Negro veteran or particularly the Negro who grew to manhood after the war and who is deprived of job opportunities, who is turning to boxing and dominating it.

History of various sorts crowded Considine's stories, but his were not dull recitations of facts. In the manner of a true historian, he breathed life into his stories and made the context and background vital to the tale. History was, after all, a part of the full story, and Considine was a storyteller in the fullest sense.

Considine enjoyed his career as much as he enjoyed telling stories. He wrote that "my past thirty years have been crowded with the kind of opportunities and breaks all reporters dream about." He said he had "a box seat near a world stage whose boards resound to the trod of a cast of characters unmatched in this century. The dramatic personae include the glorious, inglorious, thrilling, boring, noble, despicable, kind, wicked, just, sadistic, immoral, transient."

He noted that technology could never take the place of good reporting, clever description, and careful consideration of all facets of a sparkling story. Drawing typically on a literary metaphor from the Bible, he said: "But however exotic the technology, reporters always will have to gather in the wheat from the chaff of every blessed day's news, editors will have the eternal task of separating that harvest, and those who live the charmed life of commentators will rise and fall on their interpretation of what the news means."

◆

A "PACKAGE OF COILED VENOM"

The account of the Joe Louis-Max Schmeling boxing match was arguably Considine's best ever, featuring one of the best sports leads ever written. Considine was proud of the story and quoted it in full in his autobiography.

The story was not, however, easily written. As the fight approached, Considine's boss was angry at him. Reporter Damon Runyon, wanting to keep his rival away from ringside, had spread the rumor that Considine wanted his boss' job. The boss heard the rumor and believed it. Considine, in despair, was told that he would not be assigned to the fight. However, at the last minute, his boss relented and allowed him to cover it as a feature.

"When [the fight] was finished, and the ecstasy of the stadium had swept over and inoculated the reporters at ringside," Considine recalled, "Dan [his boss] turned to me and shook my hand warmly. It was like a reprieve from the Governor."

The story overflows with action-packed adjectives and descriptions. One might think that such writing would be flabby; but in fact, thanks to the colorful nature of Considine's descriptions, the story has a lean, sweaty, muscular tone to it, much like the boxers. It hits the reader with just the right shades of color and meaning.

[THE LOUIS-SCHMELING FIGHT]
Bob Considine
International News Service
June 22, 1938

Listen to this, buddy, for it comes from a guy whose palms are still wet, whose throat is still dry, and whose jaw is still agape from the utter shock of watching Joe Louis knock out Max Schmeling.

It was, indeed, a shocking thing, that knockout—short, sharp, merciless, complete. Louis was like this:

He was a big lean copper spring, tightened and retightened through weeks of training until he was one pregnant package of coiled venom.

Schmeling hit that spring. He hit with a whistling right-hand punch in the first minute of the fight—and the spring, tormented with tension, suddenly burst with one brazen spark of activity. Hard brown arms, propelling two unerring fists, blurred beneath the hot white candelabra of the ring lights. And Schmeling was in the path of them, a man caught and mangled in the whirring claws of a mad and feverish machine.

The mob, biggest and most prosperous ever to see a fight in a ball yard, knew that here was the end before the thing had really started. It knew, so it stood up and howled one long shriek. People who had paid as much as $100 for their chairs didn't use them—except perhaps to stand on, the better to let the sight burn forever in their memories.

There were four steps to Schmeling's knockout. A few seconds after he landed his only real punch of the fight, Louis caught him with a lethal little left hook that drove him into the ropes so hard that his right arm hooked over the top strand, like a drunk hanging on to a fence. Louis swarmed over him and hit Max with everything he had—until Referee Donovan pushed him away and counted one.

Schmeling staggered away from the ropes at that, dazed and sick. He looked drunkenly toward his corner, and before he had turned his head back Louis was on him again, first with a left and then with an awe-provoking right that made a crunching sound when it hit the German's jaw. Max fell down, hurt and giddy, for a count of three.

He clawed his way up as if the night air were as thick as black water, and Louis—his nostrils like the mouth of a double-barreled shotgun—took a quiet bead and let him have both barrels.

Max fell almost lightly, bereft of his senses, his fingers touching the canvas like a comical stewbum doing his morning exercises, knees bent and tongue lolling in his head.

He got up long enough to be knocked down again, this time with his dark unshaven face pushed in the sharp gravel of the resin.

Louis jumped away lightly, a bright and pleased look in his eyes, and as he did the white towel of surrender which Louis' handlers had refused to use two years ago tonight [when Max beat Joe so badly] came sailing into the ring in a soggy mess. It was thrown by Max Machon, oblivious to the fact that fights can no longer end this way in New York.

The referee snatched it off the floor and flung it backwards. It hit the ropes and hung there, limp as Schmeling. Donovan counted up to five over Max, sensed the futility of it all, and stopped the fight.

The big crowd began to rustle restlessly toward the exits, many only now accepting Louis as champion of the world. There were no eyes for Schmeling, sprawled on his stool in his corner.

He got up eventually, his dirty gray and black robe over

his shoulders, and wormed through the happy little crowd that hovered around Louis. And he put his arm around the Negro and smiled. They both smiled and could afford to— for Louis had made around $200,000 for two minutes and four seconds and Schmeling $100,000.

But once he crawled down in the belly of the big stadium, Schmeling realized the implications of his defeat. He, who won the title on a partly phony foul, and beat Louis two years ago with the aid of a crushing punch after the bell had sounded ending a critical round, now said Louis had fouled him. That would read better in Germany, whence earlier in the day had come a cable from Hitler, calling on him to win.

It was a low, sneaking trick, but a rather typical last word from Schmeling.

•◦

CONFIDENT EX-CHAMP "SMELTED BLOOD"

Considine covered all types of news, but his forté was sports —and he was at his peak in writing about boxing. He understood not only the sport but the fighters also.

In the following story about a comparatively minor match, he revealed the character of the opponents within the context of a straight fight story. The account of the fight is in itself a worthy story with a descriptive narrative that takes the reader to the scene. The reader also learns, however, something about the personalities of the two men who fought.

Max Baer, the former champ, had won his title in 1934 by beating Primo Carnera. The following year, however, he had lost the crown on a unanimous decision to James Braddock, who subsequently lost it to Joe Louis. The latter retained it for 11 years, until 1948. Baer never got a chance to fight Louis for the championship; and in 1940, at the age of 31, he was thought to be washed up.

Patrick Comiskey, Baer's opponent in the following story, was the pride of the Irish and at only 19 years of age was thought to be the best "white hope" for taking the crown from Louis. Going into the fight, he had a record of 28 wins and only one loss. His supporters figured his bout with Baer was simply a warm-up for a championship fight. With his stunning first-round loss to Baer, however, he faded from the championship scene and, like Baer, never got a chance to face Louis.

[AGING MAX BAER KO'S DROOLING KID]
Bob Considine
International News Service
September 27, 1940

JERSEY CITY, N.J.—A cocky, confident Max Baer turned back the clock of his boxing life here tonight, and with a burst of the savagery he once possessed he knocked out Patrick Edward Comiskey in the first round.

On the floor twice, once from a winging one-two punch, and again when he suddenly genuflected while Referee Jack Dempsey was trying to push the frantic Baer away, Comiskey finished up draped over the loose, dirty ropes. Through sick, glazed eyes he saw Dempsey shove Baer away from him and hold up Max's hand—thus stopping the fight after 2:39 of the round had elapsed.

It was the first time the 19-year-old Comiskey had been knocked out, and the second fight he had lost in 30 starts as a pro. He had won 25 of these by knockouts, and when he was introduced tonight to the rabidly pro-Comiskey crowd, he was called the "next No. 1 challenger for Joe Louis' title."

But Baer never let him get started. He not only broke the Comiskey bubble but nearly fractured the heavyset kid's jaw and came out of the fight unscathed himself.

Twenty thousand spectators sat stunned as Baer, a 5-to-7 underdog in the betting, turned in his furious job. Baer himself seemed unaffected.

All the animal that had been in Baer's face, and all the brute in his eyes, suddenly evaporated as Dempsey lifted his hand in victory. Baer put his arms around the drooling Irish kid and hugged and kissed him like a repentant motorist picking up a battered jaywalker. Baer seemed on the point of tears as he led the stricken kid back to his corner.

But once he had attended to that errand of mercy, Baer went berserk. He bounded happily around the ring. Amid a popping of flashbulbs, he was presented with a large silver belt—symbolic of what promoter Jack Kearns called the "white heavyweight championship of the world."

Full of confidence, Comiskey started the match by splattering Max's intent face with flicking left jabs. His highly touted right-hand punch, which most experts agreed would soon make Max quit, was cocked menacingly. Baer gave ground, and his apprehensive corner screamed, "Get down, Max. Get low."

Baer gave ground around the ring until the two men reached Comiskey's corner. Then a heavy feint and skip by Max backed Pat into the corner, and Baer went after him like a tiger with winging shots for the head.

Pat's face turned bright red, but he fought his way out of the trap and made Max give ground.

Gaining confidence, Pat started a right for Baer's open face. But Max, overweight but hard, beat him to the punch with a left hook that staggered Pat. Dazed, the younger man came back uncertainly and ran flush into Max's overhand right to the jaw. The punch knocked Comiskey heavily to the canvas. He got up at two, dizzily; and Dempsey, trying to get in there to rub off Pat's gloves, was nearly crushed by Baer's charge. Pat went down again, without being hit, and Jack took up the count at "three" and got up to "six."

When Comiskey arose, Baer then hit him with lefts and rights to the head and body. Comiskey pawed feebly, then sagged back over the roped and half turned, so that his face looked down unseeing. He was in no condition to continue—and for the time being his career is ended, and he is just another kid who was rushed in there against a smoothie too soon.

"Experience counted this time," Max pointed out in his dressing room, as he pranced around, kissing everybody within reach on top of the head.

"I sucked him in, trying for the short right shot, the first time, and he just got out of the way, but I knew then, I'd catch him the next time. And, boy, how I did—didn't I?"

Although Mrs. Baer previously had put her foot down against any future fighting for Max, except for tonight's tussle for which he received a guarantee of $30,000, the word from the Baer camp was that the former king of the playboys had "smelted blood" and wanted action. As a result, promoter Mike Jacobs indicated he would talk over a possible bout for Max with Louis in Chicago next spring.

Comiskey had no alibis tonight, except that he acted "like

a wild, scrambling young fool when I got hit.

"Maxie tagged me with a short left early in the fight," he recalled, "and it stung. So I rushed back at him, swinging wildly, like a sap. I want a return bout, and I guarantee it won't happen again."

A thoroughly chilled crowd of 19,758 contributed a gross gate of $68,575, according to figures released after the fight by New Jersey Commissioner Abe Greene.

14

H. R. KNICKERBOCKER

A RINGSIDE SEAT TO HISTORY

In 1934 H. R. Knickerbocker, an American correspondent for the International News Service, interviewed President Thomas G. Masaryk of Czechoslovakia in the old Hradzin Palace in Prague. He asked the 84-year-old leader if he worried about Adolph Hitler, who had gained totalitarian control over Germany and hinted that he hungered for more territory. Masaryk said Hitler's aggression and violence did not distress him because "every revolutionary movement such as the Nazis' has its period of ecstasy." But, the aged president explained, that ecstasy soon would subside, and the two countries would live together in peace.

"I went away with my first example of the fact that no man over seventy ever seems to be able to understand Hitler," Knickerbocker recalled. He was among the first journalists to warn about Hitler by reporting the violent events leading up to his takeover of the German government.

Four years later, the journalist returned to Czechoslovakia and was one of three American correspondents who watched as German tanks and troops overran the small Balkan country and put it under Nazi rule. With the Germans in control, the Gestapo seized the trio and charged them with spying for the Czech government. All three reporters were sentenced to death. Knickerbocker had spent ten years working out of Berlin, and the red-haired Texan knew "Hitler and the Nazis and the Germans" better than he knew "any politician, political party, or people in the world."

This knowledge may have saved his life in Czechoslovakia. The Gestapo surrounded the journalists, and some
began poking them with machine guns. The correspondents
barked out names of all the high-ranking Nazi officials
they knew, including the Führer. The Gestapo officer, they
threatened, would face grave penalties if the journalists
were harmed. The officer finally relented, freed them, and
gave them a half tank of gas for their car.

This was not the first or the last time Knickerbocker
would risk his life for a story. During his 26-year career as
a foreign correspondent, he covered world events with a style
Alexander Woollcott compared to that of the man who made
international reporting famous. "Not since I first met
Richard Harding Davis five-and-twenty years ago,"
Woollcott said, "have I myself encountered any journalist
whose panache so completely fitted in with my slightly romantic notions about the profession."

From the 1890s to World War I, Davis had a front-row
seat while reporting wars and conflicts throughout the
world. From 1923 until 1949, Knickerbocker tramped from
Berlin to Peking, Moscow to Melbourne, and London to
Jakarta. He wrote about generals, dictators, and peasants.
But like Davis, he was best known for covering wars. He referred to his job as taking a "ringside seat" to witness history. "Wherever you find hundreds of thousands of sane
people trying to get out of a place," he said, "and a bunch of
madmen struggling to get in, you know the latter are newspapermen."

His writing was as straightforward as his reporting, its
style suited to a journalist who was, according to James E.
Abbe, "quick at sifting current facts [and] quick at detecting
the relevant from the irrelevant." Abbe, a specialist on international reporting in the 1930s, listed Knickerbocker first
among the most prominent foreign correspondents of his
time. The lanky journalist was one of the fastest at writing
and sending dispatches. Correspondents used a code, known
as "cablese," that shortened word length and thus saved
money on transcontinental cable transmission. Knickerbocker was usually the first back to the bar after breaking a
big story in Berlin. "His is the quintessence of casualness,
the ultimate pose of all good reporters," Abbe declared.

This outer casualness belied an inner fury that emerged

in his writing. The tone of his prose was no less forceful than the passionate fire and brimstone sermon of an itinerant preacher. It was the style of a teacher trying to translate complicated events by using examples his readers could understand. Unlike many of his contemporaries and journalistic forebears, Knickerbocker wrote in the objective, journalistic style most common today. He frequently used statistics, quotations, and examples in his writing. Having studied journalism at Columbia University in New York, he observed the modern rules of his craft, allowing the people, the circumstances, and the eyewitness details to tell the story for him.

Along with his professional training, his upbringing in Yoakum, Texas, also influenced his writing. He was born Hubert Renfro Knickerbocker on January 31, 1898, the son of a Methodist minister. He spent his first years of college wanting to become a psychiatrist or a physician. He earned a bachelor's degree from Southwestern University in Georgetown, Texas. Later, he drove a milkwagon in Austin for awhile before selling his franchise to study psychiatry in New York City. His move to journalism was purely economical: the reporting class was the only one he could afford to take.

After attending Columbia University, he signed on with the Newark *Ledger,* where he was remembered for conducting a vice crusade. In 1923 he traveled to Berlin to continue his study of psychiatry. He took a part-time job working for United Press and soon dumped his studies to cover Germany's economic turmoil and political upheaval. His decision could not have come at a more important time. An Austrian vagabond named Adolph Hitler had begun to organize a political movement that would one day endanger the world. The first time Knickerbocker saw him, he broke out laughing:

> Even if you had never heard of him you would be bound to say, "He looks like a caricature of himself." The moustache and the lock of hair over the forehead help this look, but chiefly it is the expression of his face, and especially the blank stare of his eyes, and the foolish set of his mouth in repose. Sometimes he looks like a man who ought to go around with his mouth open, chin hanging in the style of a

surprised farm hand. Other times he clamps his lips together so tightly and juts out his jaw with such determination that again he looks silly, as though he were putting on an act.

This was Knickerbocker's style, using an economy of words that worked in unison like a machine. He wrote to answer questions. In one of his books, *Is Tomorrow Hitler's*, he used a question-answer format throughout the entire text. His news stories sometimes sounded mechanical, but others were masterful in their clarity and conciseness. That style was most apparent in his news cables, but it also was evident in magazine pieces, such as a story he wrote for *American Magazine* in 1941 entitled "Why Doesn't Somebody Kill Hitler?" It read:

I saw [Hitler] once quail before nothing more lethal than a loud voice. It was in Munich during his trial for treason. Hitler had been bullying the witnesses unmercifully. General von Lossow, who regarded Hitler with contempt, and who headed the Bavarian Reichswehr, which had suppressed the Putsch [Hitler's first attempt to take over the country], took the stand. Hitler stood up and yelled a question. The general, a tall man with shaven head and steel jaw, pulled himself up to his full height. Pointing his long forefinger in Hitler's face as though it were a spear, he shouted like a drill sergeant to a dumb recruit. As the general's voice rose to a bellow that shook the courtroom, Hitler trembled, collapsed, and fell back in his seat as though he had been struck a physical blow.

Like Hitler, Knickerbocker was a relative unknown in 1923. He watched the former army corporal fail in his first attempt to gain power during the Beer Hall Putsch in Munich. He reported on the Nazi leader's trial for treason and interviewed him after the government released him from the Lansberg prison. By the time Hitler came to power nearly a decade later, Knickerbocker had become one of the highest-paid and most-respected journalists in Germany. During the winter of 1931-1932, he wrote 90,000 words about the horrors of German suffering during the Depression. His stories were translated and compiled into a book that became a best seller in Germany. One of the best examples of his writing was a vivid account describing the plight of Berlin's homeless. That story is reprinted in this anthology. Knickerbocker used a subtle approach to reporting the conditions of the homeless throughout the story, and this restraint served to magnify the tragedy as the journalist touched on the human side of the story.

In the United States, Knickerbocker achieved fame in 1930 for a series of articles on the Soviet Union. He had spent six weeks traveling the country and investigating the Communists' ambitious five-year plan to industrialize the nation. The series was awarded the Pulitzer Prize in 1931. Again, Knickerbocker was at his best when describing the irony of a situation through the words of the people. This anthology includes one of the stories from the series. Most of the sentences are short. The contrast is clear. Another story from the series dealt with a Soviet claim that a socialist-planned system is superior to a capitalistic system. Knickerbocker took the question "Is it better?" and spent the story answering it. The best-written lead of the series came from a story about Russian inflation. Employing a nice play on words that explained volumes about the financial situation in the country, it read:

Short of everything except money, the Russian people have one humorous reflection to make on the Five-Year Plan. If it has treated them badly, it has treated the rouble much worse. But the prospects for the eventual improvement of the condition of the people are hopeful—for that of the rouble dubious.

Despite the Soviet Union's authoritarian regime, it became a popular place for American correspondents to visit, a status symbol among the elite. While working out of Berlin, Knickerbocker made several trips there and, on one of them, recorded one of the biggest scoops of the era. Stalin, who had come to power in the 1920s, was one of the most feared men in the world, and even high-ranking officials refused to talk to reporters about him. Outside of the Communist infrastructure, very little was known about Stalin. Knickerbocker figured if the head of the Supreme Soviet would not talk about himself, maybe his mother would. So he traveled to Soviet

Georgia and became the first American correspondent to interview a member of Stalin's family—his mother.

"The mother of Russia's man of steel looked very small when she came through the big double doors leading from her bedroom," Knickerbocker wrote. "Gray-haired, slender, dressed in gray woolen Georgian peasant costume, she peered at us pleasantly through silver-rimmed spectacles. She listened a moment as I explained my desires, her firm smile expanding at the mention of Stalin."

As usual, Knickerbocker found irony in the interview. He noted how the mother spoke little Russian, preferring her native Georgian language instead. The people of Georgia despised Russia, the journalist said, and yet a Georgian now determined "the course of the nation, and seventy-two million Russians listen." Knickerbocker allowed the flow of the conversation to bring out the most remarkable part of the interview. He asked if the mother dreamed her son would ever "become what he is today?"

"Well, no! You must know that we had planned quite other things for Soso [Stalin's Georgian nickname]. His father, Vissarion—well, if his father had lived he might have made a cobbler of Soso. You see, my husband was a cobbler, and his father and his father's father, and as far back as we could remember, all his folks had been cobblers. Peasant cobblers. And his father said he would make a good cobbler out of Soso. But his father died when Soso was eleven years old.

"And then"—she paused and cast another smile at her friend, who smiled back—"And then, you see, I didn't want him to be a cobbler. I didn't want him to be anything but"—she paused again—"a priest."

"Yes," she declared, more firmly, "I did dream that one day Soso would finish his studies and become a priest. That's what I dreamed."

Knickerbocker returned to Germany and continued to report from Berlin until 1933, when Hitler expelled him. The International News Service assigned him to cover Italy's invasion of Ethiopia. In October 1935, *Time* noted that Knickerbocker was reporting from Addis Ababa. "Last week," according to the magazine, "the psychiatric eye of

Newshawk Knickerbocker observed 'people...laughing, hooting, singing—half mad....Women weep and seek to quiet their nerves, overwrought by months of waiting for war.'"

In the late 1930s, Knickerbocker began reporting on the Spanish Civil War. He and another correspondent, Webb Miller, were imprisoned by Fascist leader Franco's lieutenants despite having written fair stories about the rebel uprising in Spain. If not for some good fortune, he and Miller would have fallen victim to the Fascist revolt. Later, he covered the German invasion of Czechoslovakia and the Battle of Britain.

While stationed in London, he reported one of the biggest scoops of the war. Basing his story on reliable sources, he wrote about the British naval victory over the French fleet at Oran. His story hit American newspapers before other correspondents learned about the battle from Winston Churchill, who announced the victory in a speech at the House of Commons. The British Broadcasting Company asked the International News Service for permission to rebroadcast Knickerbocker's story to England.

In 1942 Knickerbocker, then chief of the foreign service of the Chicago *Sun*, was in Melbourne, Australia, when General Douglas McArthur arrived from the Philippines. His story told of the "harrowing seven-day trip by sea and air" in which McArthur, his wife, four-year-old son, and staff had hidden on islands during the day and traveled by night. He also recorded the response of Royal Australian Air Force officers to McArthur's appointment as commander of the Allied forces in the Pacific. "It's dinkum. It's excellent," they said. "It's the best thing that's happened since the war began."

In 1943, while traveling with Allied armies near Naples, Italy, Knickerbocker reported the fall of Mussolini from power and the failure of the Italian government to surrender before the country became a battleground. He continued to cover the war for the New York *Sun* until 1945.

In 1949 he embarked on a new career and a new adventure, writing about the development of Communism in Asia. He and a group of about twenty-five journalists were returning from covering a war in Indonesia when their KLM plane crashed into a mountainside in India during a heavy rainstorm. Thus, nature had accomplished what Hitler's Gestapo had failed to do eleven years earlier. The July 13, 1949, New York *Times* included Knickerbocker's name at the top of a news story for the last time. It was appropriate that the reporter who had covered the news so many years would make news on his last assignment.

◆

USSR AS A LAND AT WAR

In the decades following the Bolshevik revolution in Russia, the Soviet Union attracted America's best foreign correspondents. It was a prestigious assignment to report from Russia, especially considering the difficulties inherent in gaining entrance into the country and the speed with which the government could expel journalists. In 1930 Knickerbocker spent seven weeks traveling throughout the Soviet Union investigating the Communists' ambitious Five-Year Plan to industrialize and improve the nation. By examining minute details, he showed who was benefiting from the heralded plan. One segment of the population was working and barely able to find what it needed. The state, on the other hand, enjoyed the fruits of the common man's labor. Without coming right out and saying it, Knickerbocker showed the hypocrisy of the Five-Year Plan. The series was awarded the Pulitzer Prize in 1931. Reprinted here is one of the stories from the series.

THE FIRST FIVE-YEAR PLAN
AND ITS POSTULATES
H.R. Knickerbocker
New York *Evening Post*
November 17, 1930

The Soviet Union is a land at war. This is a first and a last impression. It was my first impression after a journey of seven weeks to the farthest outposts of the Five-Year Plan, a journey of more than 10,000 miles along the industrial front from the Ural Mountains to Caucasia.

Moscow, Nijny-Novgorod, Cheliabinsk, Ufa, Samara,

Stalingrad, Gigant, Berblud, Rostof, Baku, Tiflis, Ciaturi, Batum, Yalta, Sebastopol, Dnieprostroy, Stalina and the Don Basin—all these are salients in the war for industrialization that today holds Russia in a feverish grip. In all these, to a varying but always an impressive degree, I found an atmosphere of militant struggle, a nation under arms living figuratively but effectively under martial law and subsisting on the short rations of a beleaguered state.

It is a war that, according to the Plan, will come in October, 1933, not to an end but to a brief moment of stock taking. That year will mark the formal close of the first period of the most gigantic economic project in history, which was begun in October, 1928, an attempt over night to industrialize the most backward land in Europe, to make of vast Russia a self-contained entity, an impregnable fortress for Communism. The officers in the war are the 1,300,000 members of the communist party. The soldiers are the entire population. The chief weapon is 64,000,000,000 roubles of capital investment. The specific objectives are double-power oil, coal and steel production, triple metal production, quadruple machine production—in short to multiply at least by two the total output of all industry and collectivize all farms.

No matter whether the result will be a success, partial success or failure, the world, intelligent of the consequences, will watch the results of this grandiose scheme with anxious interest. Today two years have passed of the Five-Year war for industrialization and the Soviet Union stands midpoint in its headlong course toward its lately adopted audacious goal of accomplishing the Plan in four years instead of five. The whole department of the Government Planning Commission is already working upon a fifteen-year plan to succeed the present one. For the slogan is not merely, "Overtake," but "Outstrip the leading capitalist nations." It is too early now to wonder or worry about the fifteen-year plan. But now, after two years of the Five-Year Plan, is perhaps the most advantageous time yet afforded for an estimate of the progress achieved, an estimate that should at the same time throw light on the whole complex of problems that has arisen in connection with the execution of the Plan, to puzzle or disturb the outside world.

This record of observation will carry its own answer to many questions. Is the Plan succeeding to such an extent that solvency is guaranteed for credits to the Soviet Union? Is it succeeding to such an extent that the Soviet Union is likely to become a dangerous competitor? Is the Soviet Government still master of the Plan, or has the Plan mastered the Soviet Government? To what extent has the Plan been able to determine the Soviet Union's foreign trade policy and is dumping an integral part of that policy? What part does forced labor play? What of costs? How is the population taking the privations and how severe are they?

On these and a score of other pertinent questions my reconnaissance just completed over the principal salients has provided a stock of eye-witness material that at least has the value of being fresh and immediate to the issues uppermost in the mind of the outside world. It has provided the first view of the series of largest industrial undertakings of the Plan never before visited by a foreign correspondent. It has provided a cross-section not alone of familiar Moscow, but the whole of European Russia and that portion of Asia that is most significant. Finally, it has provided data on the one point that of late has most agitated the "bourgeois" world—the problem of Soviet dumping. Dumping, by the narrowest definition, is selling abroad large quantities of goods below the cost of production. To make a charge of dumping has always been easy. Every domestic manufacturer is inclined to raise the cry when his prices are undercut by a foreign competitor. But to establish the fact of dumping has always been difficult because reliable information on the cost of production is rarely included in Chamber of Commerce reports, annual corporation statements or—Soviet trade statistics.

Mileage, however, coverage of the ground, personal visits to points of production yielded information of interest on the costs of certain Soviet commodities. Gathered on the spot, this information shows that in specific cases investigated, of wheat, rye, anthracite coal and oil, Soviet costs of production and delivery are by any ordinary standard of measurement, and taking the rouble at par, higher than the market price at which they are forced to sell. In the capital, Moscow, the Soviet authorities deny this. In the field and on the front, the Soviet managers of factories, mines and farms have given the *New York Evening Post* data that tend strongly to prove it. not vague generalized data, but precise figures per ton of coal, per gallon of oil, per bushel of wheat and rye and in roubles of railroad miles and sea charges. The same sort of information tends to exonerate the Soviet Union of dumping manganese, at least in its sales, to the United States. This much for facts. What they may mean, how they came about, whither they may lead for the Soviet Union and for the outside world and to what degree conclusions to be drawn from them may be modified by the factor of the uncertainty of Soviet currency are questions for discussion in their place. First, to the survey of what the Plan has done for or to the population to date.

It must begin with Moscow. If it ends there it will be misleading. This city is inhabited by 2,200,000 persons and there are among them at least 2,000,000 different views of the Five-Year Plan. The 200,000 Moscow Communists present in the daytime astonishing agreement on all its phases. If they harbor any dissentient views, it is at night under their bed-covers. On this, or any other Russian topic, feeling runs too high for objectivity to get a hearing and any observer may be assured that his observations will be scored in one camp or another as mistaken or mendacious. This is one of the risks one must take on the exploration of Russia under the Five-Year Plan.

My entry into Soviet Russia was hardly typical of a country where food or the lack of it is the chief topic of conversation. I was just congratulating myself on goods when there came an invitation to dinner. My first meal on Russian soil was something to be approached with trepidation. On the menu were caviar of the highest quality, big gray malasol, several sorts of smoked river fish of a kind that used to attract international gourmets to Moscow in the old days, an extremely palatable cream soup with pirozhki, light pastry filled with chopped meat, three kinds of roast poultry and game, young pullets, pheasants, a rare bird called tsesarka resembling a pigeon, watermelon, pears, stuffed raspberries, baked wine sauce, cheese and a huge stand of luxurious fruit. The cook was the former chef of the Grand Duke Nikolaj Nikolaivitich, one time commander-in-chief of the Imperial Russian Army. The meal was in a special car. The hosts were Colonel and Mrs. Hugh Cooper of New York. As chief consulting engineer for the Soviet Government's $100,000,000 hydro-electric project below the Dnieper River rapids and as one of the very few foreigners whom

Joseph Stalin really likes, Colonel Cooper enjoys certain privileges.

That was an interlude of diversion from Russia's reality. That reality could be anticipated in the dining car at breakfast. Two eggs, a tiny pat of butter, zwieback and tea, luxuries all too little appreciated by one unaware that the rations to come were to cost three roubles, about $1.50. The waiter had no change. He passed around paper slips in place of kopecks. Four more hoarders of silver coin had just been shot in Moscow, but the sturdy Russian kopecks had refused to be scared out of hiding. They still reposed by millions in countless peasant socks. Green apples, small and gnarled, were the sole offering of peasant women in the wayside stations. Gone were the roast chickens, sandwiches of great amber-grained caviar, pickled cucumbers, butter, milk, eggs, all these not of olden times but of just three years ago. The stations were as bare as a picked bone.

An hour and fifteen minutes late, we arrived at Moscow to jolt over its cobblestones down to the hotel. But no, cobblestones have disappeared. Moscow has presented a new contradiction and none could be more typical of the era of the Plan. The streets are paved, miles of them, and in the best asphalt. On the ride to the hotel alone there are more paved streets than were in all Moscow in 1927. But to ride over them costs just five times as much. Droshky fares have quintupled in price.

Along the streets are scores of new buildings, flat-facaded, glass-fronted office buildings, great complex workers' flats and the horizon that once was dominated by the blue and golden and starry domes and lacy crosses of Moscow's countless churches is punctured now by smokestacks. The picture is disfigured; the charm has begun to fade and the beauty of old Moscow to recede.

On the paved streets by the new buildings goes afoot a population that has given up a good deal more than the romance of Muscovy. They swarm along the sidewalks and overflow and scatter along the thoroughfares. Their monotone of gray, the uniformity of their unsmiling haste is the same as ever. They move, perhaps, a trifle faster. There seems to be a trace more of nervousness in them. "Permit me, citizen," is chopped a shade shorter than before. And there are tens of thousands more of them. The five-day week has done that. Freeing one-fifth of the population every day, it has made every day a holiday for nearly a half million in Moscow. They are forever on the go.

"We work harder on our day off," said one man, "than we do on our jobs. On our days off we have to look for something to buy. And it wears out our shoes." Shoes! Euphemistic expression. Not since the days of famine, civil war and intervention have there been such fantastic substitutes for footwear as are now common in this city. Here a man, his wife and their two children go by, all four shod with frayed canvas sneakers, the soles long ago worn out and stuffed for the day with thick cardboard. There go two youths each wearing on their feet chopped off ancient rubber boots. An ill-clad, bearded man has wrapped his feet in rags. A peasant is barefooted. Cast your eyes on the sidewalk and wait for a good pair of boots to go by. Lift your eyes. Nine cases out of ten it will be a Red army soldier or one of the uniformed troops of the G.P.U. state political police. Of all the women passing, one-third are wearing tattered but recognizable women's shoes and the other two-thirds some sort of makeshift. The most popular are house slippers. The cobblers do a frantic trade and accept no repair work for delivery under three months.

For a moment the footgear looks worse than the clothing. But the frost has come and overcoats are slow to appear. The cold nips, men shiver. But war is war. They say every man is a soldier and troops must do their duty. Promised from the cooperatives is one coat apiece for the workers, or cloth for a coat this winter some time. Mistrustful, some Muscovites, who have lost their old coats or worn them until they have fallen apart, are planning to cut up carpet. Some have no carpet.

Down the street comes the sound of music. A parade is in progress. The head of the column swings around the corner. Two companies of G.P.U. officers, fresh from military academy graduation. Their uniforms, immaculate, are made from the best cloth. Their overcoats fall to their ankles in warm, thick folds.

In this war there are troops and troops.

❧❦

GERMANY'S POVERTY

In the early 1930s, Germany's population suffered through rampant inflation and unemployment. The poverty and turmoil caused by this economic debacle allowed the Communists and Nazis to gain strength and thrive. Knickerbocker had lived in Germany for nearly ten years. He understood the language and the people. The following story reflects not only his strength as an observer but his grasp of the political unrest hidden below the surface. The account follows Knickerbocker's trek through the dark world of German poverty. At one point, two old women begged for his coffee. Walking around another corner brought the journalist into a run-down hotel, with people crowded into each dingy abode, which he described as "a good room for a suicide." The story ends with Knickerbocker disproving the notion that the German welfare dole was enough to support a family.

WINTER 1931-1932
H.R. Knickerbocker
International News Service
1932

The midnight moon in the Froebel Strasse stood high over the gas tanks, shed silver on the blocklong bulk of Berlin's Night Refuge for the Homeless. A lamp burned in the warden's office. Not another light showed in the building. Too late to enter.

It was no lark to spend a night as a homeless tramp in Berlin, and the exploration of the question "How great is Germany's poverty?" ceased to be amusing when the winter wind cut through my rags. Max and Hans and Otto and I hurried past long lines of barracks. In them were part of the army of Germany's jobless.

Today there are approximately 5,000,000 of them. The public treasury, the Federal Government, the States, the communes and the cities spend around $750,000,000 a year for the support of the 5,000,000 and their families and the 1,200,000 short-time workers who, earning less than the dole, are furnished the difference to enable them to live.

Through Berlin's famous "model slum" district we wandered. The streets do not look like slum streets. They are wide and clean. From the outside they are streets of luxury compared to the East Side tenement streets of New York. In the "Ruecker Klause," a tavern, music clanged loudly. A piano player beat the keys of an upright without a front; a violinist and a drummer belabored their instruments heavily. At the tables sat groups of hard-eyed youths and girls.

The girls snatched the beer from our hands. Nobody else had a glass before them on the table. A "comrade" came over and explained that this was a resort of fugitive reformatory inmates, all under age, all jobless, all, he declared, hungry.

In the "Mulack Klause" two old women begged our coffee from us. Further down the Mulack Street, in a refuge and inn for members of a smiths' guild, the back room was full of men, reading tattered sheets of newspapers or just sitting. None had a drink or anything to eat before him. A band of three musicians came in, a French horn, a cornet and clarinet. They blew lustily a pre-war military march, but when they finished nobody had a pfennig for them.

The Mulack Refuge had beds only for union members. In the "Zarowka," low-ceilinged cellar across the street from the Schlesischer Bahnhof, a squat, dark woman showed us beds. Five to a room, the beds were filthy, had no sheets. A mark—25 cents—apiece was too expensive. We moved on to the "Hotel Metropole," stood shivering before a dark hall until the porter answered our ring.

"Got fifty-four guests," he muttered, "eighty pfennigs apiece. See for yourself." He tossed us a key.

We climbed five flights of stairs, found room ninety-six, observed five beds, considered the bedclothes gray with dirt, noted a cracked jar, remarked it would be a good room for a suicide, and departed. It was 3 o'clock.

Before Max's dwelling he paused to show us where he had hung a huge red banner of defiance to the police the day the shooting started. In Max's kitchen, scrubbed, clean, neat, his wife rolled the youngest member of the household into the hall, and essayed to explain how she managed to feed her husband, her five children, aged four months, four, six, nine and eleven years, and herself on her husband's unemployment dole of 15 marks 35 pfennigs, $3.80 a week. While she made a pot of imitation coffee, she talked.

"First, what I have to take out before food: max gets 85 pfennigs a week for tobacco. We have to pay 3 marks a week back rent; 70 pfennigs for gas; 50 pfennigs a week for installment payments on a sweater for Max, and 30 pfennigs a week for rent towels; 1 mark 30 for newspapers and 1 mark party dues. That makes 6 marks 80 pfennigs and leaves 8 marks 20 pfennigs—$1.95 a week to feed seven people."

"But why," I exclaimed, "why 1 mark 30, nearly 10 per cent of your income, for newspapers?"

"There is the *Rote Fahne,* the *Rote Post* and the *Arbeiter Illustrierte Zeitung.* As good Communists, we must read the party press."

This seemed to me the most remarkable example of several things. But most remarkable of all was the utterly matter of fact way she mentioned that out of an income of fifteen marks eighty-five pfennigs, two marks thirty, or 15 per cent went to the party.

"And how do you buy food for seven people a week with eight marks, twenty pfennigs?"

"Bread and potatoes," she replied. "Mostly bread. On the day we get the money we buy sausage. Can't resist the temptation to have a little meat. But the last two days of the week we go hungry. That is, mostly it's Max that goes hungry."

It is pertinent to observe that Max's unemployment dole amounting to a round sixty-three marks a month is, because of the five children, considerably above the average. According to the Labor Office, Neukoelln, the average dole received throughout the Reich by an unemployed worker with wife and child is fifty-one marks a month. According to this official source, rent, light, heat and indispensable incidentals come to an iron minimum of 32 marks 50 pfennigs a month. This leaves 18 marks 50 pfennigs, or $4.16 for food for three persons a month.

Until I undertook this investigation, I shared the opinion widely held at home that the German dole provided a living for its recipients. It even seemed probable that a good many persons would prefer to live on the dole than to go to work. I also held the opinion that the Russian employed worker had less to eat than the German unemployed worker. All these opinions have been revised in the face of the observed facts in Berlin. The dole at its present level in Germany is not enough to live on; too little to die on.

15

ERNEST HEMINGWAY

The Novelist Who Went to War

A line of Spanish infantry buried their faces in the dirt as heavy machine-gun and rifle fire peppered their positions at the top of a ridge. With them lay a middle-aged American writer who recorded in vivid detail the attack they had just made.

"The men, bent double, their bayonets fixed, were advancing in the awkward first gallop that steadies into the heavy climb of an uphill assault," he wrote in a news dispatch. "Two men were hit and left the line. One had the surprised look of a man first wounded who does not realize the thing can do this damage and not hurt."

The writer spoke from experience. Nearly twenty years before, a mortar shell exploded three feet from him, killing the Italian soldier standing next to him and riddling him with more than 200 pieces of shrapnel. But he was an 18-year-old kid then, hungering for the action and adventure of war. Now he was a renowned novelist with a family. Why was he risking his life covering a civil war in Spain? Because the journalist, Ernest Hemingway, had a passion for Spain almost as strong as his love for writing. "Never risk anything," he told his brother, Leicester, "unless you're prepared to lose it completely."

Hemingway wanted to experience the events he wrote about—whether he was writing as a journalist or a novelist. "It's very hard to get anything true on anything you haven't seen yourself," he wrote in his book *Green Hills of Africa*. He based some of his greatest works of fiction upon his experiences as a journalist.

Hemingway was born July 21, 1899, at home in Oak Park, Illinois. His father practiced medicine, and his singer mother taught voice lessons. His father took him hunting and fishing, while his mother nagged him to play the cello. As an adult, with a six-foot frame and a muscular build, Hemingway embraced the life of a sportsman and abandoned music. Though never a stellar athlete, he loved competition. Some of his first writing dealt with sports, and he gained fame at Oak Park High School for writing Ring Lardner-like letters for the *Trapeze*, the student paper. Lardner, a sportswriter-humorist, wrote a series for the *Saturday Evening Post* consisting of letters home from Jack Keefe, a fictitious White Sox rookie with a pea brain and a big ego. Hemingway patterned his *Trapeze* column after Lardner's style of sardonic humor.

After high school, Hemingway traveled to Missouri, where a rich uncle helped him land a job as a cub reporter on the Kansas City *Star*. The first rules of the *Star's* "Style Book" admonished reporters to "Use short sentences. Use short first paragraphs. Use vigorous English. Be positive, not negative." In an interview with the *Star* in 1940, Hemingway lauded the old stylebook's emphasis on clarity, conciseness, and accuracy. "Those were the best rules I ever learned for the business of writing," he declared. "I've never forgotten them. No man with any talent, who feels and writes truly about the thing he is trying to say, can fail to write well if he abides with them."

That Hemingway read the style manual and sought to heed its wisdom illustrates his desire to develop and improve his writing talent. In the stories that he wrote for the *Star*, his strengths as a novelist were already apparent. He was no ordinary cub reporter. His keen ear for dialogue, for example, caught a colorful exchange between an anxious volunteer and a sergeant outside an Army recruiting station:

A stout, red faced man wearing a khaki shirt was the first up the stairs.

"I'm the treat 'em rough man," he bawled. "That cat in the poster has nothing on me. Where do you join the tankers?"

"Have to wait for Lieutenant Cooter," said the sergeant.

"He decides whether you'll treat 'em rough or not."

Another story headlined "At the End of the Ambulance Run" opened with an anecdote that introduced a series of vignettes about life in the hospital emergency room:

> The night ambulance attendants shuffled down the long, dark corridors at the General Hospital with an inert burden on the stretcher. They turned in at the receiving ward and lifted the unconscious man to the operating table. His hands were calloused, and he was unkempt and ragged, a victim of a street brawl near the city market. No one knew who he was, but a receipt, bearing the name of George Anderson, for $10 paid on a home out in a little Nebraska town served to identify him.
>
> The surgeon opened the swollen eyelids. The eyes were turned to the left. "A fracture on the left side of the skull," he said to the attendants who stood about the table. "Well, George, you're not going to finish paying for that home of yours."
>
> "George" merely lifted a hand as though groping for something. Attendants hurriedly caught hold of him to keep him from rolling from the table. But he scratched his face in a tired, resigned way that seemed almost ridiculous, and placed his hand again at his side. Four hours later he died.

One of the stories that the youthful Hemingway wrote for the *Star* was so well written that it impressed the city editor and sparked enthusiastic predictions about his journalistic future. The story, written during the last month Hemingway worked in Kansas City, contrasted a prostitute with people attending a YWCA dance. The young reporter started the story with, "Outside, a woman walked along the wet streetlamp lit sidewalk through the sleet and snow." Six paragraphs later, the ending returned to the solitary figure.

> The pianist took his seat again and the soldiers made a dash for partners. In the intermission the soldiers drank to the girls in fruit punch. The girl in red, surrounded by a crowd of men in olive drab, seated herself at the piano; the men and the girls gathered around and sang until mid-

night. The elevator had stopped running, and so the jolly crowd bunched down the six flights of stairs and rushed waiting motor cars. After the last car had gone, the woman walked along the wet sidewalk through the sleet and looked up at the dark windows of the sixth floor.

Kansas City provided Hemingway his first brushes with danger. While covering a fire, he slipped inside fire lines to "see what was going on." Sparks fell all over a new brown suit and burned it full of holes. During a shootout between detectives and internal revenue agents, he watched from under a nearby Ford.

Always wanting to see and experience the action, not just hear about it, Hemingway tried to join the Army in hopes of fighting in Europe in World War I, but was rejected because of poor eyesight. He then volunteered as a Red Cross ambulance driver. Upon arrival in Paris, he paid his taxi cab driver to take him and another former *Star* cub reporter, Theodore Brumback, to a place being shelled by the German artillery.

The Red Cross assigned him to Italy, where after a few months' service, he edged too close to the front lines while handing out chocolate to Italian soldiers. A shell struck nearby, wounding him and killing two soldiers nearby. Brumback said Hemingway acted heroically, aiding a more seriously wounded Italian soldier before allowing stretcher bearers to evacuate him.

While recovering from his wounds, Hemingway wrote short stories that American publishers later rejected. Having gained some fame, however, from having been the first Yankee wounded in Italy, he found opportunities to speak about his war experiences. Through one of his lectures, he met Ralph Connable, a powerful businessman from Toronto, Canada. Connable used his influence to help the 20-year-old Hemingway obtain a job as a feature writer for the Toronto *Star Weekly*. Gregory Clark, the features editor, was an ex-infantry major who would become Hemingway's close friend. Initially, Clark failed to find much impressive about the tall, overweight youth who walked with a limp and appeared "shy, anxious, and restless." Neither did the newspaper's editor expect Hemingway to develop into anything out of the ordinary. They were right—at first—as he churned out ordinary copy during his first year with the *Star Weekly*.

Then things changed as Hemingway began writing about topics that excited him. His stories about fishing and camping sparkled from his clear observations and descriptions. Of rainbow trout fishing, he wrote, "It is a wild and nerve-frazzling sport, and the odds are in favor of the big trout who tear off thirty or forty yards of line at a rush and then will sulk at the base of a big rock and refuse to be stirred into action by the pumping of a stout fly rod aided by a fluent monologue of Ojibwayian profanity. Sometimes it takes two hours to land a really big rainbow under these circumstances." Later in the story, he described the disappearance of a grasshopper:

> The hopper floats spraddle-legged on the water of the pool an instant, an eddy catches him, and then there is a yard-long flash of flame, and a trout as long as your forearm has shot into the air and the hopper has disappeared.

The richness of Hemingway's language grabs the reader and thrusts him into the scene. Note the use of alliteration, "flash of flame," and the comparison, "a trout as long as your forearm." The word pictures also gain motion from his use of active verbs: "floats," "catches," "shot," and "disappear."

In 1921 Hemingway moved to Paris, where he worked as the Toronto *Star Weekly's* European correspondent. Paris proved a fertile training ground for his fiction as well as for his non-fiction. In only his early twenties, he produced copy with the depth and insight of a grizzled veteran. Yet, he was always the student. He sought out the company of the best foreign correspondents and learned from them. While covering the Lausanne Conference, he talked writing and politics with William Bolitho, a correspondent for the New York *World*. Bolitho, Hemingway declared, taught "[me] many things that were the beginning of whatever education I received in international politics."

The muckraker Lincoln Steffens also acted as a mentor. While covering the Genoa Conference, Hemingway received from Steffens a course in writing. One night Hemingway, reading a cable he had written, said, "Stef, look at this cable: no fat, no adjectives, no adverbs—nothing but blood and bones and muscle. It's great. It's a new language." The Genoa experience changed the way Hemingway wrote.

In Europe, Hemingway crafted stories ranging from human interest pieces about skiing in Switzerland to breaking news stories about the war between Greece and Turkey. At times he experimented with repetition and other stylistic techniques, but mostly his stories focused on how events affected the common people. A story about runaway German inflation ignored the complexities while telling about a young entrepreneur:

> The boy in a Strasbourg [France] motor agency where we went to make some enquiries about crossing the frontier, said, "Oh yes. It is easy to get over into Germany. All you have to do is go across the bridge."
> "Don't you need any visa?" I said.
> "No. Just a permit stamp to go from the French." He took his passport out of his pocket and showed the back covered with rubber stamps. "See? I live there now because it is so much cheaper. It's the way to make money."

Using the effect of German inflation on the boy to introduce his story, Hemingway recalled his trip into Germany, where ten French francs were exchanged for 670 marks. He ended his story by describing a scene in a German pastry shop packed with French tourists looking for a cheap meal. His last paragraph painted a telling picture of what was happening at the German border:

> As the last of the afternoon tea-ers and pastry eaters went Strasbourg-wards across the bridge, the first of the exchange pirates coming over to raid Kehl [Germany] for cheap dinners began to arrive. The two streams passed each other on the bridge, and the two disconsolate looking German soldiers looked on. As the boy in the motor agency said, "It's the way to make money."

Hemingway's Toronto *Star* dispatches combined what was beautiful and ugly about Europe in the early 1920s. He wrote about the exhilaration and excitement of running with the bulls in Pamplona, Spain, but also included the tragedy of a boy who stumbled in the street in front of the galloping animals. "The first bull lowered his head and made a jerky, sideways toss," crashing the boy against a fence while the crowd roared.

Later, in a letter to his father, Hemingway explained why he included the good and the bad, the moral and immoral in his fiction. His explanation also summarized what he wanted to do with his journalism:

> I'm trying in all my stories to get the feeling of actual life across—not to just depict life—or criticize it—but to actually make it alive. So that when you have read something by me you actually experience the thing. You can't do this without putting in the bad and the ugly as well as that which is beautiful. Because if it is all beautiful, you can't believe in it. It is only by showing both sides—three dimensions and if possible four—that you can write the way I want to write.

In a 1935 column in *Look* magazine, Hemingway tried to tell a young writer how to capture the details that make a good story:

> Listen now. When people talk, listen completely. Don't be thinking what you're going to say. Most people never listen. Nor do they observe. You should be able to go into a room and when you come out know everything that you saw there and not only that. If that room gave you any feeling, you should know exactly what it was that gave you that feeling. Try that for practice. When you're in town, stand outside the theatre and see how the people differ in the way they get out of taxis or motor cars. There are a thousand ways to practice. And always think of other people.

This attention to details appeared in his dispatches from the Spanish Civil War (1936-1939). His reporting of the war was biased by his devotion to the Loyalist forces of the government fighting against Francisco Franco, whose Fascist forces eventually defeated the Loyalists. Still, his dispatches for North American Newspaper Alliance represent some of his finest journalistic prose. They provided vivid glimpses of the war and its soldiers. As World War I had inspired his novel *A Farewell to Arms*, the Spanish Civil War provided the material used in *For Whom the Bell Tolls*.

By 1940 his fame as one of America's best novelists was secure, but he still returned to journalism in 1944 to cover World War II. His stories for *Collier's* magazine lacked the passion of his Spanish Civil War reports, but they contained quotations and descriptions that made readers feel as if they were riding in the Jeep with Hemingway. His stories were long, following a rambling magazine-style journalism.

Hemingway made a distinction between his journalistic and fiction writing. "A newspaper man," he wrote in 1931, learns his trade writing against deadlines, "writing to make stuff timely rather than permanent....No one has the right to dig this stuff up and use it against the stuff you have written to write the best you can." Hemingway the journalist wrote to describe something happening that day so readers could picture it in their imaginations. A month later, he said, they will forget it. The tools he employed, though, to create an image of the battle of Teruel, when he longed for a spade "to make a little mound to get my head under," would be as effective today as they were in 1937. His advice to a young writer in 1935 explains the underlying objective he had for each of his stories.

Watch what happens today. If we get into a fish, see exactly what it is that everyone does. If you get a kick out of it while he is jumping, remember back until you see exactly what the action was that gave you the emotion. Whether it was the rising of the line from the water and the way it tightened like a fiddle string until drops started from it, or the way he smashed and threw water when he jumped. Remember what the noises were and what was said. Find what gave you the excitement. Then write it down making it clear so the reader will see it too and have the same feeling that you had.

In an article for *Look* magazine in 1956, Hemingway described journalism as "that writing of something that happens day by day, in which I was trained when young, and which is not whoring when done honestly with exact reporting."

∎

WAR'S INNOCENT VICTIMS

As a foreign correspondent for the Toronto *Star*, Hemingway traveled to Turkey, where the Turks and Greeks were battling for control of a Turkish empire fragmented by World War I. Caught in the crossfire was Turkey's Christian minority, which was terrorized and even slaughtered by the Muslim Turks. Because the war started soon after World War I, the Allies were reluctant to become involved. For Hemingway, the scene of refugees fleeing the horrors of war would become an all too familiar sight. His reports from Constantinople re-created vivid images of war refugees that later would show up in his fiction.

A SILENT, GHASTLY PROCESSION
Ernest Hemingway
Toronto *Daily Star*
October 20, 1922

Adrianople.—In a never-ending, staggering march the Christian population of Eastern Thrace is jamming the roads towards Macedonia. The main column crossing the Maritza River at Adrianople is twenty miles long. Twenty miles of carts drawn by cows, bullocks and muddy-flanked water buffalo, with exhausted, staggering men, women and children, blankets over their heads, walking blindly along in the rain beside their worldly goods.

This main stream is being swelled from all the back country. They don't know where they are going. They left their farms, villages and ripe, brown fields and joined the main stream of refugees when they heard the Turk was coming. Now they can only keep their places in the ghastly procession while mud-splashed Greek cavalry herd them along like cow-punchers driving steers.

It is a silent procession. Nobody even grunts. It is all they can do to keep moving. Their brilliant peasant costumes are soaked and draggled. Chickens dangle by their feet from the carts. Calves nuzzle at the draught cattle wherever a jam halts the stream. An old man marches bent under a young pig, a scythe and a gun, with a chicken tied to his scythe. A husband spreads a blanket over a woman in labor in one of the carts to keep off the driving rain. She is the only person making a sound. Her little daughter looks at her in horror and begins to cry. And the procession keeps moving.

At Adrianople where the main stream moves through, there is no Near East relief at all. They are doing very good work at Rodosto on the coast, but can only touch the fringe.

There are 250,000 Christian refugees to be evacuated from Eastern Thrace alone. The Bulgarian frontier is shut against them. There is only Macedonia and Western Thrace to receive the fruit of the Turk's return to Europe. Nearly half a million refugees are in Macedonia now. How they are to be fed nobody knows, but in the next month all the Christian world will hear the cry: "Come over into Macedonia and help us!"

◆

THE ACRID EXPERIENCE OF WAR

In the 1920s, Hemingway traveled to Spain to write about the bullfighters of Pamplona. Falling in love with the country and its people, he continued to return to Spain throughout his career. When civil war broke out in 1936, he raised money and solicited recruits to fight for the Loyalists, who represented the democratically elected government. He traveled to Spain himself to report on the war for the North American Newspaper Alliance. His emotional bond to the Loyalists tainted his journalistic objectivity, but his writing and reporting could not be faulted. The underlying partisanship tended to heighten the emotional impact of the stories.

A NEW KIND OF WAR
Ernest Hemingway
NANA Dispatch
April 14, 1937

Madrid.—The window of the hotel is open and, as you lie in bed, you hear the firing in the front line seventeen blocks away. There is a rifle fire all night long. The rifles go tacrong, capong, craang, tacrong, and then a machine gun opens up. It has a bigger calibre and is much louder, rong, cararong, rong, rong. Then there is the incoming boom of a trench mortar shell and a burst of machine gun fire. You lie and listen to it, and it is a great thing to be in bed with your feet stretched out gradually warming the cold foot of the bed and not out there in University City or Carabanchel. A man is singing hard-voiced in the street below and three drunks are arguing when you fall asleep.

In the morning, before your call comes from the desk, the roaring burst of a high explosive shell wakes you, and you go to the window and look out to see a man, his head down, his coat collar up, sprinting desperately across the paved square. There is the acrid smell of high explosive you hoped you'd never smell again, and, in a bathrobe and bedroom slippers, you hurry down the marble stairs and almost into a middle-aged woman, wounded in the abdomen, who is being helped into the hotel entrance by two men in blue workmen's smocks. She has her two hands crossed below her big, old-style Spanish bosom, and from between her fingers the blood is spurting in a thin stream. On the corner, twenty yards away, is a heap of rubble, smashed cement and thrown up dirt, a single dead man, his torn clothes dusty, and a great hole in the sidewalk from which the gas from a broken main is rising, looking like a heat mirage in the cold morning air.

"How many dead?" you ask a policeman.

"Only one," he says. "It went through the sidewalk and burst below. If it would have burst on the solid stone of the road, there might have been fifty."

A policeman covers the top of the trunk, from which the head is missing; they send for someone to repair the gas main and you go in to breakfast. A charwoman, her eyes red, is scrubbing the blood off the marble floor of the corridor. The dead man wasn't you nor anyone you know, and everyone is very hungry in the morning after a cold night and a long day the day before up at the Guadalajara front.

"Did you see him?" asked someone else at breakfast.

"Sure," you say.

"That's where we pass a dozen times a day. Right on that corner." Someone makes a joke about missing teeth, and someone else says not to make that joke. And everyone has the feeling that characterizes war. It wasn't me, see? It wasn't me.

The Italian dead up on the Guadalajara front weren't you, although Italian dead, because of where you had spent your boyhood, always seemed, still, like our dead. No. You went to the front early in the morning in a miserable little car with a more miserable little chauffeur who suffered visibly the closer he came to the fighting. But at night, sometimes late, without lights, with the big trucks roaring past, you came on back to sleep in a bed with sheets in a good hotel, paying a dollar a day for the best rooms on the front. The smaller rooms in the back, on the side away from the shelling, were considerably more expensive. After the shell that lit on the sidewalk in front of the hotel, you got a beautiful double corner room on that side, twice the size of the one you had had, for less than a dollar. It wasn't me they killed. See? No. Not me. It wasn't me anymore.

Then, in a hospital given by the American Friends of Spanish Democracy, located out behind the Morata front along the road to Valencia, they said, "Raven wants to see you."

"Do I know him?"

"I don't think so," they said, "but he wants to see you."

"Where is he?"

"Upstairs."

In the room upstairs they are giving a blood transfusion to a man with a very gray face who lies on a cot with his arm out, looking away from the gurgling bottle and moaning in a very impersonal way. He moaned mechanically and at regular intervals, and it did not seem to be him that made the sound. His lips did not move.

"Where's Raven?" I asked.

"I'm here," said Raven.

The voice came from a high mound covered by a shoddy gray blanket. There were two arms crossed on the top of the mound, and at one end there was something that had been a face, but now was a yellow scabby area with a wide bandage cross where the eyes had been.

"Who is it?" asked Raven. He didn't have lips, but he talked pretty well without them and with a pleasant voice.

"Hemingway," I said. "I came up to see how you were doing."

"My face was pretty bad," he said. "It got sort of burned from the grenade, but it's peeled a couple of times and it's doing better."

"It looks swell," I said. "It's doing fine."

I wasn't looking at it when I spoke.

"How are things in America?" he asked. "What do they think of us over there?"

"Sentiment's changed a lot," I said. "They're beginning to realize the government is going to win this war."

"Do you think so?"

"Sure," I said.

"I'm awfully glad," he said. "You know, I wouldn't mind any of this if I could just watch what was going on. I don't mind the pain, you know. It never seemed important really. But I was always awfully interested in things, and I really wouldn't mind the pain at all if I could just sort of follow things intelligently. I could even be some use. You know, I didn't mind the war at all. I did all right in the war. I got hit once before, and I was back and rejoined the battalion in two weeks. I couldn't stand to be away. Then I got this."

He had put his hand in mine. It was not a worker's hand. There were no callouses, and the nails on the long, spatulate fingers were smooth and rounded.

"How did you get it?" I asked.

"Well, there were some troops that were routed, and we went over to sort of reform them, and we did, and then we had quite a fight with the fascists, and we beat them. It was quite a bad fight, you know, but we beat them, and then someone threw this grenade at me."

Holding his hand and hearing him tell it, I did not believe a word of it. What was left of him did not sound like the wreckage of a soldier somehow. I did now know how he had been wounded, but the story did not sound right. It was the sort of way everyone would like to have been wounded. But I wanted him to think I believed it.

"Where did you come from?" I asked.

"From Pittsburgh. I went to the University there."

"What did you do before you joined up here?"

"I was a social worker," he said. Then I knew it couldn't be true, and I wondered how he had really been so frightfully wounded, and I didn't care. In the war that I had known,

men often lied about the manner of their wounding. Not at
first; but later. I'd lied a little myself in my time. Especially
late in the evening. But I was glad he thought I believed it,
and we talked about books. He wanted to be a writer, and I
told him about what happened north of Guadalajara and
promised to bring some things from Madrid next time we got
out that way. I hoped maybe I could get a radio.

"They tell me Dos Passos and Sinclair Lewis are coming over, too," he said.

"Yes," I said. "And when they come I'll bring them up to
see you."

"Gee, that will be great," he said. "You don't know what
that will mean to me."

"I'll bring them," I said.

"Will they be here pretty soon?"

"Just as soon as they come I'll bring them."

"Good boy, Ernest," he said. "You don't mind if I call you
Ernest, do you?"

The voice came very clear and gentle from that face that
looked like some hill that had been fought over in muddy
weather and then baked in the sun.

"Hell, no," I said. "Please. Listen, old-timer, you're going to be fine. You'll be a lot of good, you know. You can talk
on the radio."

"Maybe," he said. "You'll be back?"

"Sure," I said. "Absolutely."

"Goodbye, Ernest," he said.

"Goodbye," I told him.

Downstairs they told me he'd lost both eyes as well as his
face and was also badly wounded all through the legs and in
the feet.

"He's lost some toes, too," the doctor said, "but he doesn't
know that."

"I wonder if he'll ever know it."

"Oh, sure he will," the doctor said. "He's going to get
well."

And it still isn't you that gets hit, but it is your countryman now. Your countryman from Pennsylvania, where
once we fought at Gettysburg.

Then, walking along the road, with his left arm in an
airplane splint, walking with the gamecock walk of the professional British soldier that neither ten years of militant

party work nor the projecting metal wings of the splint could destroy, I met Raven's commanding officer, Jock Cunningham, who had three fresh rifle wounds through his upper left arm (I looked at them; one was septic) and another rifle bullet under his shoulder blade that had entered his left chest, passed through, and lodged there. He told me, in military terms, the history of the attempt to rally retiring troops on his battalion's right flank, of his bombing raid down a trench which was held at one end by the fascists and at the other end by the government troops, of the taking of this trench and, with six men and a Lewis gun, cutting off a group of some eighty fascists from their own lines, and of the final desperate defense of their impossible position his six men put up until the government troops came up and, attacking, straightened out the line again. He told it clearly, completely convincingly, and with a strong Glasgow accent. He had deep, piercing eyes sheltered like an eagle's, and, hearing him talk, you could tell the sort of soldier he was. For what he had done he would have had a V.C. in the last war. In this war there are no decorations. Wounds are the only decorations, and they do not award wound stripes.

"Raven was in the same show," he said. "I didn't know he'd been hit. Ay, he's a good man. He got his after I got mine. The fascists we'd cut off were very good troops. They never fired a useless shot when we were in that bad spot. They waited in the dark there until they had us located and then opened with volley fire. That's how I got four in the same place."

We talked for a while and he told me many things. They were all important, but nothing was as important as what Jay Raven, the social worker from Pittsburgh with no military training, had told me was true. This is a strange new kind of war where you learn just as much as you are able to believe.

16

ANNE O'HARE MCCORMICK

TEACHER TO THE WORLD

Through three decades marked by rapid change, reporter Anne O'Hare McCormick served as a calm teacher to the world's dictators, presidents, diplomats, and ordinary citizens.

From her vantage point at the New York *Times*, McCormick watched the Roaring '20s give way to the Great Depression and then to the cataclysm of World War II. She in turn explained the news to readers across the globe, painting a brilliant background and giving detailed perspectives to her news reports.

As a good teacher to her readers, McCormick was not content to toss around raw facts and crudely crafted bits of information. Events, she thought, were part of the thickly textured pattern of human existence. A little swatch of information could not possibly cover the news. McCormick strove, then, to cover her topics with exceptional depth and thoroughness. She taught her readers about the world by giving them a broad, detailed context along with comprehensive facts and painstaking observations.

She tempered her honest, observant style with a genuine sense of kindness. The combination opened worlds to her as a reporter. Franklin Roosevelt, for instance, had vowed never to be interviewed by an individual reporter. He broke the rule, though, for McCormick and talked with her extensively. He called her "a wonderful human being." On the other end of the political continuum, Benito Mussolini also appreciated being interviewed by McCormick. The Italian dictator listened to her suggestions and solicited her opinions on world matters. Diplomats considered McCormick's reports to be "required reading."

Her fellow reporters attributed her success to her genuine, kind, feminine attitude. As C.L. Sulzberger, a fellow World War II correspondent, put it, McCormick "retained a boundless energy and feminine charm. With plain, merry face, square jaw and upturned nose, she radiated warmth and kindness; everyone loved her and, what was important for a journalist, also confided in her."

That kindness and caring developed out of family necessity. She was born in 1880 in Yorkshire, England, to Thomas and Teresa O'Hare. The young family shortly moved to Columbus, Ohio. While Anne was still in high school, Thomas O'Hare deserted the family. Anne felt she should help support her family; so as soon as she graduated from college, she went to work with her mother on the staff of the *Catholic Universe Bulletin* in Cleveland. After her family was on solid ground again, Anne married Frank McCormick, an engineer and importer who frequently traveled to Europe. Accompanying him on his business trips, she became a sharp-eyed observer of the European community. She began keeping a journal as they traveled.

Her journal grew thicker and thicker, and it occurred to her that her observations might be put to good use. She wrote a hesitant letter to Carr Van Anda, editor of the New York *Times*, in 1921. Might he be able to use some dispatches from Europe? Even though Van Anda had never met McCormick, he told her to give it a try.

By 1922, her dispatches had become a fixture at the *Times*. She was hired as a regular correspondent. Her reports from Europe were printed under the title "In Europe" until 1936, and then the name became simply "Abroad."

McCormick was forty-two years old when she began writing for the *Times*. She would cover wars and other events until she was well into her seventies, always taking time to give the detailed, tireless perspective that marked her work. She wrote her last piece only weeks before she died in 1954.

Throughout her career, McCormick took care to put her subjects at ease. She rarely took notes on interviews, explaining that notetaking "makes people nervous." She was at home interviewing people such as Hitler and Stalin, as well as men and women on the street.

She never limited her reports, however, to mere interviews. She took command of each story by studying its context and predicting its implications. Furthermore, she had a clear idea of where the news was, whether in the national capitals or at a bombed-out home where an ordinary woman swept the debris of war away.

She believed her deeply analytical style was absolutely vital in helping to maintain world freedom. She correctly explained to her readers across the globe that Hitler and Mussolini posed a grave threat to world safety, long before statesmen came to that conclusion. Anthony Eden, a British Foreign Secretary, commented in some surprise that reporters had shown much more insight than diplomats had in World War II. "And why not?" McCormick asked him, tongue-in-cheek. "After all, Mr. Secretary, diplomats are only badly trained reporters."

McCormick was one of the best trained. The Pulitzer Prize committee recognized her work by giving her the 1937 prize for foreign correspondence. While World War II still raged, she was named to the secret Advisory Committee on Post-War Foreign Policy. She also was mentioned frequently as a candidate for diplomatic posts.

She was an expert on foreign affairs because she saw them in their true depth and richness. Not content to gaze blankly on the surface of officialdom, she realized that news came from everywhere, from the common people and the great. Explaining what she looked for in the coverage of World War II, she said, "The signs were little things, the gestures of little people, yet it seemed to me then...that those individual gestures were bigger with promise for the future than great political events."

That statement reflected her writing style. Her stories from both Europe and America were peppered with observations of real people—and with her explanation of what those people and actions meant to the world.

She recognized that she had a privileged vantage point compared to ordinary men and women. She knew nothing happened in a vacuum; and in her job as a world traveler, she had every opportunity to observe the broad context that helped explain the world in upheaval. She considered it a duty to explain the deep context of everything, from incidents as serious as the bombing of Rome to topics as lighthearted as the growing popularity of Florida resorts.

She was not satisfied with merely reporting about bombing attacks on Rome, but felt obliged to put the assaults into historical perspective. "The bombing of Rome shakes the Western World," she wrote, "because it brings home with a special poignancy the schism within our civilization which is at the root of this war. At last our bombs have fallen on the triune and many-layered city that is in some way ancestral to all who share the great heritage of Western law and culture." She concluded that the bombing of Rome was an attempt to separate the cancerous Fascist Rome from the Rome that was the "cradle of Christianity."

McCormick's writing was analytical and explanatory. She wanted readers to understand exactly how news stories fit into the grand scheme of history. Her accounts, as a result, were wise counsels from one who had seen and who therefore knew.

One example of her analytical style was her report on the death of Pope Benedict XV. Far more than a mere obituary, it gave the Pope's life and death a full, colorful meaning:

> Benedict XV, the fourth Pope since the Kingdom of Italy took possession of Rome, was the first for whose death the Italian Government lowered its flags to half-mast in token of mourning.
>
> That gesture of Italy is significant. It draws attention to qualities in the dead Pontiff that were not generally recognized during his life. Benedict was little known and little considered until he died. Now a curiously clouded personality and a singularly overshadowed career suddenly emerge into the light of appraisal and take on new dimensions.

The report that followed did not mince words. McCormick said that "Benedict XV seemed one of the negative Popes....One saw him at public functions in the Vatican, drooping under his tiara...."

She went on, however, with other colorful details that shed light on the Pope's true character before his final days. She wrote from personal experience, describing the Pope in vivid, energetic language: "I remember his quick, staccato stride as he crossed his library to meet us...the swift glance with which he greeted and took us in...." She concluded that the late Pope was more important than he had seemed.

McCormick was not afraid to draw such conclusions. She objectively observed and then made a reasoned assessment. For example, after descrubing Benedict's personality and life work, she summed up his importance:

> Benedict may or may not have been a great Pope. He had two qualities in a great degree—prudence and patience. These are not the qualities of genius; but in times like these they are perhaps more mollifying to the world's angers...than more brilliant and subjugating gifts.

Along with her insistence on analyzing and explaining the deeper perspective, McCormick searched for and found a unifying theme in her stories. She wanted readers to recognize an underlying rhythm in world events. In "Bulldozer and the Woman With a Broom," for example, she saw a theme in the healing process as Europe strove to rebuild after World War II. She talked to a woman sweeping the bombed-out remnants of her home and saw in her the key to the restoration of the continent. In herself, the woman was not newsworthy, but what she represented was of tremendous importance. The story is reprinted in this anthology.

McCormick's deep analyses were rooted in her photographic descriptions. She wrote of the American South as though it were a picture postcard: "The village lay among ranging hills, in a setting of Alpine beauty; Mount Mitchell was a blurred cone in the dim distance and the nearer slopes were misty green in a spring rain." She went on to contrast that peaceful scene with the fact that the South's "old mold [was] cracking under the pressure."

Her descriptions did more than paint pretty pictures. They also set the proper mood for readers to be in when they read her stories. Their ability to do that is evident in the following passage showing how tired and harassed the U. S. Senate was as it shut down in December of 1929:

> On a weary day when the Senate was diagnosed as a case of nerves, and reckless allusions to Communists and wild

jackasses, common and preferred Senators, were cited in proof of Senatorial brain fag, it happened that an official air-tester man was called into the Chamber to analyze the exhausted atmosphere....[The test] was not intended to measure how much moisture and fresh oxygen are used up on a tariff schedule, or burned up in the heat of personal remarks. It was intended for nothing at all—alas!—but a check on the ventilating system.

But what if there were an instrument for taking sound-ings in the stale air of debate! What if some accurate gauge could register the humidity of the political atmo-sphere!...In the beginning there were forecasters in plenty to predict that this Congress would run into storms, but none to foresee that they would be so violent as to blow down party walls and tie up traffic.

Although McCormick's most notable stories were about such significant events as the potential liberation of Rome, many stories were about seemingly more mundane occur-rences. She still gave them her devoted detail and her ex-haustive analysis. For instance, she painted this vivid pic-ture of Florida vacationers:

At the height of the season,...Florida has all the fascina-tion of a moving picture, in one crowded reel, of the head-long adventure that is America. We are all here, ampli-fied and magnified—pioneer, bushwhacker, gold-digger, dreamer, loafer, bluffer, social climber—all of us that have made Our Country, Right or Wrong.

The piece was not merely a feature on Florida's resort industry. McCormick used her postcard portrait to analyze what the popularity of beach vacations in Florida really showed us about ourselves:

Of course, there is a corollary to these random impres-sions of American Winter resorts and resorters. It may be that our delight in building docks and development pro-jects in the sands where we go to play, our hilarity in money-making and our somewhat dull extravagance in money-spending are signs not only of the energy but also of the limitations of youth. Perhaps we lack the English content in pure holiday and the French seriousness in pleasure because our interests are too shallow and our experience is too circumscribed. One may draw the usual indictment. One may wonder that with all its suavity, luxury and Winter bloom Florida should remain an intellectual desert.

McCormick's careful writing style, emphasizing detail and analysis for the broader picture, was perhaps best summed up in her own statement about the duties of women in the post-World War II age. "[W]omen, and particularly American women in a time when the United States is thrust into a position of unique power and influence," she wrote, "have the soul of the nation in their keeping." She took her own advice to heart. She tried to keep the soul of the nation intact during decades of upheaval by observing, analyzing, and teaching what it all meant. Her classroom was the world. Her news reports were her textbook.

◆

"IN THE DEPTHS OF THE HUMAN SPIRIT THERE IS A CORE OF FAITH"

Christmas 1943 was the fifth Christmas since Hitler's armies had invaded Poland on September 1, 1939. Although America had not entered the war until December 1941, McCormick thought it important to show Americans that other nations had been suffering a war-torn Christmas for half a decade. As in many of her stories, her ideas were rooted in an outlook that sought to explain the overall picture of life itself.

As is obvious in the following piece, she was devoutly religious. She often covered religious topics, especially from the Vatican. In this article, she relied on the biblical Christmas story to give a thematic explanation for the meaning of war.

WHERE THE CHRISTMAS LIGHTS ARE OUT
Anne O'Hare McCormick
New York *Times*
December 25, 1943

The fifth Christmas of the war finds a large part of the civilized world exhausted, ravaged, crazed or dulled by cruelty. The "countless thousands" who suffered from man's inhumanity to man in the past have multiplied into countless millions in the present. The horror has become so vast that it is almost impersonal. Individual agony is all but lost sight of in the wholesale atrocities practiced by Nazi terror squads—men trained for terror—in occupied territory, particularly in the East. When cities are bombed, the scurrying inhabitants are only incidental wreckage in the destruction of rails and stores and forges. When children slowly starve, unable to hold out until the rescue expeditions arrive, they are hardly more than fading shadows in a dark and faceless landscape.

The President spoke yesterday of our "unseen allies," and indeed nobody can see far enough to see their faces. Nobody has a mind big enough to understand their thoughts or a heart wide enough to feel their misery. But Christmas brings it close again for the traveler who looks from this safety zone on the shattered settings of many Christmases.

Christmas is a haunted time when the scenes of yesterday blur the pictures of today. There is the English village where the waifs sang carols in lighted doorways of the old timbered cottages or the pleasant London square where the fog swept through the windows on Christmas night and added its own touch of mystery to the tree, the children's wonder and the sense of insulated security the English always felt in their snug and misty island. Village and city square live only in memory; the first bombs that fell on Britain wiped out both. The little church in Naples where the sailors crowded wide-eyed around the ancient "Presepio" is part of the wreckage of the waterfront. In Bethlehem itself the shrine that covers the cave of the Nativity is encircled by Army trucks and armored cars.

Moscow is grimmer than it was on a grim Christmas ten years ago. The dim old cathedral at Kiev filled on the Russian Christmas with the imploring, quavering voices of the old is a skeleton in a skeleton city. This year the hotel waiters will not sneak in for a stolen glimpse of the American Christmas tree, crossing themselves instinctively at the sight of the candles and the angels. If they are still alive, they can have a Christmas tree of their own even on the battlefield.

Little is felt of the old square where the Christmas market of Nuremberg was held. The tinkling toys and gingerbread men dance no more in the rainbow light cast on the snow by the stained-glass windows of the medieval church. Mines are being laid to blow up the little piazza in Rome where the children preached on Christmas afternoon. Hungry ghosts walk in Ship Lane and the street of the Coppersmiths in Athens, once filled with Christmas bustle, bargaining and laughter. The wide promenade of the Champs-Elysees, where the tight little family circles of Paris paraded primly after Christmas dinner, is now the exercise ground of the German garrison.

Nothing is as it was save Christmas itself. The shattered frames of memory's pictures are the settings of human life. They help the mind to realize the broken homes, the lost traditions, the physical degradation and moral torture human beings are enduring. At the same time we know that in places where the walls are crumbled and the lights are out Christmas will still be kept because it has to be, because it repeats year after year the one affirmation man must believe in if he is to keep on struggling.

The story of Christmas is the story of the importance of man. The idea embodied in the child born in the manger of Bethlehem is the idea of the supreme importance of the redemption of the human race. It was the incarnation in the Western World, the world of the Roman Empire, of the old Hebraic faith in the immeasurable value of the human soul.

This is the idea humanity is still fighting for. Not since the beginning of the Christian era has it been so furiously assailed and so furiously defended as it is today. For what is the naked issue of the most universal war in history but the right of man to be himself? Other issues complicate and confuse the minds of armies and nations. The fundamental antithesis is often blunted. The systems representing self-government in the most advanced form it has yet attained are fighting with one great totalitarian system against another. But underneath the mixed motives, the extreme nationalisms, the non-synchronizing conceptions of government and life that are fused in the great coalition runs a common will to resist conquest and dominion, to retain at any cost the right of nations and eventually of individuals to work out their own salvation in their own way.

No lesser aim could justify the horrors of this war. The memories and thoughts that assail us at Christmas time could not be borne unless somewhere in the depths of the human spirit there is a core of faith that the great symbolism of the Nativity is true. The Child was homeless, too. He escaped the slaughter of the innocents only by a flight into exile. He was stoned in the highways and hanged on a cross. Yet the idea lived because the spirit of man is stronger than the walls he builds or the ruin he works when he vainly seeks to destroy himself and enslave himself.

●◇

A WOMAN WITH A BROOM
SYMBOLIZES POST-WAR EUROPE

As World War II drew to a close, Europe was in shambles. Families and homes were shattered. Women outnumbered the surviving males. Bombs and gunfire had reduced ordinary dwellings to dust.

Amidst all the destruction, McCormick saw women across Europe beginning to sweep away the mounds of debris from the war. In their seemingly futile gesture, McCormick saw the hope of rebuilding. She made careful use of that theme in this piece. By so doing, she was able to focus an otherwise broad topic into a readable form.

BULLDOZER AND THE WOMAN
WITH A BROOM
Anne O'Hare McCormick
New York *Times*
March 28, 1945

Every correspondent who has been near the front has
seen the woman with the broom described by John MacCor-
mac in a dispatch from the United States Ninth Army Headquarters east of the Rhine. In a devastated town two miles
behind the fighting line he observed a woman emerge from a
cellar and, though her house was a ruin, proceed to sweep
away the dust and rubble that covered the doorstep.

This woman happened to be German, but in every war-
ravaged country the woman with the broom trying to clear
away the debris that used to be her home is as familiar and
monotonous a sight as ruin itself. In one flattened village in
Holland after another, dazed old men were standing in wa-
vering clusters in the shell-pocked fields, but the women
were working in the dooryards that a few hours before had
led to houses. Several were trying to tie their chrysanthe-
mum stalks to the poles that held them up. The chrysanthe-
mums were still blooming, bright yellow beside piles of
brick dust, and the housewives were mechanically starting
to save the one whole thing that survived the wreck of the
shattered cottages.

The Dutch, it should be remembered, have suffered terrible things in this war. The process of liberation has been
harder, slower and therefore more ruinous than in France
or Belgium, and the Germans in the occupied part of the
country have treated the population and the countryside itself, reclaimed from the sea with infinite labor, with su-
perlative cruelty—perhaps, the Netherlanders say, because
the Nazis expected more "cooperation" from them and were
goaded to fury by the obstinate resistance they met in Holland.

For Americans, living in conditions unimaginably different from those prevailing in occupied and liberated
countries, it is vital to understand the bitterness of over-
strained and underfed people who have suffered too much
and too long. It is one reason why refugee governments are
bound to be unstable and short-lived. It is why every provi-

sional regime, including the French, by far the strongest of all, seems to move in a political vacuum. It explains the "ingratitude" that irks our soldiers in the land they are fighting to free. The temper of dispossessed and hungry people, and their sudden swings from violence to apathy, constitute one of the human and—or, for they are the same thing— the political problems which Mr. Hoover, in the series of articles appearing in this newspaper, rightly rates as taking priority over all other problems.

But the woman in Evreux, in battered Normandy, was not thinking so far ahead when she appeared with her broom that bleak Sunday morning and began raising the dust in the path of General de Gaulle and the distinguished visitors from Paris. With a dash and energy as impatient as General Patton's as he sweeps across the German plain, she was making a broomstick attack upon the crumbled stones that lay atop a tiny patch of garden. She paid no attention to the cortege skirting the shell holes in the road until a woman in the party stopped to ask her what she thought she was doing with a broom in the wake of 2,000 pounds of bombs. "Who's to save the cabbages and onions if I don't? They're all that's left of all the work of all my life," she said fiercely. "And somebody has to begin clearing away this mess."

Then there was the old woman sweeping out a cowshed in the Aego Romano, near Rome. The land had been flooded by the Germans and was once more a breeding place for malarial mosquitos, banished by the efforts of fifty years. The house was gone. In a fifty-mile radius not an animal was left. The farmer, who had lost a hand in a minefield, looked at us with hopeless eyes; but the woman kept on sweeping, clearing a little space in the wreckage to begin life anew.

The woman with a broom is both symbol and promise. It's pretty futile to start attacking the ruins of great cities with a kitchen broom. Yet everywhere, before the monster bulldozers arrive to clear paths for the armies through the debris left by the bombers, women instinctively seize their brooms in this futile, age-old gesture of cleaning up the mess the men have made.

There's no assurance that they can clear it up this time, but today there are more women than men in Europe, widows of soldiers, widows of hostages, widows of the last war, and they are bound to try. In Paris an association of widows of men executed by the Germans is headed by a lovely girl widow who said months ago exactly what Miss Horsburgh, one of the two Englishwomen who will join Dean Virginia Gildersleeve as delegates to San Francisco, says of the responsibility of representatives who will assemble at the conference. "We are the trustees of the future," the French girl asserted. "We can't leave it to the next generation because they won't have seen what we have seen, and they won't understand."

It isn't chance that women are named for the first time to a conference called to set up the framework of international order. There should be more of them, for they are in the wars now, and millions of them have nothing much left but a broom. Whether they could do better than men is a question, but they are somehow angrier over destruction, and at least there's not much danger of doing worse. Certainly it's a sound and self-protective instinct that impels the men to hand over to the women a little of the responsibility for the hardest job in history.

17

ERNIE PYLE

THE MOST PRAYED-FOR MAN IN AMERICA

Ernie Pyle was probably the best loved reporter of all time.

His columns about the common soldier fighting and dying in World War II touched the hearts of his readers. More than 300 daily newspapers and 1,000 weeklies carried his columns syndicated by the Scripps-Howard chain. He wrote two books, *Here is Your War* and *Brave Men*, that were compilations of his columns. Both sold well. He was called a democratizer, uniting people of all stations, both in the fields of war and in the homes of readers in the United States. He wrote about the foot soldier and wrote from what he called "the worm's-eye view." He slithered in foxholes as deep and as dirty as those of the men he observed.

His columns from the field were letters home from the boys at war. He wrote for the soldiers who could not or would not write for themselves. He never demeaned his subjects, nor did he exalt them beyond the level they deserved. He clearly showed his readers what the war meant to the men doing the fighting and dying. A master at writing about the common soldier, he exhibited the opposite of Ernest Hemingway's adventurous approach to war. Indeed, Pyle hated war and seemed oblivious to strategy.

His folksy, chatty, sometimes humorous, but usually compassionate writing style earned him the affection of the people back home, who hoped for a chance to read about their sons and fathers in his columns. His personal accounts included soldiers' names and hometowns. Households across America spoke of him as a member of the family. It was said that he was "the most prayed-for man in the country."

From his early pre-war writing, Pyle refined two approaches to reporting. He absorbed himself completely in his subject, and he developed the uncanny ability to mix with all types of people. He had an unobtrusive approach. He mingled with the troops, observed, and became absorbed in their lives. A shy person, he still had the ability to put folks at ease. Privates and generals alike were comfortable talking to him. He rarely took notes.

Occasionally, he would write a story with a pencil while under fire in the field. His typical method, though, was to gather material from the field for several days and then return to whatever place had been set up for his fellow reporters and write several dispatches from there.

No detail was too insignificant for him to report on. He wrote about the soldiers' longings and what they did at home. He wrote about trench foot and foot powder. He wrote about doctors in the field hospitals and about the sounds tanks made as they ground up a hill. His column allowed readers to get a perspective on the vastness of the war, and he showed the diversity of the work of the soldiers. His distinguished war correspondence was awarded the Pulitzer Prize in 1943.

Pyle's talent was in his storytelling ability. He described events with clear, simple sentences. He used strong verbs and was not afraid to be poetic. He used repetition and vivid imagery. Nor was he afraid to put himself into his stories. His stories were almost diary-like because they were so personal. Many used first person. Only in a diary would one write about the color of a tin of foot powder.

It was in the details that readers could get a feeling of the routine of the soldier's day and the horror of war. People back home were attending to the details of life—getting up in the mornings, going to work, washing dishes. The details that Pyle provided of everyday living on the battlelines helped them know what it was like to be a soldier. Readers could sense that as long as Pyle was describing the mundane, their boys were doing all right.

Pyle's columns made the soldiers themselves feel important also, and they loved him for what he did. He urged Congress to pass a bill allowing soldiers to wear a stripe to show their overseas service, and he insisted that combat infantrymen receive $10 a month extra pay. The legislation gained the name "the Ernie Pyle Bill."

Pyle was a small, bald man, the only son of Indiana farmers. He was in high school when World War I started and promised his parents that he would finish school before going to war. He joined the Navy Reserves after his high school graduation, but the war ended before he could be called into active duty. He always felt dismayed that he had not been able to join his friends in the war.

He enrolled at Indiana University and was editor of the campus newspaper. He left school just before graduation to take a job with the La Porte (Ind.) *Herald*. From there he went to Scripps-Howard's Washington *Daily News* as a reporter, was made a copy editor, and then moved to New York and the *Evening World* and later the *Post*. He went back to the Washington paper in 1926 and became the country's first aviation reporter. Beginning in 1934, after an illness forced him to seek a drier climate, he began writing folksy travel pieces. He had married Geraldine "Jerry" Siebolds in 1925, and she accompanied him on his travels across the country. They crossed the continent thirty-five times, and he wrote also from Alaska, Hawaii, and Central and South America. He would travel for about a week and then stay in a hotel and write his columns. In the introduction to the book *Ernie's War*, David Nichols wrote that Pyle was "a man who enjoyed a tall tale and the company of rugged individualists— Alaskan gold miners or a squatter who painted pictures in his shack behind the Memphis city dump."

He and Jerry had a rocky marriage, but he rarely revealed that aspect of his life in his war columns, mainly because he thought his problems were insignificant when men were dying in battle. Jerry attempted suicide at least twice, and she died of uremic poisoning only seven months after Pyle was killed.

By the time of the Battle of Britain in 1940, Pyle was ready to report on what he considered a more serious topic than travel: the war in Europe. He shipped to England and wrote his first war stories from London. The dispatches were not about military strategy but about the ways the British were coping with the bombings: firemen who put out the fires; people hiding out in air-raid shelters. He wrote as if he were a guest sharing in the misery. His story from London on December 30, 1940, was poetic, describing the sight of the old city burning as "the most hateful, most beautiful single scene I have ever known."

His descriptive style carried through the rest of the war years. However, he soon lost his innocent perspective. He wrote some of his most memorable pieces while living with the men in the First Infantry Division in North Africa. There he shared the war with the soldiers and used his keen eye for detail to describe for hometown readers the soldiers' daily lives. In North Africa, he finally found a way to focus his knack for reporting the human side of life.

It was there also that he was particularly shocked by the apparent callousness of some P-38 Lightning pilots who had strafed a German truck convoy. The event marked a turning point in his writing. He began to write more seriously about the realities of war. He was fascinated with the awful dichotomy of war: basic human goodness that was displayed in peacetime changed to brutal cold-hearted killing during times of war, and the change created a dilemma for the soldiers doing the killing. That idea became a recurring theme in his war stories. His heroes were not romantic aviators or Alaskan gold-miners. They were simple men who killed other simple men because they had a job to do. In the long essay that ended *Here Is Your War*, he wrote that he saw changes in the soldiers brought about by the killing and the moral dilemma they faced each day.

His personalization of the war brought home only too powerfully the fact that real men were dying for their country. He often expressed contempt for those Americans for whom the war was an inconvenience. He was appalled that folks back home would whine about rationing or not having their loved ones with them while men were dying on foreign soil. It was this thinking that prevented him from taking well-deserved leave time from his work. He thought of his reporting as "service" as much as if he had served in the Armed Forces; and from 1943 until his death in 1945, he went home only twice for brief visits.

The effect of his increasing weariness showed in his writing style. In the beginning of the war, he had a superficial, naïve perspective on war. After months in North Africa, his reporting began to lose its spirit. He was sick of war, and his reporting reflected the attitude of a man whose outlook had hardened. He hated war and once wrote that he hoped he would be the last war correspondent.

After North Africa and Italy, Pyle went to France and reported on its liberation after the Normandy invasion in June 1944. His reporting in France showed his fatigue, and he despaired that he had lost what he called his ability to "weigh and describe" the war. He went home briefly—the last of the two trips he made during the war. The War Department urged Pyle to travel to the Pacific to boost the morale of the troops there, and, of course, Pyle complied.

The war in the Pacific was different. Instead of dirty foxholes and his beloved infantrymen, he encountered clean ship berths and sailors. His prejudice showed in his writing, and the remoteness of the Pacific outposts made his columns disjointed. The practice of Navy censors to forbid the use of sailors' names affected his writing also. He resented being in the Pacific; and, although still immensely popular, he rankled the servicemen there by writing that the real war was in Europe.

On April 18, 1945, he followed a group of Marines who had invaded the small island of Ie Shima, west of Okinawa. While Pyle surveyed the destruction on the beach, a sniper shot him, and he died instantly. He was buried on the island in a crude wooden coffin. His death followed that of President Franklin Roosevelt by six days. The country was once again thrown into mourning one of the stalwart figures of the war. Soldiers and civilian readers took his death as a personal loss, and he was eulogized throughout the country.

After the war, his body was moved to the National Memorial Cemetery of the Pacific in Punchbowl Crater, Hawaii, an ironic burial site for a reporter who so loved his dirty infantrymen in Europe.

SOLDIERS' HUMANITY IN THE FACE OF WAR

Although shocked by the killing he saw, Pyle was moved by the selflessness of the soldiers he covered. In Italy in 1944, he wrote a story that is the one most often reprinted in anthologies. It was about the death of Captain Henry T. Waskow of

Belton, Texas. Emotionally appealing, it is indicative of Pyle's style. The reader has a sense of Pyle standing back, simply observing the members of Waskow's company as they paid their last respects.

[THE DEATH OF CAPTAIN HENRY WASKOW]
Ernie Pyle
Scripps Howard Newspaper Alliance
January 10, 1944

In this war I have known a lot of officers who were loved and respected by the soldiers under them. But never have I crossed the trail of any man as beloved as Captain Henry T. Waskow, of Belton, Texas.

Captain Waskow was a company commander in the Thirty-sixth Division. He had led his company since long before it left the States. He was very young, only in his middle twenties, but he carried in him a sincerity and a gentleness that made people want to be guided by him.

"After my father, he came next," a soldier said. "He'd go to bat for us every time."

"I've never known him to do anything unfair," another said.

I was at the foot of a mule trail the night they brought Captain Waskow down. The moon was nearly full, and you could see far up the trail, and even part way across the valley below.

Dead men had been coming down the mountain all evening, lashed onto the backs of mules. They came lying belly-down across the wooden pack-saddles, their heads hanging down on one side, their stiffened legs sticking out awkwardly from the other, bobbing up and down as the mules walked.

The Italian mule skinners were afraid to walk beside the dead men; so Americans had to lead the mules down at night.

Even the Americans were reluctant to unlash and lift off the bodies when they got to the bottom; so an officer had to do it himself and ask others to help.

I don't know who that first one was. You feel small in the presence of dead men, and you don't ask silly questions.

They slid him down from the mule and stood him on his feet for a moment. In the halflight he might have been merely a sick man standing there leaning on others. Then they laid him on the ground in the shadow of the low stone wall beside the road. We left him there beside the road, that first one, and we all went back into the cowshed and sat on water cans or lay on the straw, waiting for the next batch of mules.

Somebody said the dead soldier had been dead for four days, and then nobody said anything more about it. We talked soldier talk for an hour or more; the dead man lay all alone, outside in the shadow of the wall.

Then a soldier came into the cowshed and said there were some more bodies outside. We went out into the road. Four mules stood there in the moonlight, in the road where the trail came down off the mountain. The soldiers who led them stood there waiting.

"This one is Captain Waskow," one of them said quietly.

Two men unlashed his body from the mule and lifted it off and laid it in the shadow beside the stone wall. Other men took the other bodies off. Finally, there were five lying end to end in a long row. You don't cover up dead men in the combat zones. They just lie there in the shadows until someone comes after them.

The unburdened mules moved off to their olive grove. The men in the road seeemed reluctant to leave. They stood around, and gradually I could sense them moving, one by one, close to Captain Waskow's body. Not so much to look, I think, as to say something in finality to him, and to themselves. I stood close by and I could hear.

One soldier came and looked down, and he said out loud, "God damn it." That's all he said, and then he walked away.

Another one came, and said, "God damn it, to hell, anyway!" He looked down for a few last moments and then turned and left.

Another man came. I think he was an officer. It was hard to tell officers from men in the dim light, for everybody was bearded and grimy. The man looked down into the dead captain's face and then he spoke directly to him, as though he were alive, "I'm sorry, old man."

Then a soldier came and stood beside the officer, and bent over, and he too spoke to his dead captain, not in a whisper but awfully tenderly, and he said, "I sure am sorry, sir."

Then the first man squatted down, and he reached down and took the dead hand, and he sat there for a full five minutes holding the dead hand in his own and looking intently in the dead face. And he never uttered a sound all the time he sat there.

Finally he put the hand down. He reached over and gently straightened the points of the captain's shirt collar, and then he sort of rearranged the tattered edges of his uniform around the wound, and then he got up and walked away down the road in the moonlight, all alone.

The rest of us went back into the cowshed, leaving the five dead men lying in a line, end to end, in the shadow of the low stone wall. We lay down on the straw in the cowshed, and pretty soon we were all asleep.

●◆

A REAL SOLDIER

Two stories Pyle wrote in Italy told about Sergeant Buck Eversole, and they have been reprinted here. The stories illustrated his ability to observe, to report details, his "ability to weigh and describe." They also showed his maturity and his sense of the dichotomy of war. Buck Eversole was doing his job as a soldier, just as he had done as a cowboy in Idaho and Nevada. Notice how Pyle let Eversole tell his feelings in his own words.

SGT. BUCK EVERSOLE
Ernie Pyle
Scripps Howard Newspaper Alliance
February 1944

IN ITALY, February 21, 1944—The company commander said to me, "Every man in this company deserves the Silver Star."

We walked around in the olive grove where the men of the company were sitting on the edges of their foxholes, talking or cleaning their gear.

"Let's go over here," he said. "I want to introduce you to my personal hero."

I figured that the lieutenant's own "personal hero," out of a whole company of men who deserved the Silver Star, must be a real soldier indeed.

Then the company commander introduced me to Sgt. Frank Eversole, who shook hands sort of timidly and said, "Pleased to meet you," and then didn't say any more.

I could tell by his eyes and by his slow and courteous speech when he did talk that he was a Westerner. Conversation with him was sort of hard, but I didn't mind his reticence for I know how Westerners like to size people up first.

The sergeant wore a brown stocking cap on the back of his head. His eyes were the piercing kind. I noticed his hands—they were outdoor hands, strong and rough.

Later in the afternoon I came past his foxhole again, and we sat and talked a little while alone. We didn't talk about the war, but mainly about our West, and just sat and made figures on the ground with sticks as we talked.

We got started that way, and in the days that followed I came to know him well. He is to me, and to all those with whom he serves, one of the great men of the war.

* * *

Frank Eversole's nickname is "Buck." The other boys in the company sometimes call him "Buck Overshoes," simply because Eversole sounds a bit like "overshoes."

Buck was a cowboy before the war. He was born in the little town of Missouri Valley, Iowa, and his mother still lives there. But Buck went West on his own before he was sixteen, and ever since has worked as a ranch hand. He is twenty-eight and unmarried.

He worked a long time around Twin Falls, Idaho, and then later down in Nevada. Like so many cowboys, he made the rodeos in season. He was never a star or anything. Usually he just rode the broncs out of the chute for pay—seven-fifty a ride. Once he did win a fine saddle. He has ridden at Cheyenne and the other big rodeos.

Like any cowboy, he loves animals. Here in Italy one afternoon Buck and some other boys were pinned down inside a one-room stone shed by terrific German shellfire. As they sat there, a frightened mule came charging through the door. There simply wasn't room inside for men and mule both; so Buck got up and shooed him out the door. Thirty feet from the door a direct hit killed the mule. Buck has always felt guilty about it.

Another time Buck ran onto a mule that was down and crying in pain from a bad shell wound. Buck took his .45 and put a bullet through its head. "I wouldn't have shot him except he was hurtin' so," Buck says.

* * *

Buck Eversole has the Purple Heart and two Silver Stars for bravery. He is cold and deliberate in battle. His commanders depend more on him than on any other man. He has been wounded once, and had countless narrow escapes. He has killed many Germans.

He is the kind of man you instinctively feel safer with than with other people. He is not helpless like most of us. He is practical. He can improvise, patch things, fix things.

His grammar is the unschooled grammar of the plains and the soil. He uses profanity, but never violently. Even in the familiarity of his own group his voice is always low. He is such a confirmed soldier by now that he always says "sir" to any stranger. It is impossible to conceive of his doing anything dishonest.

After the war Buck will go back West to the land he loves. He wants to get a little place and feed a few head of cattle, and be independent.

"I don't want to be just a ranch hand no more," he says. "It's all right and I like it all right, but it's a rough life and it don't get you nowhere. When you get a little older, you kinda like a place of your own."

Buck Eversole has no hatred for Germans. He kills because he's trying to keep alive himself. The years roll over him, and the war becomes his only world, and battle his only profession. He armors himself with a philosophy of acceptance of what may happen.

"I'm mighty sick of it all," he says very quietly, "but there ain't no use to complain. I just figured it this way, that I've been given a job to do and I've got to do it. And if I don't live through it, there's nothing I can do about it."

* * *

IN ITALY, February 22, 1944—Buck Eversole is a platoon sergeant in an infantry company. That means he has charge of about forty front-line fighting men.

He has been at the front for more than a year. War is old to him, and he has become almost the master of it. He is a senior partner now in the institution of death.

His platoon has turned over many times as battle whittles down the old ones and the replacement system brings up the new ones. Only a handful now are veterans.

"It gets so it kinda gets you, seein' these new kids come up," Buck told me one night in his slow, barely audible Western voice, so full of honesty and sincerity.

"Some of them have just fuzz on their faces and don't know what it's all about, and they're scared to death. No matter what, some of them are bound to get killed.

We talked about some of the other old-time noncoms [non-commissioned officers] who could take battle themselves, but had gradually grown morose under the responsibility of leading green boys to their slaughter. Buck spoke of one sergeant especially, a brave and hardened man, who went to his captain and asked him to be reduced to a private in the lines.

"I know it ain't my fault that they get killed," Buck finally said. "And I do the best I can for them, but I've got so I feel like it's me killin' 'em instead of a German. I've got so I feel like a murderer. I hate to look at them when the new ones come in."

* * *

Buck himself has been fortunate. Once he was shot through the arm. His own skill and wisdom have saved him many times. But luck has saved him countless other times.

One night Buck and an officer took refuge from shelling in a two-room Italian stone house. As they sat there, a shell came through the wall of the far room, crossed the room and buried itself in the middle wall with its nose pointing upward. It didn't go off.

Another time Buck was leading his platoon on a night attack. They were walking in Indian file. Suddenly a mine went off and killed the entire squad following Buck. He himself had miraculously walked through the mine field without hitting a one.

One day Buck went stalking a German officer in close combat and wound up with the German on one side of a farmhouse and Buck on the other. They kept throwing grenades over the house at each other without success. Finally Buck stepped around one corner of the house and came face to face with the German, who'd had the same idea.

Buck was ready and pulled the trigger first. His slug hit the German just above the heart. The German had a wonderful pair of binoculars slung over his shoulders, and the bullet smashed them to bits. Buck had wanted some German binoculars for a long time.

* * *

The ties that grow up between men who live savagely and die relentlessly together are ties of great strength. There is a sense of fidelity to each other among little corps of men who have endured so long and whose hope in the end can be but so small.

One afternoon while I was with the company, Sgt. Buck Eversole's turn came to go back to rest camp for five days. The company was due to attack that night.

Buck went to his company commander and said, "Lieutenant, I don't think I better go. I'll stay if you need me."

The lieutenant said, "Of course I need you, Buck; I always need you. But it's your turn, and I want you to go. In fact, you're ordered to go."

The truck taking the few boys away to rest camp left just at dusk. It was drizzling, and the valleys were swathed in a dismal mist. Artillery of both sides flashed and rumbled around the horizon. The encroaching darkness was heavy and foreboding.

Buck came to the little group of old-timers in the company with whom I was standing, to say goodbye. You'd have thought he was leaving forever. He shook hands all around, and his smile seemed sick and vulnerable. He was a man stalling off his departure.

He said, "Well, good luck to you all." And then he said, "I'll be back in just five days." He said goodbye all around and slowly started away. But he stopped and said goodbye all around again, and he said, "Well, good luck to you all."

I walked with him toward the truck in the dusk. He kept his eyes on the ground, and I think he would have cried if he knew how, and he said to me very quietly:

"This is the first battle I've ever missed that this battalion has been in. Even when I was in the hospital with my arm they were in bivouac. This will be the first one I've ever missed. I sure do hope they have good luck."

And then he said:

"I feel like a deserter."

He climbed in, and the truck dissolved in the blackness. I went back and lay down on the ground among my other friends, waiting for the night orders to march. I lay there in the darkness thinking—terribly touched by the great simple devotion of this soldier who was a cowboy—and thinking of the millions far away at home who must remain forever unaware of the powerful fraternalism in the ghastly brotherhood of war.

18

MEYER BERGER

For three decades Meyer Berger roamed the streets of New York City, regaling readers with tales of their hometown. "No newspaperman covered New York more competently or wrote about it with such deep affection," declared a writer for *Newsweek* magazine.

Berger entertained readers with amusing, informative, and emotional stories no matter what the topic—from Brooklyn gangsters to White House staffers. An irrepressible storyteller, he wrote some of the most memorable accounts the *Times* ever published. He poked fun at gangsters Al Capone, Dutch Schultz, and Waxey Gordon, and turned their tedious trials into dramatic copy. At times his prose slammed readers against the back of their seat, and sometimes it spirited them away on a verbal roller coaster ride. His stories captured the mood, setting, and personality of people and places.

Few details missed his observant eye. He covered events so thoroughly that he seemed to have discovered every pertinent bit. His narratives, one admirer wrote, reconstructed the sights and sounds of a "parade, an eclipse, a homicidal maniac running amok, a murder trial, a train wreck, a bank robbery, a harrowing explosion in a crowded school, or just a thunderstorm that broke a summer heat wave." Another writer called him a "painfully shy, sensitive and hard-working" reporter. Nevertheless, Berger was a master at searching out facts that others missed. A fellow reporter complained, "When Mike covers a story, it's hard to write a follow-up. There is no angle he overlooks."

The ability to move from the "big" story to the "slice-of-life" feature stood out as his strength. He could take seemingly small, commonplace people and episodes and endow them with universal importance. He had, a critic said, the talent, matched by few reporters, to "turn into gold the cutting of a zoo leopard's toenails, the gift of a violin to a homeless musician, the humdrum life in a small town that a young soldier overseas longs for."

Born in Brooklyn on September 1, 1898, Berger grew up in a slum, quitting high school after only two terms because of his family's poverty. His father, a Czechoslovakian immigrant, was a tailor; and his mother operated a candy store. They had eleven children. Meyer started hawking newspapers at eight years old and joined the New York *World* as a night messenger three years later. He ran copy between Park Row and the *World's* downtown Brooklyn offices.

The *World's* writers were some of the best in the business; and the unassuming lad feasted on the stories, personalities, atmosphere, and excitement of the newsroom. When he wasn't carrying copy, he was picking up hot coffee and sandwiches for the staff, holding the orders close to his body for warmth during cold winter nights. When copy was in, he would "stand near the long copy table in the cavernous old *World* office and watch the poker games," he recounted. "Here I absorbed all the legends of the craft, ancient and contemporary. I contracted news print fever in this way, by a kind of osmosis. Here I learned, I think, a sounder journalism than is now taught in grayer halls of learning. The men from whom I caught this fever have, for the greater part, died of it. They didn't know, but they were my faculty. I was their sole student."

He worked at the newspaper until World War I when he enlisted in the Army. Too nearsighted to pass the eye exam, he memorized the chart. Later, he said he fought in the war without ever seeing it. He served in France, rose to the rank of sergeant, and won a Silver Star. While under heavy fire, he carried four wounded men back to American lines. He was wounded in the battle and received the Purple Heart. After the war, he rejoined the *World* as a police reporter in Brooklyn. Later, he joined the Standard News Association. In 1928 he signed on as the chief rewrite man for the new

Brooklyn-Queens section of the New York *Times*. His stories on Brooklyn gangsters and murders propelled him to the main newsroom.

He made his mark with his coverage of the Al Capone tax evasion trial. It was his first out-of-town assignment. His stories on the trial were so enthralling that work in the *Times'* newsroom would stop as copy boys, copyreaders, and editors read them page by page as they came off the telegraph machines. In those stories one can find many of the techniques that accounted for the quality of Berger's writing, including the description of character through concrete details and actions, precise word choice, and the use of dynamic verbs and common, colorful language. Berger culled many of the fascinating comments originating in the trial and spliced them together for a memorable lead on one of the stories:

Capone the generous, Capone the spendthrift, lord of the great estate on Palm Island, Fla., with a cupboard-bank holding "rolls that would choke an ox," with a telephone bill for three short winters totaling $9,000; spending $7,000 for meat to feed his he-men guards, thousands for linens, drapes, cakes and macaroni, was sketched on the Federal court canvas today by a dozen witnesses imported from Florida to testify against him in his trial for income tax evasion.

It was glum Capone that started from the court chamber when the session ended at noon. He had been hit hard by the testimony. Outside the streets were wet with a depressing downpour.

Following this metaphorical lead, Berger recreated the tension in the trial by describing what a witness did rather than just what he said. "The witness smiled uneasily at Capone; but the gang chief's lips seemed pursed in anger, and his eyes indicated a rising temper," Berger wrote. The witness "did a little nervous lip work on his own account and faced the prosecutor again." In a later passage in the story, Berger described the nervous fear of the defendant. "The witness," he wrote, "hesitated, glanced fleetingly at the defendant, where the storm signals, as indicated on the facial barometer, were becoming stronger."

Six days later, Berger described the closing arguments in which the defense attorneys pleaded with a "farmer jury" to acquit Capone. "And Capone drank it in," Berger wrote. The gangster, Berger implied, was not too bright. "A mint kept his ponderous jaws moving as he gave ear to the word painting of his counsel. Even the parts about the Punic wars, about Cato, about the *Arabian Nights*, and *The Old Man of the Sea* held him in rapt attention, though there seems to be a reasonable doubt as to whether he grasped the full meaning of it all. It sounded good." In a follow-up story, Berger allowed Capone's actions to tell the story. "Throughout the proceedings," he wrote, "Capone with a far-away look in his eyes, fussed with the brief-case straps, picked at a bandage that covered his right forefinger, ran his pudgy palm across his face and watched himself jiggle his own feet. If he understood the drift of the arguments or was at all interested in what bearing they might have on his fate, he did not show it. Even his blue, pencil-striped suit was guilty of indifference. It looked baggy and relaxed." Berger's account of the trial, which was marked by factual detail mixed with interpretation and spiced with humor, was nominated for the 1932 Pulitzer Prize.

A little more than three years later, Berger sat in the gallery to watch another sensational tax-evasion trial. The star was Arthur Flegenheimer, known by friends as Dutch Schultz, one of New York's big three racketeers. Unlike Capone, whom Berger painted as a large, uneducated grouch, Schultz was "an omnivorous reader," who might have risen to great heights in some other field if he had wanted a "straight" career. Berger described him as "a broad-shouldered, well-groomed man with a pleasant manner." As with his stories about Capone, Berger showed a keen sense of detail in writing about Schultz:

"Dutch" Schultz's round face was wreathed in continual amusement in the Federal court this afternoon as a dozen Bronx detectives paraded to the stand to testify that they tapped his telephone lines in 1929-30, talked with him in his Third Avenue speakeasy, and heard him boast of controlling the window cleaners' racket in his territory, north of Manhattan.

He would not disclose the reason, when the day's session

closed, why the procession of police witnesses appealed so strongly to his sense of humor. He waved that off.

Schultz grudgingly admitted that he liked Berger's stories but was offended when Berger quoted a source as saying Schultz was a "pushover for a blonde." He confronted Berger about the line. "But it's true, isn't it?" Berger asked nervously. "Yes," Schultz said, "but what kind of language is that to use in the New York *Times*?"

Each of Berger's stories on the trial began with a summary of the day's top events and an explanation of what they meant to either side. He then gave a dramatic blow-by-blow description of the trial. These accounts, sparkling with colorful language, chronicled the rise and fall of fortunes in the trial. For example, the "up-state" jurymen "gulped down the testimony"; "the defense dikes in [the] trial...burst in Federal Court today"; and "the government then introduced a parade of Bronx citizens who seemed a bit touchy about describing the nature of their business during prohibition." In another story, Berger used colorful verbs to describe Schultz's fury and frustration when the jury failed to reach a verdict quickly:

As Schultz paced his anxious beat while daylight faded and night came on with still no verdict in the trial, which began on April 15, perspiration glistened on his forehead and wilted his white starched shirt collar.

"The suspense is awful," he said, pausing in his restless march, and his grin, when he said it, was sickly.

He devoured every rumor on how the jury was standing. Though insisting that he was "calm," he finally said:

"There's a certain amount of strain, but I can stand it."

The jury stalemated 7-5 in favor of a guilty verdict. Schultz survived the trial, but he was murdered in October of that same year.

Gangsters like Schultz and Capone were big news in the 1930s, and Berger became an expert on the subject. They were colorful characters, and Berger used common English to paint memorable images of them. Of the notorious killer Louis "Lepke" Buchalter, he wrote, "Former Lepke aides and gunmen made corpses on Catskill, Brooklyn, and Bronx landscapes. They were burned with gasoline, buried in quicklime, shot, stabbed with icepicks, garroted—all on the orders of the little man with the fawnlike stare and the uneasy and diffident front."

One of his most memorable stories dealt with the death of Brooklyn mobster Abe Reles, who fell or was pushed from the Half Moon Hotel on Coney Island in 1940. "Mr. Berger stood on the window-sill of Reles' room," wrote a critic, "and described what Reles saw and heard, and how he must have felt. It sounded quite artless, like all of Mr. Berger's prose, but that was the art in it."

Berger sailed overseas at the beginning of World War II and spent his spare time cheering up the wounded. "Mike told stories as well as he wrote them," recalled fellow *Times* reporter Devlin, "and as he reeled off anecdote after anecdote the wounded men almost forgot their pain. A nurse in an air-evacuation hospital in Europe remembered one evening when the doctor in charge of her ward said, 'You can skip the sedatives tonight. That *Times* reporter is here again.'"

In England Berger had continuing trouble with ulcers, and he returned to the States after two months. He continued to cover the war, but shifted his emphasis to the effect it was having on the people at home. After traveling with a trainload of wounded soldiers, he wrote a touching story that was reprinted in *Time* magazine. *Time* called Berger one of the "most professional of U.S. reporters." It was a story, the magazine declared, that "well & truly evoked the heartbreaking feelings of the returning soldier." Note the concrete details of Berger's observations and how they help the reader to see the scene:

In the car's faint, diffused light you see a bandaged blond head, a young arm in a stiff cast, a leg that stops short of full length. Occasional splashes of illumination from war plants along the right of way jerk over the sleeping forms, swim frantically on the ceiling, slide down the walls.

The little nurse, ghostly white in starched garb, moves quietly down the carpeted aisle. She peers anxiously at each sleeping ace, gently lifts a wounded leg or bandaged arm to replace it on the mattress. A restless soldier leans from an upper bunk and murmurs. The nurse brings a sleeping powder in water, and the soldier throws the dose down his throat, whispers thanks, sinks back to try for sleep again.

In describing the impact an army hospital had on the 9,000 residents of Phoenixville, Pennsylvania, Berger wrote a story as it might have been told by an old citizen:

Well, you see blind boys tapping their way down Main Street, finding their way into the post office, and into the stores, with instructors trailing them, and it's not easy to keep your eyes off them. You're going about your own business, and you run smack into a couple of boys with no noses, no ears and maybe only slits for mouths, like so many have, and I don't care who you are, you're bound to be startled.

Well, maybe we did stare, a little, but that was only the first few times. We learned mighty fast that staring made those boys more bitter than anything else. They'd go back to the hospital thinking, "That's the way it's going to be; wherever we go we'll be goggled at like circus freaks, or monsters," and the nurses and the doctors and the psychiatrists up there would have to work like the dickens to coax them out of it.

The story illustrates Berger's willingness to take risks, to broaden the boundaries of style, and to challenge accepted thinking.

In 1939 Berger began to write the "About New York" column. It was discontinued in 1940 because of a shortage of newsprint, but then reinstated in 1953. Although he devoted all his time to reporting, he enjoyed roaming through the city on his vacations looking for anecdotes, story ideas, and pictures. "New York couldn't run out of stories, it just couldn't," he said. "There are a million plots every day, and a million different twists to make the story." His passion for the city was reflected in the following lines:

New York's voice speaks mystery....It has a soft, weird music, a symphony of winds at high altitudes, of muted traffic in endless serpentine twisting over city hills and grades, of jet hiss and propeller thrum, of the hoarse call of tugs on many waters, of great liners standing in from the broad sea, or moving out. You hear another voice when you stand on the Brooklyn Bridge in early morning; the sigh of great smokestacks, the raspy breathing of tugs, the gull flocks, sighing wind in the bridge cables, the quivering complaint of the whole span under its moving freight.

Such writing earned Berger prestige and success, but he refused to become a prima donna. When he became a columnist, he rejected the idea of moving into his own office. Instead, he preferred to keep his desk in the middle of the newsroom, surrounded by noise, commotion, and people.

He continued, as he had done as a youth on the New York World, to roam the newsroom of the *Times'*, now helping copy boys, college students, and cub reporters feel at home on the staff. He regaled them with tales from the past and awed them with his talent.

After knocking out his first story as a reporter for the New York *Times,* John C. Devlin yelled, "Copy." But no copy boy showed up to snatch his page.

"I'll take it," said a soft voice beside him. Devlin turned to see a "spindly, bald-headed man, wearing horn-rimmed glasses." The man smiled, took the page from Devlin's hands, and walked away. The reporter at the next desk leaned over and said, "You know who that was, don't you— Mike Berger! He's pretending to be a copy boy. He wouldn't want you to get nervous on your first night here, waiting to have your copy picked up."

Berger died on February 8, 1950, at the age of sixty. One of his last columns dealt with a blind, destitute 82-year-old violinist having the opportunity to play again. "The long years on the Bowery had not stolen [his] touch," Berger wrote. "Blindness made his fingers stumble down to the violin bridge, but they recovered. The music died and the audience pattered applause. The old violinist bowed and his sunken cheeks creased in a smile."

In writing that story, Berger could have been thinking of himself. He had never studied journalism in college, but he became, as one colleague said, "a school of journalism, top drawer, all by himself."

●◇

AMERICA'S DEAD ARRIVE FROM WORLD WAR II

In 1947 Berger covered the arrival of the first war dead from Europe. His moving account appeared in the New York *Times,* over the objection of Arthur Hays Sulzberger, the publisher. Sulzberger wanted the story killed because he had wept when he read it. He fired off a memo to the managing editor forbidding him to print any "stories that make me cry." The story made many others cry and became one of the most memorable stories of the war era.

400,000 IN SILENT TRIBUTE AS WAR DEAD COME HOME
Meyer Berger
New York *Times*
October 27, 1947

The first war dead from Europe came home yesterday. The harbor was steeped in Sabbath stillness as they came in on the morning tide in 6,248 coffins in the hold of the transport *Joseph V. Connolly.* One coffin, borne from the ship in a caisson, moved through the city's streets to muffled drumbeats and slow cadenced marches, and 400,000 New Yorkers along the route and at a memorial service in Central Park paid it the tribute of reverent silence and unhidden tears.

At the service on the Sheep Meadow, chaplains of three faiths prayed for the soldier dead. Their words, and the choking sadness of taps, suspended in quivering, unseasonal heat, evoked women's sobs and caught at men's throats.

The transport *Joseph V. Connolly* broke through the haze outside the Narrows at nine A.M., a shadowy hulk all gray and tan, with a funeral wreath at her forepeak. Nothing moved on her decks. The coffin picked out for the service, guarded by men at attention, was out on the boat deck.

The *Connolly's* escort wheeled into line—the destroyers *Bristol* and *Beaty;* the gleaming white coast-guard cutter *Spencer;* five of the city's fireboats and other small craft. Seamen aboard the destroyers, ordered to man the rails, stepped to their stations and came to rigid attention. A breeze played with their hair and toyed with their kerchiefs. The ship's ensign, half-masted, stirred in the wind, and at 9:15 A.M. foam flowed from the *Connolly's* prow and the craft moved toward the harbor.

The pace was slow, a bare ten knots. Buoys tolled and lapsed into quiet. There was a stir on the *Bristol's* fantail, and Corporal Carroll Ripley, a marine, raised his trumpet; and Church Call, muted and tender, hung over the waters. Rear Admiral John J. Brady retired, opened a prayer: "O god ____" but a wind tore the invocation to tatters.

Sailors poised at the rails heard low commands, and floral tributes mounted on plywood hit the sea with loud splashes—a nine-foot cross, a great star of David, an anchor, a nine-foot American flag. Then smaller floats from various organizations. They were caught in the *Connolly's* wake.

Then there were more prayers, by Jewish and Protestant chaplains, and the words of the Twenty-third Psalm: "The Lord is my shepherd." Escorting planes hovered over the marine procession, drowned out the words. Volleys from cannon crashed and echoed over the waters.

When the prayers ended, the bugler played taps, and the quavering notes hung in the sunlit air. Then the craft plowed onward between the mist-shrouded shores in deep, dimensional silence.

Down in the lower harbor the vacant towers of Manhattan rose in the haze like white and gray tombstones towering skyward. Richmond-bound ferryboats glided in silence to port of the marine procession, their flags at half-mast. Crowds on their decks were bareheaded, and the passengers bowed as in prayer.

Then cannon boomed again, and the sound was like echoing thunder. This salute was from the *USS Missouri*, far off to port, paying its tribute of twenty-one guns. The echoes rolled, rumbling, to the horizon. Then silence closed again.

The *Connolly* turned into her berth. A young ensign poised at the *Bristol's* rail murmured to a chief yeoman: "They came in too late. The 'Welcome Home' signs and the signs with 'Well Done' are all painted out, or have faded. There's something ironic in that."

At 12:45 the coffin borne from the *Connolly* was set on a caisson. Women who saw this wept openly, and men turned away. Somewhere a bugle sounded, to move a procession of more than six thousand—servicemen, veterans, city groups.

The curbs were crowded, but here, as at sea, the silence was awesome. Nobody spoke, not even the children. Eyes were moist, and lips moved in prayer as the flag-draped coffin passed, the caisson drawn by a dark armored car with two sergeants, arms folded, high in the turret.

Mounted police led the procession. Their horses' hooves pattered lightly on the soft pavement. Far down the line came the music—the slow soft tones of the dirges—and the slow, measured cadence of slow-marching boots. No other sounds broke in, except an occasional plane, or the voice of an officer chanting the step.

The procession stopped at the Eternal Light. The great square there was hollow, and the sun struck through the withering leaves in the park. General Courtney Hodges, who had led some of the men whose bodies came home in the *Connolly's* hold, got from his car, and placed a wreath on the Light.

Then came the long march up Fifth Avenue's pavement. The crowds at the curb were moved. Some let the tears run freely. Some wiped them away. Some made the sign of the cross as the caisson rolled past them. In Fifth Avenue's canyons, muted brass played *Onward, Christian Soldiers*.

The marchers were grim. Behind the mounted police came the West Point cadets, then a battalion of middies. The boots of the Eighty-second Airborne beat out a steady step, and the sun struck lights from their helmets. There were marines and sailors, Waves and Spars and Wacs, winding slowly up midtown hill, paced by the drumbeat.

Rockefeller Center was thronged. The bells of St. Patrick's Cathedral wafted a muted knell, and the light Sabbath breezes carried it far down the street until it quivered away in the stillness.

Outside the park, a little streetsweeper held his broom stiffly with his left hand while his right hand rose in salute as the caisson rolled past him. No one smiled. Men and women stared at the streetsweeper with grave understanding, and bowed their heads to their chests in silent salute.

Out on the Meadow some forty thousand men and

women, seated, rose from the camp chairs to see the divisions wheel into place in solid phalanxes. Heat haze dimmed the apartment houses, created a blue smoky look in the autumnal trees, touched all things with smooth softness....

In a front row, a woman started up, stretched out her arms, and screamed the name, "Johnny!" The dirge lifted and fell. Then in a brief space of silence the woman screamed again: "There's my boy, there's my boy!" and other women, beside her, put comforting arms on her shoulders. She stifled her cries, but her shoulders shook.

Eight pallbearers lifted the coffin and bore it up a ramp to the catafalque. As it came to rest, the men in the copse fired one last round of the salute, and a silence, thicker than any before, fell on the meadow. Now the sobbing was even more general. Men hid their faces. Women shook with emotion....

It was four o'clock then. The sun was down in the park's western trees, and the Meadow lay under autumnal afternoon shadow. The houses on Central Park West had receded deeper in gloom, save where the sun was gold on high windows. A firing squad mounted the ramp and, upon crisp command, tore at the blanket of silence with three even volleys. A West Point bugler hung taps over the Meadow. The pallbearers came up the ramps again, four from each side, and bent to the handles. The West Point Band, with muffled instruments, played *Nearer, My God, to Thee* as the pallbearers lifted their burden and started to carry it to the caisson. Emotional tension could almost be felt in waves.

Again the mother down front shrilled, "Johnny, my Johnny," and the accents carried, and they hurt. Men bit at their lips.

The coffin, still wrapped in the flag, was set gently back on the caisson. The honor guard took up position behind it. The armored car rolled, and the caisson swayed slightly, came true, and followed. It rolled southward out of the park into the twilight, with the U.S. Army Band sending after it the sweet melancholy of the dirge *The Vanished Army*.

◆

BERSERK GUNMAN GOES ON NEIGHOBORHOOD KILLING SPREE

Berger's best-known story chronicled a deranged military veteran as he stalked a block in Camden, New Jersey, killing twelve people and wounding four. For six hours Berger retraced the steps of Howard Unruh, an angry psychopath, and then wrote a 4,000-word story under deadline pressure. The New York *Times* printed the story without changing a word. For his work, Berger received the Pulitzer Prize for Reporting in 1950. He sent the $1,000 prize money to Unruh's mother.

VETERAN KILLS 12 IN MAD RAMPAGE ON CAMDEN STREET
Meyer Berger
New York *Times*
September 7, 1949

CAMPDEN, N.J., Sept. 6—Howard B. Unruh, 28 years old, a mild, soft-spoken veteran of many armored artillery battles in Italy, France, Austria, Belgium and Germany, killed twelve persons with a war souvenir Luger pistol in his home block in East Camden this morning. He wounded four others.

Unruh, a slender, hollow-cheeked six-footer paradoxically devoted to scripture reading and to constant practice with firearms, had no previous history of mental illness, but specialists indicated tonight that there was no doubt that he was a psychiatric case, and that he had secretly nursed a persecution complex for two years or more.

The veteran was shot in the left thigh by a local tavern keeper, but he kept that fact secret, too, while policemen and Mitchell Cohen, Camden County prosecutor, questioned him at police headquarters for more than two hours immediately after tear gas bombs had forced him out of his bedroom to surrender.

The blood stain he left on the seat he occupied during the

questioning betrayed his wound. When it was discovered, he was taken to Cooper Hospital in Camden, a prisoner charged with murder. He was as calm under questioning as he was during the twenty minutes that he was shooting men, women and children. Only occasionally excessive brightness of his dark eyes indicated that he was anything other than normal.

He told the prosecutor that he had been building up resentment against neighbors and neighborhood shopkeepers for a long time. "They have been making derogatory remarks about my character," he said. His resentment seemed most strongly concentrated against Mr. and Mrs. Maurice Cohen, who lived next door to him. They are among the dead.

Mr. Cohen was a druggist with a shop at 3202 River Road in East Camden. He and his wife had had frequent sharp exchanges over the Unruhs' use of a gate that separates their back yard from the Cohens'. Mrs. Cohen had also complained of young Unruh's keeping his bedroom radio turned high into the late night hours. None of the other victims had ever had trouble with him.

Unruh, a graduate of Woodrow Wilson High School here, had started a GI course in pharmacy at Temple University in Philadelphia some time after he was honorably discharged from the service in 1945, but had stayed with it only three months. In recent months he had been unemployed and apparently was not even looking for work.

His mother, Mrs. Rita Unruh, 50, is separated from her husband. She works as a packer in Evanson Soap Company in Camden, and hers was virtually the only family income. James Unruh, 25 years old, her younger son, is married and lives in Haddon Heights, N.J. He works for the Curtis Publishing Company.

On Monday night, Howard Unruh left the house alone. He spent the night at the Family Theatre on Market Street in Philadelphia to sit through several showings of the double feature motion picture there—"I Cheated the Law" and "The Lady Gambles." It was just 3 o'clock this morning when he got home.

Prosecutor Cohen said that Unruh told him later that before he fell asleep this morning he had made up his mind to shoot the persons who had "talked about me," that he had even figured out that 9:30 A.M. would be the time to begin because most of the stores in his block would be open at that hour.

His mother, leaving her ironing when he got up, prepared his breakfast in their drab little three-room apartment in the shabby gray two-story stucco house at the corner of River Road and Thirty-Second Street. After breakfast he loaded one clip of bullets into his Luger, slipped another clip into his pocket, and carried sixteen loose cartridges in addition. He also carried a tear-gas pen with six shells and a sharp six-inch knife.

He took one last look around his bedroom before he left the house. On the peeling walls he had crossed pistols, crossed German bayonets, pictures of armored artillery in action. Scattered about the chamber were machetes, a Roy Rogers pistol, ash trays made of German shells, clips of 30-30 cartridges for rifle use and a host of varied war souvenirs.

Mrs. Unruh had left the house some minutes before, to call on Mrs. Caroline Pinner, a friend in the next block. Mrs Unruh had sensed, apparently, that her son's smoldering resentments were coming to head. She had pleaded with Elias Pinner, her friend's husband, to cut a little gate in the Unruhs' backyard so that Howard need not use the Cohen gate again. Mr. Pinner finished the gate early Monday evening after Howard had gone to Philadelphia.

At the Pinners' house at 9 o'clock this morning, Mrs. Unruh had murmured something about Howard's eyes; how strange they looked and how worried she was about him.

A few minutes later River Road echoed and re-echoed with pistol fire. Howard Unruh was on the rampage. His mother, who had left the Pinners' little white house only a few seconds before, turned back. She hurried through the door. She cried, "Oh Howard, oh, Howard, they're to blame for this." She rushed past Mrs. Pinner, a kindly gray-haired woman of 70. She said, "I've got to use the phone; may I use the phone?"

But before she had crossed the living room to reach for it she fell on the faded carpet in a dead faint. The Pinners lifted her onto the couch in the next room. Mrs Pinner applied aromatic spirits to revive her.

While his mother writhed on the sofa in her house dress and worn old sweater, coming back to consciousness,

Howard Unruh was walking from shop to shop in the "3200 block" with deadly calm, sporting Luger in hand. Children screamed as they tumbled over one another to get out of his way. Men and women dodged into open shops, the women shrill with panic, men hoarse with fear. No one could quite understand for a time what had been loosed in the block.

Unruh first walked into John Pijarchik's shoe repair shop near the north end of his own side of the street. The cobbler started up from his bench but went down with a bullet in his stomach. A little boy who was in the shop ran behind the counter and crouched there in terror. Unruh walked out into the sunlit street.

"I shot them in the chest first," he told the prosecutor later, in meticulous detail, "and then I aimed for the head." His aim was devastating—and with reason. He had won marksmanship and sharpshooters' ratings in the service, and he practiced with his Luger all the time on a target set up in the cellar of his home.

Unruh told the prosecutor afterward that he had Cohen the druggist, the neighborhood cobbler and the neighborhood tailor on his mental list of persons who had "talked about him." He went methodically about wiping them out. Oddly enough, he did not start with the druggist, against whom he seemed to have the sharpest feelings, but left him almost for the last.

From the cobbler's he went into the little tailor shop at 3214 River Road. The tailor was out. Helga Zegrino, 28 years old, the tailor's wife, was there alone. The couple, incidentally, had been married only one month. She screamed when Unruh walked in with his Luger in hand. Some people across the street heard her. Then the gun blasted again, and Mrs. Zegrino pitched over dead. Unruh walked into the sunlight again.

All this was only a matter of seconds, and still only a few persons had begun to understand what was afoot. Down the street at 3210 River Road is Clark Hoover's little country barber shop. In the center was a white-painted carousel-type horse for the children customers. Orris Smith, a blonde boy only 6 years old, was in it, with a bib around his neck, submitting to a shearing. His mother, Mrs. Catherine Smith, 42, sat on a chair against the wall and watched.

She looked up. Clark Hoover turned from his work to see the six-footer, gaunt and tense, but silent, standing in the doorway with the Luger. Unruh's brown tropical worsted suit was barred with morning shadow. The sun lay bright in his crew-cut brown hair. He wore no hat. Mrs. Smith could not understand what was about to happen.

Unruh walked to "Brux"—that is Mrs. Smith's nickname for her little boy—and put the Luger to the child's chest. The shot echoed and reverberated in the little 12 by 12 shop. The little boy's head pitched toward the wound, his hair, half-cut, stained with red. Unruh said never a word. He put the Luger close to the shaking barber's hand. Before the horrified mother, Unruh leaned over and fired another shot into Hoover.

The veteran made no attempt to kill Mrs. Smith. He did not seem to hear her screams. He turned his back and stalked out, unhurried. A few doors north, Dominick Latela, who runs a little restaurant, had come to his shop window to learn what the shooting was about. He saw Unruh cross the street toward Frank Engel's tavern. Then he saw Mrs. Smith stagger out with her pitiful burden. Her son's head lolled over the crook of her right arm.

Mrs. Smith screamed, "My boy is dead. I know, he's dead." She stared about her, looking in vain for aid. No one but Howard Unruh was in sight, and he was concentrating on the tavern. Latela dashed out, but first he shouted to his wife, Dora, who was in the restaurant with their daughter Eleanor, 6 years old. He hollered, "I'm going out. Lock the door behind me." He ran for his car and drove it down toward Mrs. Smith as she stood on the pavement with her son.

Latela took the child from her arms and placed him on the car's front seat. He pushed the mother into the rear seat, slammed the doors and headed for Cooper Hospital. Howard Unruh had not turned. Engle, the tavern keeper, had locked his own door. His customers, the bartender, and a porter made a concerted rush for the rear of the saloon. The bullets tore through the tavern door paneling. Engle rushed upstairs and got out his .38 caliber pistol, then rushed to the street window of his apartment.

Unruh was back in the center of the street. He fired a shot at an apartment window at 3208 River Road. Tommy Hamilton, 2 years old, fell back with the bullet in his head. Unruh went north again to Latela's place. He fired a shot at the door and kicked in the lower glass panel. Mrs. Latela crouched behind the counter with her daughter. She heard the bullets, but neither she nor her child was touched. Unruh walked back toward Thirty-second Street, reloading the Luger.

Now the little street—a small block with only five buildings on one side, three one-story stores on the other—was shrill with women's and children's panicky outcries. A group of six or seven little boys and girls fled past Unruh. They screamed "Crazy man!" and unintelligible sentences. Unruh did not seem to hear or see them.

Alvin Day, a television repairman who lives in near-by Mantus, had heard the shooting, but driving into the street he was not aware of what had happened. Unruh walked up to the car window as Day rolled by, and fired once through the window, with deadly aim. The repairman fell against the steering wheel. The car seemed to wabble. The front wheels hit the opposite curb and stalled. Day was dead.

Frank Engel had thrown open his second-floor apartment window. He saw Unruh pause for a moment in a narrow alley between the cobbler's shop and a little two-story home. He aimed and fired. Unruh stopped for just a second. The bullet had hit, but he did not seem to mind, after the initial brief shock. He headed toward the corner drug store, and Engle did not fire again.

"I wish I had," he said, later. "I could have killed him then. I could have put a half-dozen shots into him. I don't know why I didn't do it."

Cohen, the druggist, a heavy man of 40, had run into the street shouting "What's going on here? what's going on here?" but at sight of Unruh hurried back into his shop. James J. Hutton, 45, an insurance agent from Westmont, N.J., started out the drug shop to see what the shooting was about. Like so many others, he had figured at first that it was some car backfiring. He came face to face with Unruh.

Unruh said quietly, "Excuse me sir," and started to push past him. Later Unruh told the police: "That man didn't act fast enough. He didn't get out of my way." He fired into Hutton's head and body. The insurance man pitched onto the sidewalk and lay still.

Cohen had run to his upstairs apartment and had tried to warn Minnie Cohen, 63, his mother, and Rose, his wife, 38, to hide. His son Charles, 14, was in the apartment, too. Mrs.

Cohen shoved the boy into a clothes closet and leaped into another closet herself. She pulled the door to. The druggist, meanwhile, had leaped from the window onto a porch roof. Unruh, a gaunt figure at the window behind him, fired into the druggist's back. The druggist, still running, bounded off the roof and lay dead in Thirty-second Street.

Unruh fired into the closet where Mrs. Cohen was hidden. She fell dead behind the closed door, and he did not bother to open it. Mrs. Minnie Cohen tried to get to the telephone in an adjoining bedroom to call the police. Unruh fired shots into her head and body, and she sprawled dead on the bed. Unruh walked down the stairs with his Luger reloaded and came out into the street again.

A coupe had stopped at River Road, obeying the red light. The passengers obviously had no idea of what was loose in East Camden, and no one had a chance to tell them. Unruh walked up to the car, and, though it was filled with total strangers, fired deliberately at them, one by one, through the windshield. He killed the two women passengers, Mrs. Helen Matlack Wilson, 43, of Pennsauken, who was driving, and her mother, Mrs. Emma Matlack, 66. Mrs. Wilson's son John, 12, was badly wounded. A bullet pierced his neck, just below the jawbone.

Earl Horner, clerk in the American Stores Company, a grocery opposite the drug store, had locked his front door after several passing men, women and children had tumbled breathlessly into the shop panting "crazy man...killing people...." Unruh came up to the door and fired two shots through the wood panelling. Horner, his customers, the refugees from the veteran's merciless gunfire, crouched, trembling, behind the counter. None there was hurt.

"He tried the door before he shot in here," Horner related afterward. "He just stood there, stony-faced and grim, and rattled the knob, before he started to fire. Then he turned away."

Charlie Petersen, 18, son of a Camden fireman, came driving down the street with two friends when Unruh turned from the grocery. The three boys got out to stare at Hutton's body lying unattended on the sidewalk. They did not know who had shot the insurance man or why, and, like the women in the car, had no warning that Howard Unruh was on the loose. The veteran brought his Luger to sight and fired several times. Young Petersen fell with bullets in his legs. His friends tore pell-mell down the street to safety.

Mrs. Helen Harris of 1250 North Twenty-eighth Street with her daughter, Helen, a 6-year-old blonde child, and a Mrs. Horowitz with her daughter, Linda, 5, turned into Thirty-second Street. They had heard the shooting from a distance, but thought it was auto backfire.

Unruh passed them in Thirty-second Street and walked up the sagging four steps of a little yellow dwelling back of his own house. Mrs. Madeline Harrie, a woman in her late thirties, and her two sons, Armand, 16, and Leroy, 15, were in the house. A third son, Wilson, 14, was barricaded in the grocery with other customers.

Unruh threw open the front door with gun in hand and walked into the dark little parlor. He fired two shots at Mrs. Harrie. They went wild and entered the wall. A third shot caught her in the left arm. She screamed. Armand leaped at Unruh, to tackle him. The veteran used the Luger butt to drop the boy, then fired two shots into his arms. Upstairs Leroy heard the shooting and the screams. He hid under a bed.

By this time, answering a flood of hysterical telephone calls from various parts of East Camden, police radio cars swarmed into River Road with sirens wide open. Emergency crews brought machine guns, shotguns and tear gas bombs.

Sergeant Earl Wright, one of the first to leap to the sidewalk, saw Charles Cohen, the druggist's son. The boy was half out of the second-floor apartment window, just above where his father lay dead. He was screaming, "He's going to kill me. He's killing everybody." The boy was hysterical.

Wright bounded up the stairs to the druggist's apartment. He saw the dead woman on the bed, and tried to soothe the druggist's son. He brought him downstairs and turned him over to other policemen, then joined the men who had surrounded the two-story stucco house where Unruh lived. Unruh, meanwhile, had fired about thirty shots. He was out of ammunition. Leaving the Harrie house, he had also heard the police sirens. He had run through the back gate to his own rear bedroom.

Edward Joslin, a motorcycle policeman, scrambled to the porch roof under Unruh's window. He tossed a tear-gas grenade through a pane of glass. Other policemen, hoarsely calling on Unruh to surrender, took positions with their machine guns and shotguns. They trained them on Unruh's window.

Meanwhile, a curious interlude had taken place. Philip W. Buxton, an assistant city editor on *The Camden Evening Courier*, had looked Unruh's name up in the telephone book. He called the number, Camden 4-2490W. It was just after 10 A.M., and Unruh had just returned to his room. To Mr. Buxton's astonishment, Unruh answered. He said hello in a calm, clear voice.

"This Howard?" Mr. Buxton asked.

"Yes, this is Howard. What's the last name of the party you want?"

"Unruh."

The veteran asked what Mr. Buxton wanted.

"I'm a friend," the newspaper man said. "I want to know what they're doing to you down there."

Unruh thought a moment. He said, "They haven't done anything to me—yet. I'm doing plenty to them." His voice was still steady without a trace of hysteria.

Mr. Buxton asked how many persons Unruh had killed.

The veteran answered: "I don't know. I haven't counted. Looks like a pretty good score."

"Why are you killing people?"

"I don't know," came the frank answer. "I can't answer that yet. I'll have to talk to you later. I'm too busy now."

The telephone banged down.

Unruh was busy. The tear gas was taking effect, and police bullets were thudding at the walls around him. During a lull in the firing, the police saw the white curtains move and the gaunt killer came into plain view.

"Okay," he shouted. "I give up. I'm coming down."

"Where's the gun?" a sergeant yelled.

"It's on my desk, up here in the room," Unruh called down quietly. "I'm coming down."

Thirty guns were trained on the shabby little back door. A few seconds later the door opened and Unruh stepped into the light, his hands up. Sergeant Wright came across the morning-glory and aster beds in the yard and snapped handcuffs on Unruh's wrists.

"What's the matter with you?" a policeman demanded hotly. "You a psycho?"

Unruh stared into the policeman's eyes—a level, steady stare. He said, "I'm no psycho. I have a good mind."

Word of the capture brought the whole East Camden populace pouring into the streets. Men and women screamed at Unruh, and cursed him in shrill accents and in hoarse anger. Someone cried "lynch him," but there was no movement. Sergeant Wright's men walked Unruh to a police car and started for headquarters.

Shouting and pushing men and women started after the car, but dropped back after a few paces, discussing the shootings, and the character of Howard Unruh. Little by little the original anger, born of fear, that had moved the crowd, began to die.

Men conceded that he probably was not in his right mind. Those who knew Unruh kept repeating how closemouthed he was, and how soft spoken. How he took his mother to church, and how he marked scripture passages, especially the prophecies.

"He was a quiet one, that guy," a man told the crowd in front of the tavern. "He was all the time figuring to do this thing. You gotta watch them quiet ones."

But all day River Road and the side streets talked of nothing else. The shock was great. Men and women kept saying: "We can't understand it. Just don't get it."

19

MARGUERITE HIGGINS

Tenacious Pursuer of News

The only woman to win a Pulitzer Prize for war correspondence, Marguerite Higgins aggressively pursued her stories on the battlefronts of Europe, Korea, and Vietnam.

Being a woman presented both handicaps and advantages in her work as a reporter. She did not expect special treatment because of her gender, but she was not ashamed to trade on her femininity if that got her the story. As *Newsweek* magazine said, "If Maggie Higgins elbowed other reporters in her dogged pursuit of the news, it was not because she was out to prove, as a crusading feminist, that women are equal to men. She did it because she believed the public has the right to know."

Her aggressiveness spilled over into her writing. She used strong, graphic language to describe scenes of war. She put the reader in the midst of battle, usually because she herself had been in the action. There was nothing soft about her writing style.

Yet, Higgins herself admitted her strength was in her newsgathering, not her writing. "For those who have the yen for reporting, but no gift with a metaphor, let me encourage you with the assurance that my writing was far from brilliant," she said in her autobiography, *News is a Singular Thing*.

There is, however, much to be said for her writing craftsmanship. She took her excellent reportorial skills and transferred the information she gathered into highly readable copy. Her writing was consistently good, although not always brilliant. She chose the right words, used active voice, illustrated her points with clear description—employed all the devices of the journalist in plying her trade. She filled her writing with concrete details and active verbs that transported the reader into the thick of battle. Her analytical pieces, exhibiting her sharp logic and intuition, carried the reader through the complexities of politics and war.

Recognizing that her writing was weaker than her reporting, she made a point of taking time and care to craft her stories. "Partly because I am a naturally slow writer and partly because of the fear of making an error," she explained, "it used to take me longer than most correspondents to accomplish the same thing. So in order to compete I just had to stick at it longer....I am not particularly quick mentally, but I am stubborn."

Her fear of errors came about because of her fear of her first city editor, L.L. Engelking, of the New York *Herald Tribune*. That fear caused her to check and double-check her stories so that she never had to tell "Engel" that she forgot to ask how to spell a name or had made a mistake. As a result, she earned a reputation for accurate reporting and earned the respect of the people she interviewed and of her fellow correspondents. During her career, she received more than fifty awards, including the Pulitzer and the Army campaign ribbon for outstanding service in World War II.

It was her determination and her accuracy that got her overseas in 1944. She was the only child of an Irish-American father and the French woman he married when he was a soldier in World War I. Born in Hong Kong in 1920, she spoke Chinese and French until the age of twelve when her family moved to Oakland, California. She graduated cum laude from the University of California and was editor of the campus paper. Just out of Columbia University's Graduate School of Journalism, she was hired by the *Herald Tribune* to be a local reporter. Her lifelong ambition, though, was to be a foreign correspondent, and she applied time and again for overseas duty, only to be turned down. She appealed to Helen Rogers Reid, the paper's publisher. Reid knew Higgins' reputation for tenacity and thoroughness, and soon Higgins found herself in France.

"I was a ruthless city editor with myself," she recalled. "Each day I read every single French paper, as well as

Agence France Press, the French wire service. Then I would assign myself to check the validity of every major news development....I went to the ministry or individual involved, and probed until I found out to my own satisfaction precisely what the facts were."

She also learned from her work on a metropolitan daily that accuracy and details are important to a story. She learned that reporters must be prepared. She lamented that such care and thoroughness are no longer taught to journalism students: "...Above all, you learned to do your homework: find out in advance as much as humanly possible about the individual or issue involved in a potential story so as not to waste time asking obvious questions that could be answered by any reference book or newspaper library.

"Aren't reporters taught this any more?" she asked with chagrin. "Time after time in touring the United States on lecture tours, I've been confronted by reporters who start off with some such question as 'Let's see now, is it the Associated Press you work for?' Like anybody else, my reaction to such lack of preparation is to wonder why the reporter bothers with the interview at all if he is going to handle it so carelessly."

While in Europe, Higgins covered the liberation of Buchenwald and of Dachau, two of the most notorious of the Nazi concentration camps. Some writers credited her with the actual liberation of Dauchau, saying she convinced the Nazi soldiers still inside the camp to surrender. Higgins herself said she and Sgt. Peter Furst of *Stars and Stripes* collected the guns of twenty-two soldiers after she persuaded them in German to surrender. Correspondents had difficulty conveying the facts of the Holocaust convincingly to readers in the United States, but Higgins took a powerful, straightforward approach. Rather than cover up the horrors she saw, she provided concrete details of the sites of the ovens and tortures that the prisoners endured.

While in Europe, she was prolific, filing 1,500 to 3,000 words a night. She often worked twenty hours a day. Her hard work paid off. After the war ended, she stayed on to cover the Nuremburg trials. She became the *Herald Tribune's* Berlin bureau chief in 1947 at a very young twenty-six. She then covered the beginning of the Cold War, was arrested twice by both the Russians and the Poles, and reported the Soviet blockade of Berlin.

Higgins' real success did not come, however, until the war in Korea. She was sent to the Tokyo bureau in 1950. Unhappy with the transfer, she protested the assignment—but, with what she called "her Irish Higgins' luck," she happened to be one of the first correspondents to report on the early days of the Korean War. While there, she was one of six correspondents to win the Pulitzer Prize covering the war.

However, she almost was prohibited from working in Korea. Lt. Gen. Walton H. Walker, convinced that women did not belong in a combat zone because they were too delicate for the hardness of war and of soldiers, ordered her out of North Korea in July 1950. She appealed to Gen. Douglas MacArthur, declaring that she was covering the war as a correspondent, not as a woman. MacArthur responded, "...Marguerite Higgins is held in highest professional esteem by everyone." She was allowed back in Korea. Carl Mydans, a *Life* magazine photographer covering the war, said Higgins had three campaign fronts in Korea: the war itself, her rivalry with competing correspondents, and the struggle to prove that being a correspondent had nothing to do with being a woman.

She and fellow *Herald Tribune* correspondent Homer Bigart battled for the front page. Their rivalry was the talk of the war because of the risks the two took to get their stories. Bigart resented sharing coverage with a woman; Higgins was determined to prove that she belonged in the war area. Their rivalry eventually ended in mutual respect.

The cause of the rivalry was Higgins' aggressiveness. She spurred Bigart and her other male competitors to work hard. She woke up earlier, slept less, and wrote more, forcing the others to come up with better stories than they would have if she had not been there. Such comments as one by *Time* magazine—"As an all-round journalist, News-hen Higgins may not be up to her *Tribune* colleague, Homer Bigart,...or with some of the other crack correspondents in Korea"—just spurred her to work harder, sometimes twenty-four hours a day.

There was resentment among the correspondents, too. "Higgins is about as winsome as a maddened adder," said one competitor. "[She won't] let anything get in the way of her ambition to spend each day on the front page of the New York *Herald Tribune!*" Among other things, some reporters re-

sented her friendship with Gen. MacArthur. He once invited
her forward on the plane on her return to Korea. He gave her
information about ground troops that others felt she got because she was a woman. She admitted that being a woman
had its drawbacks, but she also had the advantage of getting
more attention.

While she knew that, however, she refused to allow or to
ask anyone to treat her any differently. One Army colonel
wanted to send her back because of "trouble." "Trouble," she
replied, "is news, and the gathering of news is my job." She
once wrote, "I have since observed that many minorities—
including women correspondents—have a tendency to wear
chips on their shoulders, and these frequently consist of taking the attitude that you are bound to be gypped out of an appointment or a promotion solely on the grounds that you are a
woman, or a Jew, or a Negro. This attitude offers great and
comforting opportunities of fooling yourself because it pre-
vents your facing up to the fact that just possibly the reason
you aren't going to receive a certain promotion is that your
talents aren't up to it."

Higgins did more than perhaps any other woman to
prove that women can be correspondents and do the job as
well as any man. Her bravery and aggressive approach to
reporting clearly served her well enough to cover wars.

Despite the controversy surrounding her willingness to
trade on her femininity, journalists still respected her
work. Said one competitor: "Maggie was a cross between Al-
ice in Wonderland and Eleanor Roosevelt. She regarded the
world with wide-eyed excitement, then rolled up her sleeves
determined to do something about it."

Her coverage of the Korean war action, most of which she
reported first-hand, was spectacular. She traveled about in
her Jeep, becoming a familiar figure in her muddy gray
tennis shoes, baggy pants, khaki shirt, and fatigue cap. Normally, she carried only her typewriter and a musette bag
with her personal articles and food, and she often slept on the
ground. Her stories were exciting and made clear to readers
that she was in the thick of things. Said Col. Richard
Stephens of the 21st Infantry Regiment: "We've learned
Maggie will eat, sleep and fight like the rest of us, and that's
a ticket to our outfit any day." She once helped at a temporary
aid station by holding plasma bottles for the wounded men

while the station was being shelled. She provided readers with a sense of her routine with this lead to one of her stories: "A reinforced American patrol, accompanied by this correspondent this afternoon barreled eight miles through enemy territory....The jeep flew faster than the bullets which knicked just in back of our right rear tire."

Along with her personal effects, she sometimes carried a carbine. "Most correspondents," she explained, "carried arms of some kind. The enemy had no qualms about shooting unarmed civilians. And the fighting line was so fluid that no place near the front lines was safe from sudden attack."

Often her editors did not know where she was. Once after an unusually long silence, they finally received a delayed dispatch across the wire describing the landing at Inchon. Higgins was with the fifth wave of Marines. Both she and Bigart received front-page play with their stories on the landing. Higgins' story is reprinted in this anthology.

She was outspoken in her stories and did not shrink from telling the truth about the sometimes wastful loss of life in Korea. Some authorities accused her and other correspondents of "giving aid and comfort to the enemy." She said she was only "telling the brutal story about the licking our troops were taking."

While some generals and authorities distrusted her, the soldiers loved her. Tall and attractive, she was waved at and applauded everywhere she went. Jimmy Cannon of the New York *Post* said, "Riding in a jeep with Maggie is like being a jockey on Lady Godiva's horse."

After the war, she returned to the United States and became the *Herald Tribune's* roving reporter and a columnist. She covered the rebellion in the Belgian Congo in the early 1960s and was the first *Tribune* reporter to stay in Stanleyville since Henry Stanley found Dr. David Livingston in 1877. She filed two exclusive stories: an account of Indian troops arriving in Leopoldville and an interview with rebel leader Antoine Gizenga. "Gizenga is," she wrote in her straightforward style, "timid, suspicious, and indecisive." She persuaded him to let her do the interview by convincing him that talking to a reporter would be to his advantage.

With the buildup of American military strength in Vietnam, she once again was at the front lines, by this time writing a column for *Newsday* with a hard anti-Communist stand. Said *Time* magazine: "She knew how to take a cool, levelheaded look at world affairs, and she disdained those commentators who were addicted to 'romantic nonsense.'"

In the fall of 1965, having contracted leishmaniasis, a rare tropical disease, she left Vietnam. She died of the disease in January 1966.

●◆

CHARLIE COMPANY HOLDS OUT AGAINST HUGE ODDS

Higgins covered some of the battles in Korea from the midst of the action. When not eyewitnessing the fighting, she exercised a sharply honed sense for gathering the kinds of details that would allow her to reconstruct the action as if she had seen it in person. That was the case with the following story about a small company of American soldiers who were trapped by a North Korean attack.

In an attempt to recreate the episode, Higgins relied on direct quotation from one of the participants and on the use of concrete details of the setting and the action. The result was a report imbued with a story-telling quality and an example of how a thorough job of gathering details is a key to good writing.

[GI'S HOLD OFF KOREAN ONSLAUGHT]
Marguerite Higgins
New York *Herald Tribune*
August 17, 1950

With U.S. 34th Infantry Regiment, On Central Front in Korea—The circular grain-filled mill was completely surrounded, and there were only nine men left in Charlie Company (C Company) who could still shoot. Forty wounded were stacked in the middle of the room.

It went straight back to Indian-fighting covered-wagon warfare; only the gimmick here was that the Korean enemy had superior fire power.

"And yet, by God, we somehow held them off for ten hours until our tank broke through and got us. It was the roughest thing I've heard of in this war."

This was Lt. Charles Payne, of Neosho, Mo., speaking. He is the only officer still around to tell the tale, perhaps the most dramatic of the war. Lt. Payne has a good basis for comparison, for he has been continuously in action since the first day of American participation in this war, when I saw him lead a bazooka team into action.

The Communist onslaught against the trapped American company was only one remarkable incident of the current American attempt to wipe out the enemy bridgehead against the Naktong River here.

"The main reason we stood them off, I think, was because we had given up all hope of getting out," Lt. Payne said. "Once we had accepted death as inevitable, everybody calmed down. It even became kind of exciting instead of just plain terrifying. We would ration out ammunition—we took it from the dead, the dying and the wounded—and go from window to window, waiting to fire till each man was sure he could really hit something."

The last-ditch stand of Charlie Company in the grain mill on the Naktong River road developed out of a counterattack in which it was sent to rescue another hard-pressed unit.

"The enemy let us go right down the road past their positions, then closed in on us from all sides," Lt. Payne said. "Most of us took shelter under a bridge about 100 yards from the mill. We had lots of wounded down there. Finally, they started shooting under the bridge. They had machine guns, automatic weapons, rifles, everything on us. I told the walking wounded to make a dash for the mill, and the rest of us ran with them, trying to give cover as best we could. The guy running next to me got it just as we reached the mill."

The mill had thin walls, but big bags of grain afforded Charlie Company shelter from the bullets peppering the building. The remnants of the company reaching the mill had one Browning automatic rifle, carbines and M-1s.

"We stacked the wounded in the middle, two and three deep," Lt. Payne continued. "It was pretty awful as the day wore on because we ran out of water and first-aid kits.

"A few died. There was one guy kept begging me to shoot

him all day. After the tank came we got him down to the aid station, and they were trying to get a helicopter to take him back because he would never have survived the ambulance ride. I don't know what ever happened to him.

"In the mill they kept hitting the oil cans and the oil in the machinery. It was pretty terrible because the hot liquid kept dropping down on the wounded there in the middle of the room."

Lt. Payne, the battalion executive officer, assigned the men to windows with ammunition to use only when they were sure of a killing.

"In the first minutes it was pretty panicky in there. A couple of guys made a break for it across the rice paddies, and got it. Then we knew there was no alternative; so we were stuck. We decided to go down fighting. Pretty soon the guys were saying, 'Look at that one step into the firing,' and just try to get as many of them as we could dust off, and stuff like that. I knew they had steadied and everything was O.K."

The Koreans kept coming at the building in waves of a dozen or more, but accurate fire threw them back.

"There was a brief period when we thought they had given up," Lt. Payne recounted. "We saw them marching away from us in formation. I told the guys not even to breathe. But the wounded kept groaning. That chilled you, because you thought it might divert them back to us. But later we found that they had just gone around to come at us another way."

Charlie Company took refuge in the mill at 8 a.m. At 6:30 p.m., when help came, a substantial number of wounded had died from their old wounds, and there were new wounds inflicted by enemy guns and grenades.

"We could see the tank coming towards us, opening up on machine gun positions, with blasts tossing Reds into the air, and boy, were we happy," Lt. Payne said.

"Lt. Albert Alfonso of Honolulu and his company were with the tank, and they came through, firing from the hip. The Reds kept firing, but we got everybody out and back down the road."

Lt. Payne, a very lucky guy, is the only staff officer of his battalion still at the front and still pressing his luck. The rest were killed or wounded.

MARGUERITE HIGGINS

MARINES STORM KOREAN SEA WALL

Higgins believed in reporting from the spot where battle action was heaviest. She got to do that with her most famous story from the Korean War. It is reprinted below, detailing the U.S. Marines storming the sea wall at the city of Inchon. The story clearly demonstrates Higgins' ability to put readers in the middle of the action—using, for example, illustrations familiar to them—and her great powers of observation. Notice also her use of concrete details, vivid verbs, and economical language.

MAGGIE HIGGINS LANDS AT INCHON
Marguerite Higgins
New York *Herald Tribune*
September 18, 1950

WITH THE U.S. MARINES AT INCHON, KOREA, SEPTEMBER 15 (DELAYED)—Heavily laden U.S. Marines, in one of the most technically difficult amphibious landings in history, stormed at sunset today over a ten-foot sea wall in the heart of the port of Inchon and within an hour had taken three commanding hills in the city.

I was in the fifth wave that hit "Red Beach," which in reality was a rough, vertical pile of stones over which the first assault troops had to scramble with the aid of improvised landing ladders topped with steel hooks.

Despite a deadly and steady pounding from naval guns and airplanes, enough North Koreans remained alive close to the beach to harass us with small-arms and mortar fire. They even hurled hand grenades down at us as we crouched in trenches, which unfortunately ran behind the sea wall on the inland side.

It was far from the "virtually unopposed" landing for which the troops had hoped after hearing of the quick capture of Wolmi Island in the morning by an earlier Marine assault. Wolmi is inside Inchon harbor and just off "Red Beach." At H-hour minus seventy, confident, joking Marines started climbing down from the transport ship on

≈ 297 ≈

cargo nets and dropping into small assault boats. Our wave commander, Lieutenant R.J. Schening, a veteran of five amphibious assaults, including Guadalcanal, hailed me with the comment, "This has a good chance of being a pushover."

Because of tricky tides, our transport had to stand down the channel, and it was more than nine miles to the rendezvous point where our assault waves formed up.

The channel reverberated with the ear-splitting boom of warship guns and rockets. Blue and orange flame spurted from the "Red Beach" area, and a huge oil tank, on fire, sent great black rings of smoke over the shore. Then the fire from the big guns lifted, and the planes that had been circling overhead swooped low to rake their fire deep into the sea wall.

The first wave of our assault troops was speeding toward the shore by now. It would be H-hour (5:30 p.m.) in two minutes. Suddenly, bright orange tracer bullets spun out from the hill in our direction.

"My God! There are still some left," Lieutenant Schening said. "Everybody get down. Here we go!"

It was H-hour plus fifteen minutes as we sped the last two thousand yards to the beach. About halfway there the bright tracers started cutting across the top of our little boat. "Look at their faces now," said John Davies of the Newark *News*. I turned and saw that the men around me had expressions contorted with anxiety.

We struck the sea wall hard at a place where it had crumbled into a canyon. The bullets were whining persistently, spattering the water around us. We clambered over the high steel sides of the boat, dropping into the water and, taking shelter beside the boat as long as we could, snaked on our stomachs up into a rock-strewn dip in the sea wall.

In the sky there was good news. A bright, white star shell from the high ground to our left and an amber cluster told us that the first wave had taken their initial objective, Observatory Hill. But whatever the luck of the first four waves, we were relentlessly pinned down by rifle and automatic-weapon fire coming down on us from another rise on the right.

There were some thirty Marines and two correspondents crouched in the gouged-out sea wall. Then another assault boat swept up, disgorging about thirty more Marines. This went on for two more waves until our hole was filled and Marines lying on their stomachs were strung out all across the top of the sea wall.

An eerie colored light flooded the area as the sun went down with a glow that a newsreel audience would have thought a fake. As the dusk settled, the glare of burning buildings all around lit the sky.

Suddenly, as we lay there intent on the firing ahead, a sudden rush of water came up in to the dip in the wall, and we saw a huge LST [Landing Ship, Tank] rushing at us with the great plank door half down. Six more yards and the ship would have crushed twenty men. Warning shouts sent every one speeding from the sea wall, searching for escape from the LST and cover from the gunfire. The LST's huge bulk sent a rush of water pouring over the sea wall as it crunched in, soaking most of us.

The Marines ducked and zigzagged as they raced across the open, but enemy bullets caught a good many in the semi-darkness. The wounded were pulled aboard the LSTs, six of which appeared within sixty-five minutes after H-hour.

As nightfall closed in, the Marine commanders ordered their troops forward with increasing urgency, for they wanted to assure a defensible perimeter for the night.

In this remarkable amphibious operation, where tides played such an important part, the Marines were completely isolated from outside supply lines for exactly four hours after H-hour. At this time the outrushing tides—they fluctuate thirty-one feet in twelve-hour periods—made mud flats of the approaches to "Red Beach." The LSTs bringing supplies simply settled on the flats, helpless until the morning tides would float them again.

At the battalion command post, the news that the three high-ground objectives—the British Consulate, Cemetery Hill, and Observatory Hill—had been taken arrived at about H-hour plus sixty-one minutes. Now the important items of business became debarking tanks, guns, and ammunition from the LSTs.

Every cook, clerk, driver, and administrative officer in the vicinity was rounded up to help in the unloading. It was exciting to see the huge M-26 tanks rumble across big planks onto the beach, which only a few minutes before had been protected only by riflemen and machine gunners. Then came the bulldozers, trucks, and jeeps.

It was very dark in the shadow of the ships, and the unloaders had a hazardous time dodging bullets, mortar fire, and their own vehicles.

North Koreans began giving up by the dozens by this time, and we could see them, hands up, marching across the open fields toward the LSTs. They were taken charge of with considerable glee by a Korean Marine policeman, Captain Woo, himself a native of Inchon, who had made the landing with several squads of men who were also natives of the city. They learned of the plan to invade their home town only after they had boarded their ship.

Tonight, Captain Woo was in a state of elation beyond even that of the American Marines who had secured the beachhead. "When the Koreans see your power," he said, "they will come in droves to our side."

As we left the beach and headed back to the Navy flagship, naval guns were booming again in support of the Marines. "This time," said a battalion commander, "they are preparing the road to Seoul."

Marguerite Higgins' articles are reprinted with permission of the I.H.T. Corporation and Mrs. John Hay Whitney.